# History of Evangelical Christianity in Russia

# HISTORY OF EVANGELICAL CHRISTIANITY IN RUSSIA

by

Albert W. Olema, B.A., B.S., M.Th., D.D.

## TABLE OF CONTENTS

## INTRODUCTION

### Who Are the Russians?

The question, who are the Russians, has been asked by many people. The first ethnic background of the Russian people was given by the Hebrew prophet Ezekiel about 2,600 years ago. In Ezekiel 38:2 the prophet writes of "...Gog, of the land of Magog, the prince of Rosh, Meshech, and Tubal. ..." This refers to the ancient people who were called, Rosh, Meshech, and Tubal.

In Genesis chapter 10 we have the so-called "Table of Nations." In the light of Genesis 10:2, three of the forefathers of the ancestral tribes of the modern Russian people can be traced back to Japheth, the son of Noah. Magog was the second son of Japheth, Tubal the fifth son, and Meshech the sixth son. Rosh is not descendant from this family.

The three names mentioned in this family tree are not fiction, but they have turned up in many archaeological discoveries of the early ancient history. The reason for this is obvious. The families of these forefathers adopted their names as tribal names. The family descended from Magog became known as the tribe of Magog, but the ancient Greeks called them Scythians. The Scythians is the principle part of the people who make up modern Russia.

Herodotus, the fifth century B.C. Greek philosopher and historian, mentions Mesech and Tubal in his writings. The ancient Greek historian identified them with a people named Sarmatians and Muschovites. These peoples at that time lived between the Caspian Sea, the Don River, and the Sea of Azov. By the third century B.C. their territory extended from the Baltic to the Black Sea, and from Vistula to the Volga River. The Sarmatians are believed to have been the ancestors of the Slavs.

The Greek name Moschi derived from the Hebrew name Meshech is the origin of the name for the city of Moscow.

Rosh was a designation for the tribes then north of the Taurus mountains, dwelling in the area of the Volga River. The Byzantine and Arabic writers have mentioned a people called Ros and Rus, dwelling in the country of Taurus, and reckoned among the Scythian tribes. In this name and tribe is the first historical trace of Russ or Russia.

The nomadic tribes in Russia were in constant warfare. Conflicts among the Slavs became so violent and devastating that by the middle of the ninth century they voluntarily concurred to choose a foreign prince who could unite them into one strong nation. Accordingly, they sent messengers overseas to invite a ruler from among a Norse tribe called Russ. Rurik of this Scandinavian tribe settled in Novgorod, about 110 miles south-southeast of Leningrad. He became sole ruler of the whole domain in 862, which is considered as the beginning of the Russian Empire.

In 988 Prince Vladimir of Russia accepted the Greek Orthodox religion as the State religion. The people were forced to receive baptism. Thus the Russian State Church consisted of unconverted heathen. For several hundred years there was no preaching of the gospel nor any spiritual movement.

In 1788 began the Mennonite migration to the Ukraine. In the middle of the past century began a mighty spiritual awakening which spread into many parts of the Russian Empire.

In 1917 the Communists took over Russia. The Soviet regime would wish to put in the place of religion, philosophical materialism and the allegiance to the State. Of the 270 million Russians, only about 16 million are card-carrying Communists. The Soviets have failed to stamp out Christianity in Russia. Christianity is still on the march, and the new converts continue to replace the losses caused by natural death and official persecution.

I am also very thankful to the publishers whose publications I have been able to use. Please note: the dates listed following the names of rulers in this volume refer only to their length of reign. All the pictures of the cities in the Soviet Union were taken by the author.

*Albert W. Olema*
*Dallas, Texas, U.S.A.*
*1983*

# CHAPTER I

## WESTERN PROTESTANTISM ESTABLISHED IN RUSSIA

### Protestantism Allowed to Enter Russia by a Miscalculation on the Part of the Emperors

The Church of Russia had always been the most isolated branch of the European Christian community. From the 13th century to the middle of the 16th century it had no contact with the Western Christendom. When Russia reentered the society of European nations, the Orthodox Church was still a stranger to the Western world. The Russian upper classes who admired Europe and its culture in most cases felt superior to their own religion and took less notice of the Church life in the West, being unaware of any problem as to relations between Eastern and Western Christians.

The Russian State Church permeated every phase of Russian life, personal, social and national. The majority of Russians identified themselves as members of the Church, and though as individuals they might be skeptics, agnostics and even atheists, few of them broke away entirely from the Orthodoxy which more than any other, expressed the character of the Russian people and their essential unity. Every Russian home was adorned with holy ikons. The ikons were also displayed at railway stations, public offices, shops and taverns. Every person was baptized and confirmed. Most Russians went to confession at least once a year and received Holy Communion, were married in the Church, and expected to be buried with Orthodox rites. In almost all Russian homes a number of Christian customs and ordinances were observed, especially those connected with Holy Week and Easter. This close and intimate relation between daily life and the Church extended throughout the entire nation.

Church processions attracted huge crowds and were widespread, as were pilgrimages and other religious demonstrations. Monasteries and shrines were numerous all over the country, and everywhere one was confronted by manifestations of Church life. There was no place for any other religious philosophy in the Orthodox circles. The

Reformation movement with various Protestant sects, according to the Orthodox opinion, was just a series of heretical doctrines so far from the true Orthodoxy that it did not pose any danger of pollution.

Western Protestantism owes its spread in Russia to a fundamental miscalculation on the part of the Emperors. They were on their guard against the Catholics whom they feared threatened Creco-Russian piety. However, the Emperors saw no danger from the Protestant side, because the heresies of Luther and Calvin were so far away from Orthodoxy that they could be no contamination. Whenever possible, and almost as a matter of policy, the Muscovite government summoned Protestant foreigners to Russia in preference to Catholics.

Palace of Peter the Great

## First Lutheran Church Built in Moscow in 1575

Some Lutherans were interested in Russian affairs and determined to break the old tradition of isolation. The Russian government was favorable toward the Western Protestants and made no difficulties for them to come to Russia, where they could practice their own religion. As a remarkable illustration of Russian tolerance towards Protestantism, it may be mentioned that in 1575 Ivan the Terrible permitted the building of a Protestant church in Moscow, at a distance of only one mile from the Kremlin.

Later on, Protestantism gained ground and made numerous converts. The just-mentioned religious force finally became a proselytising religion in Russia, even if it did not spread to the Orthodox in its original Lutheran and Calvinist forms. It was a naturalized and nationalized Protestantism, and although the Great-Russians remained comparatively immune to it, the same cannot be said of the Ukrainians and other nationalities. However, there were Lutheran churches in practically every large town of European Russia.[1]

The first Reformed (Calvinist) church was built in Moscow in 1629. Emperor Peter the Great made a determined and definite move toward the West when he founded the new capital of St. Petersburg in 1703 and started some fundamental reforms. In this great and important undertaking, he felt the urgent need of people who could help him in this important work. For this reason the Emperor opened the door wide to the foreigners who would come and help him. Those who accepted the call came and brought with them new customs, philosophy, ideas and new religious influences. The majority of the foreigners who came at that particular time to Russia were Germans, of whom many were members of the Lutheran Church.

The Lutherans were not persecuted by the Orthodox Church, because they were foreigners and enjoyed the protection of the ruler and his government. However, in 1645 they were branded by the Orthodox Church as heretics. The same year the Orthodox leaders and the Lutheran leaders held several discussions at Moscow to determine whether or not the Lutherans were actually Christians. The main controversy was that of baptism. The Lutherans baptized by sprinkling, but the Orthodox Church baptized by immersion. The Lutherans defended the validity of their baptism, but the Muscovites rejected it. The Orthodox became convinced that the Lutherans were far more dangerous heretics than the Catholics because they rejected several sacraments, the regular priesthood, apostolic succession, relics, and fasts. On the other hand, most of these Lutherans were Lutherans by name only without any personal experience of salvation. However, in the 17th century there were some Lutheran ministers who did proclaim the message of salvation, of whom Pastor Quirinus Kuhlmann (1651-1689) was one. This humble servant of God came from Breslau, Germany. He was dissatisfied with the mere form of the Lutheran Church, and in particular with the indolence of the Church, and began

1. Walter Kolarz, **Religion in the Soviet Union** (New York: St. Martin's Press Inc., 1961), pp. 245, 250.

to preach the gospel to the Russians. Kuhlmann was arrested on the charge that he was preaching a new religion to the Russian people, different from the Orthodox faith; and on May 26, 1689, he was brought to court for a trial. From the records of the examinations in the court, it is evident that his convictions were founded on the truth of the gospel, although he states in his answers that he came to Russia to preach the gospel at the bidding of an angel who appeared to him in a dream. He was pronounced guilty for preaching heresy to the Orthodox people. The judges sentenced Kuhlmann and his followers to death at the stake. The sentence was carried out a few days later.[2]

Novgorod

## Pietism in the Russian Empire

To understand the spread of Pietism in the Russian Empire, it is necessary to see its beginning from the right perspective. In the middle of the 17th century, a spiritual movement got started in some of the Catholic and Reformed churches in France, Switzerland and Holland. Through the activities of a converted Roman Catholic priest, Jean de Labadie (1610-1674), many people were saved. In the Catholic

[2] N.I. Saloff-Astakhoff, **Christianity in Russia** (New York: Loizeaus Brothers Publishers, 1941), pp. 73-74.

churches these groups of the converted people were called "congregations" or "brotherly-union." Labadie taught that the preaching of the gospel and faith in Christ was the only means of salvation and foundation for holy living. In his meetings they read the Bible and learned about the way of the holy living.

At one of the holy meetings in Switzerland, a young man, Philip J. Spener (1635-1705), was awakened who later became the father of Pietism. At this time there was another spiritual movement which got started before the mainstream of Pietism and manifested its transforming power in many of the Catholic and Reformed churches. In the Catholic churches the movement became known as Jansen's Influence. This spiritual movement endorsed the Pauline doctrine of sin and of grace and opposed sternly the Jesuits.

In many of their meetings people spoke in tongues. This wonderful spiritual activity was condemned and destroyed by the Catholic Church.

In the Reformed Church in Holland, the revival fire was started by William Teelinck (1579-1629). Studying in England, he came into contact with Puritans, and their holy lives influenced Teelinck. He returned to Holland as a gospel preacher, and a vigorous spiritual movement was kindled through him.

Later Labadie joined the Reformed Church in Holland because of his failure to reform the Catholic Church. Because of some controversy with the Roman Catholic Church, Labadie later separated himself from the Catholic Church and established his own free congregation. He taught about the unity of the people within his own circles and about the believer's spiritual priesthood. In 1670 at one of the Communion services, one saint began to speak in tongues, and soon almost the whole group present began to speak in tongues. A part of the congregation did not like it and separated from Labadie's church. After his death, his congregation abandoned Labadie's doctrine of separation and began to spread the gospel in other regions.

In the year of 1670, Philip J. Spener began with his meetings in the homes. In those meetings he applied the doctrine of 1 Corinthians chapter 14 as the basis for the believers' gatherings. In those gatherings people were not allowed to criticize nor condemn others; but people were exhorted to sing, pray and to read the Bible. Any one of the believers who had a special light of any Scripture passage could speak for the upbuilding of the body of Christ. At those meetings people confessed, asked questions and related experiences to others.

Spener stressed the absolute necessity of personal repentance and conversion. Thus a true spiritual movement got started which took on a worldwide phenomenon – known in church history as Pietism.

Spener's work was carried on by August H. Francke (1663-1727) of Germany, who was converted in 1687. The main features in his Christian life were faith and love. In 1695 by faith he began to build important institutions. He built an orphanage where at his death were about 130 orphans. He established many schools in Halle, Germany, of lower and higher learning. Around 1727 about 2,200 children studied in those schools. The students were mostly of the poor class, and many got one free meal a day. Thus Halle became the main center for the spread of Pietism, which is often called Halle's Pietism. Francke founded also a foreign missions organization, and missionaries were sent to the foreign fields. Pietism spread in two ways.

1. It spread from Halle into many countries, producing great results in conversions.

2. Later it begot the Herrnhut or Brethren movement, which is known all over the world.

Pietism entered the Russian Empire by the German immigrants who settled down in the Russian cities. Among those immigrants spread Halle's Pietism. Many of the Pastors of those immigrant congregations were Pietists and preached the gospel of Jesus Christ. Preaching to the Russians was forbidden, but through the schools its influence reached the Russians as well. During the Northern War (1700-1721), Pietism spread in a mighty way among the Swedish war prisoners. Some of Charles XII officers were from the Baltic countries and spoke German. Thus Pietism entered Russia and Finland, which was incorporated into the Russian Empire in 1808. The most important leader of Pietism in Finland was Pietary Schaefer (1660-1729).[3]

When Poland was divided under Catherine the Great in 1772, 1793 and 1795, Austria acquired a considerable part, namely Galicia and Bukoviina. The Ukrainians who were living in those areas were strongly encouraged in their national and literary development. This was characteristic of the tension between the Austrian Monarchy and the Russian Empire. The Austrian government did everything possible to persuade those on the other side of the frontier of its liberality. In so doing, it strengthened the desire of the Russian Ukrainians for the West.

It is important to note that besides St. Petersburg, also the

[3] Juhani Kuosmanen, **Heratyksen Historia**, (Tikkurila: Ristin Voitto, 1979), pp. 98-101, 106. Translated from Finnish by Albert W. Olema.

Ukraine maintained relations with Halle, Germany. Pietism was not wholly foreign to the Ukrainians. Their popular religious philosopher and poet, Grigori Skovoroda (1722-1794), is supposed to have studied in Halle from 1751 to 1753. Francke himself was dead by that time, but his son and son-in-law Freijlinghausen were caring for his spiritual heritage. After his return, the eccentric Skovoroda wandered about the country with his Bible, attacking both the monasteries and rationalism. He had certain similarities with his contemporary Johann G. Hamann (1730-1788), the wise man of the North, and he exemplifies the spiritual openness of the Ukrainians. One of Skovoroda's sayings: "The world tried to seize me, but it could not hold me," characterizes his Pietism. Taras Shevchenko (1814-1861), national poet of the new Ukraine, who was a powerful influence upon Ukrainian national feeling, also liked to quote from the Holy Bible.[4]

### Spirit of Praying Movement and Renqvistism in Finland

In the year of 1756 in the village of Santtion was a young lady, Liisa Erkintytar, who read Sundie Dentin's "True Experience of Conversion," realized her need of the forgiveness of sins, and was saved by the grace of Jesus Christ. As a result of this conversion, later on a great revival broke out in Santtion village and spread throughout the county of Kalannin, known as the Spirit of Praying Movement. In a short period of time, one-third of the people in the just-mentioned county were saved.

Liisa was a great woman of prayer and delivered short speeches. This revival spread like "prairie fire." In this revival, the gifts of the Spirit were manifested, such as speaking in tongues, visions and people predicting endtime events. By 1759 this revival had invaded many parts of Finland. Abraham Achrennius (1706-1769), a converted Lutheran minister, became an excellent leader of the Spirit of Praying Movement. 1810 and 1817, 1827 – 1828 were years of great revivals and almost the entire nation of Finland was influenced by this movement. The most outstanding leaders of this time are Matti Pukanhaava (1770-1833) and Matti Paavola (1790-1859). In 1831 the Spirit of Praying Movement was opposed by the government and a foundry worker, Mikko Rostedt, was fined 96 rubles.[5]

4. Hans Brandenburg, **The Meek and the Mighty**, (London & Oxford: A.R. Mowbray & Co., Ltd., 1976), p. 58.

5. Kuosmanen, **op. cit.**, pp. 98-106, 110-116.

The Herrnhut movement began in Finland in 1734. The most important leader of this movement in its history was Elias Lagus (1741-1819). However, the Herrnhut Brethren revival did not become a nationwide phenomenon though the spiritual blessings were great. In the beginning of the 19th century, Herrnhut fell into oblivion. Thus at the time of the annexation of Finland by Russia in 1808, several revival movements were brought into the Empire. The Finns contributed considerably to the evangelistic work in Russia.

Another mighty revival began in 1797 in the village of Savojarven. Two Christian families were working in the hayfield when the Holy Spirit fell upon those righteous souls. They began to speak in tongues and to prophesy. The most outstanding leader of this spiritual movement was Paavo Ruotsalainen (1777-1852). In 1819 the revival fires entered North Karelia, producing great results in conversions. In those meetings, speaking in tongues and prophecy was often manifested. The most powerful preacher of this time was a Lutheran minister, Niilo K. Malmberg (1807-1858), who was saved in St. Petersburg in 1828 by the testimony of some of the followers of Gossner.

In 1817 Henrik Renqvist (1789-1866) began with revival meetings in Liberi, North Karelia. A powerful spiritual movement got started by him which later on became known as Renqvistism. He was a Lutheran minister and preached the gospel of Jesus Christ. However, the State Church of Finland did not appreciate his evangelistic activities and sent him in 1824 to Svartholmen fortress to be Chaplain at the fortress prison. During the next 10 years of his ministry, a great number of inmates were saved. In 1835 he moved to Sortavalaan where he lived about 30 years. In 1836 began a great spiritual revival as a result of his ministry at that place, which spread fast, like a mighty wave, into many communities. Hundreds of people were saved. In some communities, half of the population was saved by the power of the Holy Spirit. 1841 was the greatest year of this revival movement. Over 10,000 people were saved through the ministry of this humble servant of God.[6] (There were several other great revivals in Finland before 1900).

## Francke's Influence on Emperor Peter the Great

The first changes of the Russian way of life came with the reforms of Peter the Great (1689-1725). In his impetuous way, he opened the

6. Ibid., pp. 147-153.

country up to Western influences in order to overcome the backwardness in cultural and technical spheres which Russia had inherited through the 240 years of the Mongol occupation (1240-1480). Piety certainly was not one of Peter's outstanding qualities. Yet at the same time, the Emperor acquired a deep trust in August H. Francke and his works. Peter was obviously impressed by his work with schools, particularly the emphasis on technical education.

Peter gladly allowed Francke's pupils to come to Russia as educators, teachers and Pastors. The first Russian secondary school was a pietist foundation. The first president of the St. Petersburg Academy of Sciences was a friend of August Francke. During the Northern War (1700-1721) the Baltic lands of Livonia and Estonia, which formerly belonged to Sweden, were annexed to Russia in 1710. Many of the Baltic Germans, including a number of his ministers, were of Pietist orientation. Johann Arndt's (1555-1625) books of "True Christianity" and many of the writings of Francke were translated into the Russian language. The Emperor himself read them.

Francke's first emissary was Scharschmidt, who came from Quedlinburg. Although Francke's hope for an ecumenical connection with the Orthodox Church was not realized, nevertheless Scharschmidt fulfilled a valuable service. He traveled through the length and breadth of Russia, gathering and looking after the scattered Evangelical Christians of Western origin. The existing Lutheran congregations in Moscow, Arkhangelsk, and soon in the new capital received Pietist preachers and teachers.

After Francke realized that the Orthodox Church was to remain closed to him, he turned his attention to the Swedish officers who had been transported to Siberia together with almost the whole army of Charles XII after the battle of Poltava in the Ukraine in 1709. In Tobolsk in Siberia, through a voluminous correspondence and large shipments of Bibles, Christian literature and considerable sums of money which Francke collected for the prisoners, there began a revival among the Swedes. A school was even established there. When the war prisoners returned to Sweden, they bore living testimony to the saving power of Jesus Christ.

Francke also had an indirect influence upon Finland, which was incorporated into the Russian Empire in 1808. His writings reached Russia in large quantities. It was in St. Petersburg that the strongest concentration of the Protestant element was to be found until the collapse of the Empire in 1917. In 1900 there were up to a hundred thousand Protestants in the Russian capital which was about 10 percent of the total population. The Lutherans had 15 congregations with twelve churches, the reformed had six churches, and there was also a meeting room of the Herrnhut Brethren. These congregations had outstanding primary and secondary schools, hospitals and old people's homes.[7]

St. Isaac's Cathedral. Completed in 1858. Now a museum.

### The Wurttemberg Revival Spreads into Russia

Around 1800 a revival movement got started in Wurttemberg, Germany, through the peasant Michael Hahn (1758-1819). The new revival movement spread among many of the peasantry and in the towns. This was combatted by the State Church which was ruled by rationalism. The experiences of war, as so often in church history, had strengthened the eschatological hope. The great Swabian theologian John A. Bengel (1687-1752) in his exposition of Revelation once calculated the date of Jesus' return and indicated the year 1836 as very probable. The exigencies of war, the general inflation and the manyfold

[7] Brandenburg, op. cit., pp. 15-19.

oppression of the believers – all this seemed to many to be a sign of the beginning of the anti-Christian era.

Added to this, Dr. Jung-Stilling (1740-1817), the original and romantic Christian writer, popularized Bengel's expectations and pointed to the East, where the harassed community of the endtime was to find a place of refuge. Jung-Stilling even spoke of Smarkand beyond the Caspian Sea. People's minds were aroused; even the Emperor Alexander I (1801-1825) was religiously awakened.

Thus alongside adventures and fortune-hunters, hundreds of German Christian farmers moved to Russia, Bible in hand, to religious freedom – although there was a ban on evangelism among the Russians. Sufficient land was given to each family, complete self-administration, their own churches and schools, tax exemption for 10 years, 500 rubles interest-free loan, their own courts and police, were the promises made to the new settlers.

Later they found that promises were not kept: Rights that had been guaranteed were restricted or cancelled completely. The situation of the first settlers was grim. During the next 100 years there was bread in abundance and many became prosperous. German settlements expanded from one generation to the next.[8]

### The Early 18th Century Revival in North Russia

The Moravian Brethren movement – also called the Herrnhut Brethren – was started by Count Zinzendorff (1700-1760) of Moravia and reached the Baltic countries, Latwia and Estonia in 1729, the northern provinces of the Russian Empire. In 1729 a Lutheran Pastor, the Rev. Mr. Kruner in Riga, Latwia, invited laborers from Konigsberg, Germany, to work for him. Three of the newly arrived workers were fine believers. Brother Christian David with two men from Germany began to preach the gospel in Riga. However, the piety of the Brethren was not acceptable to the Pastor and the Brethren moved on to Wolmar. They were received by the wife of General Hallort, who treated them very kindly. In Wolmar, Latwia, they had good success in winning souls to Christ.

In 1729 the Brethren arrived in Estonia where they were welcomed by the peasants. The preaching produced good results in this northern province of Russia. Although the Herrnhut movement started

8. Ibid., pp. 20-21.

in Estonia as early as 1726, it was three years later that the movement began to spread. About the year 1738 a preacher, F. W. Biefer, a Herrnhut presbyter, initiated a most successful evangelistic work in Tallinn. Soon the movement moved into the country where pietistic Lutheran Pastors held pastorates. He was able to provide an impetus toward forming groups of the Brethren.

In 1740, the first house of prayer of the Brethren was erected in Estonia. In 1742, 78 Brethren and Sisters went to the first Communion service and formed an independent congregation. The exact number of the converts cannot be established, but the revival took on a nationwide phenomenon, and by 1742 the organized membership was over 10,000, and in 1850 about 70,000 with 250 houses of prayer.

In 1698, students from Estonia matriculated at the University of Halle, Germany. They were from Parnu, Tallinn, Saaremaa and Narva. Among these students were those who were later to become Pastors in Estonia and Livonia, who played a significant role in the spiritual awakening in these countries.

A Lutheran Pastor from Estonia, the Rev. Mr. Eberhard Gutsleff (1700-1749) studied at the University of Halle, Germany, where he met the famous Pietist August H. Francke. Gutsleff accepted his viewpoints and was converted. When he returned to Estonia he became an eloquent gospel preacher. In 1737 he became superintendent of the Lutheran work in Saarema (Oesel), the greatest island of Estonia. There he found a few Pastors and families of nobility who accepted the new evangelical doctrine. The revival started by him in Saaremaa spread rapidly into many communities. In one community crowds were so large that the meetings had to be held in open air. He allowed the Brethren to preach in the Lutheran churches and was a great friend of the Herrnhutters. He allowed the believers to testify, to sing and to praise the Lord aloud. The impact of the revival was of such magnitude that from 1740 to 1745 the courts of Saaremaa did not have a single crime to resolve.

In the beginning of the 18th century, preparations were made in Estonia to publish the scriptures in the vernacular. The final accomplishment of the publication of the New Testament in the North Estonian dialect is essentially the merit of Heinrich Gutsleff (1680-1747). This printing started in 1713, but technical difficulties delayed the process; and it was not until the summer of 1715 that the New Testament was delivered to the public.

In 1728, a committee was formed to translate the Old Testament into the Estonian language. Anton T. Helle (1683-1748) moved into the foreground to undertake the translation work. He had begun with the translation of Genesis already in 1726. The undertaking of the translation work was sanctioned officially in 1731.

A great part of the money for the publication of the Estonian Bible came from General H. von Bohn, the Governor-General of Livonia, but Zinzendorff acted as a mediator.

In the beginning of the reign of Empress Elizabeth Petrovna (1741-1762), a strong opposition movement was started by the unfriendly Lutheran Pastors and the nobility. In 1743 the Russian government forbid all evangelical activities in the Baltic countries, and throughout the Russian Empire houses of prayer were closed, literature confiscated, and Christians persecuted. In 1747 three preachers, Gutsleff, Holterhoff, Fritzsche and a Herrnhut physician Dr. D. C. Krugelstein of Tartu, were brought to St. Petersburg to give an account of their activities. Gutsleff was not able to endure the rough prison life, and in February of 1749 he died as a martyr at the Peter and Paul fortress. Krugelstein and Fritzsche died in 1760 in the same prison. Only Holterhoff survived and was freed in 1762.

On February 11, 1764, Empress Catherine II (1762-1796) granted permission to the Brethren to engage in their religious activities. Because of the great opposition on 1742-1763, this spiritual movement never gained the same momentum. However, in 1817 when all the rights of the Brethren were restored, the movement began to expand again. In 1818 the number of the Brethren had increased to 31,000 (with a few congregations in Latwia) in up to 144 congregations. After the rights of the Brethren were restored, and they were legalized by 1850, their membership grew to 70,000 in 250 congregations. In 1818 there were about a thousand Estonian and Latwian workers in 144 communities.[9]

## The Herrnhut Brethren in South Russia

In 1765 there came into being a small colony at the bend of the Volga, roughly where Stalingrad lies today, at the border with the Kalmyk stepps. The Brethren named this colony Sarepta after the small river Sarpa, with reference to I Kings 17:9. The ground was unsuitable for grain growing, but there was a lot of good water and thus a

9. Dr. Arthur Voobus, **Studies in the History of the Estonian People**, (Wettern, Belgium, Cultura Press, 1974), pp. 10, 70, 98-99, 103-128, 141-143, 158.

Paul & Peter Fortress

possibility for market gardening. The settlers also developed an exemplary activity in the realm of local industries.

From here the Brethren wanted to evangelize the Kalmyks, but they had small success from their efforts. Emperor Nicholas I (1825-1855) restricted their activity very much, and the Brethren community lost their privileges one by one; and in the 1890s Sarepta ceased to be a proper Herrnhut community. However, Sarepta found a place where it could work fruitfully – the German colonies of the Volga. Already in 1764 a Herrnhut Brother of Swiss origin, Jean Jannet, had become Pastor in one of these colonies. He soon made conduct with Sarepta and opened up for them a way into the colonies. The first wave of revival here on the Volga goes back to the Brethren.

Over a period of 57 years, Sarepta sent 18 missionaries to the colonies, until denominational narrowness on the part of the Lutheran Church leadership in St. Petersburg brought about a ban on their work in 1825. The Brethren sowed a good seed, which maintained its effectiveness and strength for generations. However, the Brethren reached only 20 out of the 73 colonies with intensive work. They visited a further 23 occasionally, another 23 only rarely, the rest never.[10]

10. Brandenburg, op. cit., pp. 23-24.

## The Great Mennonite Migration to the Ukraine

The followers of Menno Simons (1492-1559), a converted Roman Catholic priest from Holland, were called Mennonites. Being persecuted in Holland, the Mennonites fled to Germany but were soon heavily oppressed because of their refusal to bear arms and fight in war. Persecutions forced them to look for refuge in some foreign country. The contemporary history reveals four reasons for the Mennonite Immigration.

1. Problems of land expansion.
2. Opposition to military service.
3. Peculiar religious views.
4. Invitation and welcome from Russia.

During the reign of Empress Catherine II, a Mennonite delegation came to Russia. By that time, large areas of Southern Russia had been freed from the last remnants of the Tatars, but vast steppes were still totally uninhabited. The first Mennonites who immigrated to the Ukraine in 1788 came from Danzig region which had been their place of refuge. They settled on Khortitsa, a long, narrow uninhabited island in the River Dnieper. In 1772 Danzig became part of Prussia, and Frederick the Great (1740-1786) denied the freedom from military service, which they had held to be essential to their concept of religion. To preserve that freedom, the Mennonites never hesitated to leave their old surroundings and to settle in strange and unknown lands. It was the promise of that freedom made by Empress Catherine II of Russia, a full-blooded German Princess herself, that encouraged them to migrate to the Ukraine.

Her Majesty's government accepted the Mennonites favorably. Land in Southern Russia was given to them and divided into sections of about 200 acres per family. The farmers were exempted from taxes for a certain number of years, and the young men were not obligated to bear arms and fight in war. Having received the land and the promise of full freedom to arrange their social life at will, with full religious liberty, the Mennonites in turn promised that they would spread no religious propaganda among the Russian population. This liberty encouraged many Mennonites to move to Russia where they could enjoy freedom of worship. A few years after the Mennonite migration to Khortitsa, the second and more important Mennonite center came into being on the River Molochna, now in the Zaporozhe Province of the Ukraine. The first Mennonites settled there in 1803-1804. The names which they gave to some of the villages they established reflect the grace and peace they believed they had found in their new homes in the Ukraine. By 1836 there were 46 villages on the Molochna and by 1863 the number had risen to 57. The island of Khortitsa and the Molochna region were the home of the Mennonite mother-colonies. The high birthrate in these original Mennonite settlements soon necessitated the foundation of the daughter-colonies to absorb the surplus population.[11]

In 1853 a number of Mennonites moved from the Ukraine to the Volga, where another important Mennonite center emerged. New settlements were also established in the North Caucasus region along the Kuban river in 1868. Several daughter colonies were established in Siberia.

The Mennonites formed a special sociological group and were most valuable citizens who did a great deal of opening up agricultural land and for the development of industry. They also performed useful work in education. This group experienced a continual expansion of the area of settlement and of economic wealth. The Mennonites kept their promise not to do religious work among the Russian population, and they were not permitted to accept any one outside of their own group into their church membership, even should he desire so.

They were bound by this promise during all their history in Russia. Yet they had a very strong spiritual influence upon the Russians surrounding them and eventually helped to spread the Evangelical Protestant movement in that country. In the beginning of the 19th century some from among them broke the old tradition and took an active part in evangelistic work among the Russians. Many Russians were converted and became witnesses among their own people.[12]

### The Mennonite Brethren Church Founded in 1860

In the course of time, many of the Mennonites who settled in Russia had elapsed into a cold religious formality. They maintained an outward form of religion in order to retain all of the material benefits to be derived by virtue of membership in the colonies. This led to a

11. Kolarz, **op. cit.**, pp. 275-276.

12. Robert S. Latimer, **With Christ in Russia** (London: Hodder and Stoughton, 1910), p. 183.

protest movement against the deadening formalism of the Old Mennonites which resulted in seven Mennonite sects in Russia.

In 1845 the dissatisfied Mennonites invited a Lutheran Pastor, Rev. Mr. Eduard Wust (1818-1859) from Wurttemberg, Germany, to minister to them. He promoted evangelism, mission festivals, and prayer

**The former Royal Palace, completed in 1762. Now Hermitage Museum.**

meetings. This revival preacher labored for 14 years in South Russia and left a harvest of saved Lutherans and Mennonites.[13]

Brotherly love drove Wust in 1849 to St. Petersburg, in order to have fellowship with those who had been touched by the revival there. He travelled further to Tallinn, Estonia, where he visited Pastor August Huhn (1807-1871) at the old Oleviste church, who was laboring there with similar blessing to Wust in the south of Russia. Huhn's memorable ministry was continued decades later by Traugott Hahn (1848-1939), the elder. It is interesting to notice how the long distances of Russia did not prevent the Brethren from seeking and finding one another. Otherwise Wust remained in the south of the Empire. He also traveled through the Crimea, where he preached in Simeferopol and organized mutual fraternal visits.[14]

13. Steve Durasoff, **The Russian Protestants Evangelicals in the Soviet Union: 1944 — 1964.** (Rutherford, Madison, Teaneck, Fairleigh Dickinson University Press, 1969), pp. 33-34.

14. Brandenburg, **op. cit.**, p. 44.

On January 6, 1860, 18 families in Gnadenfeld drew up a document to start a new church, and the Mennonite Brethren Church was officially founded.

The German Baptist leaders influenced the Mennonite Brethren from the very beginning. The German emphasis on revival methods, internal conversion, and immersion as the only correct form of baptism aided in the further separation of the Mennonite Brethren from the Old Mennonites.

In 1869 John G. Oncken (1800-1884), a German Baptist leader, visited the Ukraine and spent 10 days visiting newly established unorganized groups and assisted in the ordination of Abraham Unger as elder, who became the leader of the new movement.

The Mennonite Brethren churches enjoyed close relationship with the first Russian Baptists in South Russia, and the Pastors of both denominations shared in a reciprocal ministry, conducting baptismal immersions for members of the other fellowship when found more convenient, and the two fellowships partook of the Lord's Supper together.

Both denominations labored faithfully among the Russians, sowing the seed of evangelism in South Russia which later on aided in the spread of the great revival in the Ukraine.[15]

Before 1914, there were about 100,000 Mennonites in Russia – a fifth of all the Mennonites in the world. Despite their severe losses through World War II, Stalin's persecution, and emigration overseas, by 1971 there were still an estimated 60,000 Mennonites in the Soviet Union.[16]

One faithful worker among the Mennonites was evangelist Jakob Kroeker (1872-1948) who was born in Gnadenthal, a Mennonite colony. Later, his family moved to Crimea near Simferopol, where he was saved at the age of 13 and became a zealous Christian. After graduating from the Baptist Seminary in Hamburg, Germany, he was encouraged by the German Mennonites to be an itinerant preacher, in which capacity he travelled Russia from the north to the deepest south – through the Caucasus right up to the Turkish border.

In this capacity he preached the gospel until 1910, when he moved to Germany.[17]

15. Durasoff, op. cit., pp. 33-34.

16. Brandenburg, op. cit., pp. 22-23.

17. Ibid., pp. 150-151.

## The Hutterian Brethren in Russia

The Hutterian Brotherhood (a wing of Anabaptists) was named after Jacob Hutter (1496-1536) who was burned at the stake on February 25, 1536, at Innsbruck in the Tyrol (Austria), Central Europe. This Brotherhood was often opposed because of their stand for the biblical truths. The chief cause of their persecution was their rejection of the principle of a union between Church and State, and disapproval of the practice of the infant baptism which was indispensable for the maintenance of the prevailing State Church.[18]

The Hutterian Brethren were often forced by the persecution to flee from one place to another suffering privations and misery. In the middle of the 18th century again the Brethren were severely oppressed and harassed with ill treatment in Moravia and other countries dominated by the State Church.

In the spring of 1769 the Brotherhood had moved to Wallachia when the war broke out between Russia and Turkey (1768-1774) and the district was occupied by the Russian army. The Brethren appealed to the Russian General Sametin for help. He manifested a friendly interest in the persecuted people and advised them to emigrate to Russia. The General supplied them with the necessary passport and a wagon with a pair of oxen for the journey. In April, 1770, the little company set out.

In the province of Moldavia they met the Russian Field Marshal Count Peter Romanzov (1725-1796) and were permitted by the Russian Commander to settle on one of his states at Wischenka on the River Desna in the province Tscherinogov in northern Ukraine. The Count promised them freedom of religion and gave them money for the journey. In the beginning of August 1770, they reached Wischenka. Here the Brotherhood soon attained a position of considerable prosperity. Pottery, weaving, and metalworking were highly developed. In July 1771, the first worship service was held in the newly built house.[19]

The Brotherhood in Wischenka informed the Count about the fate of the many Hutterian Brethren still in prison in Siebenbuergen and other towns. A delegation was sent by the Brotherhood to Austria to

18. "The Hutterian Brethren, 1528 — 1928," **The Mennonite Quarterly Review,** (April 1928), pp. 83, 87.

19. "The Hutterian Brethren, 1528 — 1928," **The Mennonite Quarterly Review,** (January 1929), pp. 82-83.

petition the release of the imprisoned Brethren. The Empress Theresa (1740-1780) finally granted the release of all those who had been imprisoned for their faith and permitted them to emigrate to Russia. Several families availed themselves of this privilege and left for the Ukraine. They were brought to Wischenka at the expense of Count Romanzov, where they arrived in January 1773.[20]

By 1842 the entire Hutterian colony in the Ukraine numbered 78 families. During 1873 and 1879 all the Hutterian Brethren emigrated from Russia to the United States and settled in South Dakota.[21]

### The Influence of Prince Golitsyn

Prince Alexander Nikolayevich Golitsyn (1773-1844) came from an old Russian noble family. One of his ancestors had been tutor to Peter the Great. He himself was brought up in Empress Catherine's page corps. His gifted nature caused him to be made playmate to Catherine's two oldest grandsons, Grand Prince Alexander and Grand Prince Constantine (1779-1831), sons of Emperor Paul I (1796-1801).

The date of his turning to the biblical gospel and his conversion cannot be established. Golitsyn's friendship with the future Emperor Alexander I began in their childhood. When Grand Prince Alexander was married to Princess Luise Auguste (Elizabetta Alekseievna 1779-1826) of Baden, at the age of 17, Golitsyn, 21, became his valet. At the age of 23 he was already chamberlain. The Emperor had two children. Mariya Aleksandrovna (1799-1800) Grand Duchess of Russia, and Elizabeta Aleksandrovna (1806-1808) Grand Duchess of Russia.

When Alexander came to the throne in 1801, he called his childhood friend into the State service. When the position of Oberprokuror of the Holy Synod became vacant, the Emperor made him chairman, representative of His Majesty in the highest Orthodox Church body. This appointment seems to have led to Golitsyn's awakening. For the first time in his life he began to study the New Testament and experienced conversion. In 1810 Golitsyn also became head of the new administration for the affairs of foreign denominations. In this capacity he also had to take care of the interests of the Lutheran and Reformed Churches. Finally in 1818 he was

[20] "The Hutterian Brethren, 1528 — 1928," **The Mennonite Quarterly Review,** (January 1930), pp. 104-105.

[21] "The Hutterian Brethren, 1528 — 1928," **The Mennonite Quarterly Review,** (January 1929), p. 88.

entrusted with the newly established Ministry of Religion and Education. He was then releaved from his duties as Oberprokuror. He was one of Alexander I's most respected Ministers. Later, when the Bible Society was founded, he became the president of it. In 1812 Prince Golitsyn advised the Emperor to read the Bible, which he had not even seen before then, but which he now appreciated and also read. Alexander considered the Bible as the thing most suited to his needs, and the Divine Spirit also became his inward teacher and interpreter of truth.[22]

### The Bible Influence upon Alexander I

In 1812 when the information reached St. Petersburg that Napoleon's army had entered Moscow, a general panic came upon the inhabitants; and many of the people fled from the capital. Emperor Alexander I was prepared to go with an army to oppose the French Emperor. Prince Alexander Golitsyn at that time was repairing his palace, having many men employed for that purpose. While the people were fleeing, Prince Golitsyn continued calmly to work at his palace.

Some envious persons told the Emperor what the Prince was doing and that he must be a traitor. The Emperor went to see the Prince, inquiring about the reason why he was working in that way while so many people were fleeing. "Oh," said the Prince, "I am here in as safe a place as any I could flee to. The Lord is my defense; in Him I trust." "Whence have you such confidence?" replied the Emperor. "Who assures you of it?" "I feel it in my heart," answered the Prince, "and it is also stated in this divinely inspired volume" – holding forth the Bible to the Emperor. By some inadvertent motion of the hand, the Bible fell upon the floor – open. The Prince asked the Emperor to allow him to read to him at that very place which the Bible had opened to. It was Psalm 91 which the Prince then read to his Sovereign, who stood for a while astonished.

The army during that time was marching out of the city. It was the usual custom that when the Emperor was to be absent a longer time, the last place the Emperor visited was the great cathedral. The scripture portion which was read on that occasion was again the 91st Psalm. The Emperor sent for the priest and queried: "Who told you to choose of that particular passage of Scripture today?" The priest

22. Brandenburg, op. cit., pp. 26-27.

replied that nobody had told him, but that he had prayed asking the Lord to give a passage from the Word which would encourage the Emperor, and he felt that Psalm 91 was of the Lord for him.

The Emperor proceeded some distance on his way, and late in the evening he desired that the Bible be read to him. When the person who came in for that purpose began, he also read Psalm 91. The Emperor, interrupting him, queried: "Who told you to read this? Has Golitsyn told you?" The reply was that nobody had directed him, but that he had desired that the Lord would direct him to read what was most appropriate for the occasion, and accordingly he had selected this portion of scripture. The Emperor felt astonished at this and paid the greater attention to what was read, believing that this must have been the Lord's ordering. His Majesty was very solemnly impressed, and from that time he read a chapter every morning and evening privately from the Bible. Thus the Russian Emperor Alexander I was started in the Christian course.[23]

### The Influence of Baroness von Kruedener upon Alexander I

In order to understand Alexander I's religious developments, it is necessary to describe the influence of an important woman upon him. Juliane von Kruedener (1764-1824) was born in Riga, daughter of the noble landowner Baron Vietinghoff. On her mother's side she was the granddaughter of Field-Marshall Munnic (1683-1767), a man famous in his day, an officer of German descent who in the first half of the 18th century reformed the Russian army according to the Prussian model. At the age of 18 Juliane was married against her will to the Russian diplomat Baron Kruedener who was 20 years her senior and twice divorced. She lived a frivolous life in many of the world's capitals.

The turning point for her was a conversation with a Herrnhut shoemaker in Riga, who was measuring her for new shoes. It made a deep impression on the Baroness that this quiet one in the land, living in poverty, could give such joyful testimony to his happiness in life through faith in Jesus Christ. Juliane came to a deep repentance and conversion. She now dedicated her life to the Lord Jesus Christ. The Baroness helped the poor and wretched and gave a living testimony to the Lord. She was one of the first to point to the great social injustices of her time and fearlessly demanded that the governments introduce aid

23. **Quaker Biographies,** Issued by the Representatives of the Religious Society of Friends for Pennsylvania, New Jersey and Delaware, 1916, pp. 204-205.

programs. The Baroness used her own considerable means unstintingly for the benefit of the poor.

The first meeting between Alexander I and Baroness Kruedener took place after the Vienna Congress (1814-1815). Driven, as she believed, by God's command, this energetic woman forced an audience with the Emperor in Heilbronn. After the first conversation, she was permitted to accompany Alexander to Heidelberg. She had powerfully pointed him to the Saviour of sinners. The Baroness von Kruedener strengthened the Emperor Alexander in his Christian faith for years. Later he listened to other influences as well.[24]

Leningrad

24. Ibid., pp. 31-33.

## CHAPTER II

## QUAKERS IN THE RUSSIAN EMPIRE

### Quaker Influence Upon Peter the Great

The first personal encounter the Quakers, or Friends, had with any Russian was that with Peter I, Emperor of Russia, at the end of the 17th century. In January 1697, the young Emperor arrived in London to learn what he could first-hand of the science of shipbuilding in the Thames dockyards. On his arrival, he lodged for a time at York Buildings, later renting John Evelyn's house at Deptford, which he left in a woeful condition. Word of his arrival had reached some Friends at least, for Gilbert Molleson (1660-1730), who had a kinsman in the Emperor's service, determined to seek an interview very shortly after his appearance in the English capital. Molleson was the brother-in-law of Robert Barclay (1648-1690), who in 1678 had written the famous "Apology for the True Christian Divinity," which was held forth and preached by the people, scornfully called Quakers, the followers of George Fox (1624-1691). Molleson was desirous to have an audience with Peter the Great, and by some means to present a copy of the Apology to the Emperor. He did not reveal his plans to any of the Friends, but asked one other, Thomas Story (1663-1742) to accompany him on his errand.

The two Friends arrived at York Buildings one cold January morning, met a man upstairs in a long gallery who proved to be an English merchant trading with Russia, who frequently acted as interpreter to Peter the Great during his time in London. Meanwhile, in a room opening off the gallery, two men, very plainly dressed, were pacing up and down in conversation. Mr. Thomas Story recognized one of these as the Emperor, the other he learned later was the General, Prince Menshikov (1673-1729). Knowing that Peter the Great could not bear to be stared at, the Quakers took no notice of him, but gazed steadily out of the window at the other end of the long gallery, wearing their hats in true Quaker fashion. The Emperor looked curiously and intently at these two strange figures, and presently addressed the English merchant to whom they had been speaking. Thus the Quakers had their first opportunity to talk to a Russian through an interpreter. Thomas Story in the conversation went on to rebut the charge that "Quakers were of little use to the State. On the contrary, they were of help to any kingdom or government, for the principles of their religion prohibited idleness and excited industry. Being husbandmen, concerned with all manner of husbandry and improvements, as likewise in manufacturing and merchandising, do not want, but rather abound." He related that "the Friends do not fight in the war, but pay taxes to Caesar, who of right can use the money to what purpose he be pleased, to peace or to war."

**Palace of Peter the Great, 20 miles from Leningrad on the Finnish Gulf.**

After having heard the reply of the two Friends, Peter took several turns up and down the gallery, reflecting; and then he stood before the Quakers and looked steadfastly upon them, who pretended that they did not know who he was. Thomas Story then remarked that they had heard that there was a person of great dignity and distinction living in York Buildings, a stranger who was very inspectious into the state of affairs and things in general. Doubtless he might also be inquisitive in matters of religion, they had brought him some books concerning the Society and its faith which would give him a full and correct account of Quaker principles. Two copies of Barclay's Apology in the Latin version were produced and handed to the Emperor.

The interview took place early in the week, and the following Sunday the Emperor, dressed very plainly as a simple Englishman, and with a company of his attendants, arrived unheralded at the Quaker meeting for worship in Gracechurch Street, with the Muscovy merchant in his following to act as interpreter again. A Friend, Robert Haddock, was speaking when the Emperor entered and had no idea of who it was coming thus late to the gathering. Haddock's theme was the cleansing of Naaman, and in the course of his remarks he addressed these strangely pertinent words to the company: "If you wert the greatest king, emperor or potentate upon earth, thou art not too great to make use of the means offered by the Almighty for thy healing and restoration if thou ever expectest to enter his kingdom, into which no unclean thing can come." The Emperor left before the service was quite ended. Peter the Great spoke only Russian and German and could not understand the sermon, but his interpreter tried to do his best to render the gist of the spoken message to the Ruler of the Russians.

As the report of the visit got around, the Morning Meeting, a body of London Friends which supervised all Quaker publications, determined that a formal deputation of Friends should be sent to wait upon the Russian Monarch at his lodgings in Deptford. William Penn (1644-1718), who was fluent in the German tongue, was included in this number. Some copies of Quaker books in "High Dutch" (German) were to be taken for presentation to the Emperor. The Quakers were met with a cordial reception, and according to William Penn, who spoke fluent German, the meeting was satisfactory to both sides. As a result of this second conversation, the Emperor attended the Quaker meeting at Deptford on several occasions, behaving as a private person, and very social.

In the course of his talk with William Penn, Peter the Great had desired to know in a few words what the Quakers thought and practiced so that he might distinguish them from other men and sects. The reply which Mr. Penn sent to the Emperor is very profound. "They teach that men must be holy or they cannot be happy; that they should be few in words, peaceable in life, suffer wrongs, love enemies, deny themselves, without which faith is false, worship formality, and religion hypocrisy."

The hours of stillness in the austere meeting house at Deptford must have made some impression on the enigmatic, brutal personality of the Emperor. Fourteen years later, in 1712, in the course of the Great Northern War against Sweden, Peter the Great entered the town of Friedrichstadt in Holstein and asked the Mayor of the city if there were any Quakers among the inhabitants. He was told that there were a few and that an officer had billeted 30 of his soldiers in their meeting house. The Emperor sent an order that the men were to vacate the meeting house at once and asked the Quakers if they would call together a meeting for worship which he could attend. At 2 o'clock in the afternoon the meeting started; and the Emperor, Prince Menshikov of Moscow, General Dolgurucky and several other of his Dukes, Generals and Secretaries of State, and other great men attended. The house of prayer was thronged, and the Emperor ordered the door to be shut when the room was filled. Those who could not get in listened through the open windows.

After a time of silence, Philip Desair preached the doctrine of truth among them and all sat very quiet, especially the Emperor. He sat very gravely all the time of silence; and all the others, being awed by his example and presence, did so likewise. But the Moscovite Lords and Generals, not understanding the German language, had what was declared interpreted to them by Peter, who with much gravity and seriousness, commended what he heard, saying that whoever could live according to that doctrine would be happy. The Friends presented him with Barclay's Apology and Catechism, this time in German, which the Emperor declared he would have translated and printed in Russian. However, the Emperor and his party were greatly impressed by the worship service. The Emperor's path did not again cross the by-ways of the Quakers.[1]

### Quaker Physician in the Court of Catherine the Great

Fifty years later came a second tenuous contact between the Quakers and the rulers of Russia. The most dreaded disease of the 18th century – smallpox – which took a heavy toll on human life, was greatly curbed by inoculation. At that time, Dr. Thomas Dimsdale (1712-1800) became very famous in the field of medicine, especially inoculation. He himself came from an old Quaker family, lived in Hertford and practiced medicine.

The Empress of Russia, Catherine the Great, determined to introduce this method of treating smallpox into her realm, where its ravages were particularly severe. The Russian Minister in London was

1. Richenda C. Scott, **Quakers in Russia**, (London: Michael Joseph LTD., 1964), pp. 34-39.

instructed to make private inquiries for the best and most experienced British doctor to undertake the task. Dr. Dimsdale was recommended as the best, and in July 1768 he left for Russia with his son Nathaniel. In St. Petersburg, Dr. Dimsdale met the Empress, who treated him very graciously with great confidence. She wanted to be the first inoculated against smallpox in Russia.

Three healthy children were then inoculated from a mild case of smallpox, to provide the necessary fluid for injecting the Empress. She desired that the inoculation should be carried out in the strictest secrecy and refused to have any other doctors in attendance. When the Sovereign felt ready to undergo the operation, she sent a carriage for Dimsdale late at night and without warning. For five days no word of the inoculation was allowed to be published, and tradition says that a series of fast post horses was maintained in readiness at Catherine's behest, in case the injection proved fatal the doctor could get swiftly out of the country in all safety. Within three weeks she had fully recovered, and there were great rejoicings in the capital of Russia.

The Grand Duke, heir to the throne, a delicate boy of 14, was inoculated by Dr. Dimsdale in November the same year. This undertaking was also very successful. The reputation of the English doctor stood high, and members of all the noble families of the capital flocked to him for the prick of the needle. Honors and awards were loaded upon him. He was created a Baron of the Empire and was appointed physician to the Empress and a Councillor of State with the rank of Major-General and an annuity of 500 pounds. In addition, Catherine presented him with a miniature of herself and a gift of 10,000 pounds. In 1769 the doctor left for England but returned once more to Russia in 1781 to inoculate Catherine's two young grandsons, Alexander and Constantine. His wife, who at that time was with him, nursed the princes till their recovery from the treatment, and was termed by the princes their "English Mamma."[2]

### Quaker Influence upon Alexander I

The next ruler of Russia who had many contacts with the Quakers of England was Alexander I, who succeeded to the throne in 1801. There were to be several contacts, some enduring throughout the last 10 years of his reign, between Friends and this versatile inconsistant

2. Ibid., pp. 40-43.

**The front of the Royal Palace in Leningrad**

Emperor of the Russians. Three men were to have great influence upon Alexander I. The first was William Allen (1770-1844) of London, a manufacturing chemist and scientist. He was known in a dozen philanthropic circles as a man of outstanding ability and clear-sighted leadership. The second was Stephen Grellet (1773-1855), who was born in France but lived in England. He could speak with courage to the poor and with equal courage and effect to the crowned heads of Europe, to the light and cynical followers of the court, the leaders of fads and fashions in society.

Throughout the summer of 1813 and the first three months of 1814, Stephen Grellet was travelling in the ministry through France, Switzerland and Germany. In Frankfurt, Germany, he watched the wagonloads of wounded rumbling into the city after a battle on the Rhine, blood pouring down their wheels, men left lying for hours in the sun or rain till bedding and shelter could be found for them. Upon his arrival in England on April 1, 1814, he began to pray that God would make it possible for him to speak to the rulers of Europe to settle their differences in a peaceful way.

It was at this time that he heard that the Emperor of Russia, Alexander I, and the King of Prussia, then in Paris, were going to come to London. At the Yearly Meeting held in May, Allen told the Society about his intention to have an audience with the Emperor of Russia. An address was to be prepared to be presented to the rulers when they came. In the middle of June 1814, Alexander I and Fredrick William III (1797-1840) King of Prussia, reached the capital and the approach was made. To the people of Western Europe, Alexander appeared as the liberator from the Napoleonic yoke, a sudden meteor of hope flashing into the European skies. On June 13, 1814, the Quakers drew up two addresses for presentation to Alexander I of Russia and the King of Prussia. The address to Alexander expressed the appreciation of Friends for his efforts in the cause of peace and for promoting the circulation of the Bible throughout his dominions.

William Allen and Luke Howard (1772-1864) were appointed to arrange for a deputation to wait upon the Emperor and the King of Prussia. They at once approached the Russian ambassador in London, Count Kristopher A. Lieven (1774-1839) and were cordially received by him. On Sunday morning the Emperor expressed a wish to attend a Quaker meeting for worship that day, and the Count had fetched Mr. Allen to accompany him. They called at Curzon Street for the Emperor, his sister Ekatarina Pavlona (1788-1819), the Grand Duchess of Oldenberg, her son Alexander (1810-1829) the young Duke of Oldenberg, and her husband, Wilhelm I (1816-1864) of Wurttemberg, and drove to Westminster Meeting in St. Martin's Lane.

Alexander and his party sat down among the silent Friends, conducting themselves with great seriousness. When the meeting was brought to an end, the Emperor shook hands very affably with those near him and with those Friends lining his way to the door. William Allen was asked by Alexander to wait upon him the next three days with John Wilkinson (1783-1846).

On the following evening when Mr. Allen saw Count Lieven to confirm the details, he pressed for the inclusion of Stephen Grellet, to which the Count reluctantly agreed.

On June 21 these three Friends were admitted to Alexander's presence in the Pulteny Hotel. The Emperor stood to receive them. He was quite alone, dressed in a plain suit of clothes; and with a look of benignity, seemed to meet the Quakers as friends rather than strangers. The address from the Society of Friends and some Quaker books were handed to him. The Emperor stood, and the Friends stood around him in the middle of the room, answering to the best of their abilities the questions he eagerly put to them on the doctrine and practice of the Quakers. The conversation was carried on partly in French, partly in English, which the Emperor spoke and even pronounced well.

Alexander talked of his own experience of the guidance of the Holy Spirit and worship as an interior, spiritual exercise, stating that to him

Summer Palace of Peter the Great

outward forms and observances were but secondary matters. In his own personal prayers he had grown uneasy at the constant repetition of set words, which were not always applicable to his state of mind at the moment, and came to frame his own petitions according to his sense of need at the time, and had found sweet peace in this practice.

Several times in the course of the interview he took one or another by the hand and was much moved by some words spoken to him in French by Stephen Grellet, and told John Wilkinson how fully he had united in spirit with his prayer in the meeting for worship on Sunday. He had desired to have this opportunity apprehending that he was one in sentiment with the Friends; and though, from his peculiar situation, his practice must be different, yet the religion of Christ being one, and His worship spiritual, the Emperor believed that in this they might all unite.

Stephen Grellet raised the plight of those African peoples who were still suffering under slavery and asked that their cause might be remembered at the peace conference. Alexander assured him they would not be forgotten and he would do all he could to safeguard their interests. Then William Allen took up the question of popular education, so near to his heart, outlining briefly the work of the British and Foreign School Society in England, which reached to the poorest in the land, and pointing out all that the Emperor could do in this direction in his own country.

Alexander's interest was caught; he agreed that it was a matter of the utmost importance. In all, the interview lasted about an hour; and when the deputation left, the Emperor stated that if any Friends visited St. Petersburg on a religious account, let them not wait for any introduction, but come direct to him. He remarked that he would never forget this opportunity, and as the Friends withdrew, shook hands with each in turn, saying: "I part from you as from friends and brethren."

When at Portsmouth a week later, ready to sail for Russia, the Emperor suddenly expressed the wish to visit any family of the Quaker persuasion that could be found in the neighborhood. Lord Sidmouth (1757-1844) arranged for him to go to the home of John Glaisyer (1776-1844) in Brighton, but when the imperial carriage arrived, the crowd which had gathered to see the Russian Emperor was so great that it was impossible for the coachman to get to the house. Alexander did not give up his desire. Shortly afterwards, as he was driving along the road to Dover, he noticed two people in Quaker dress standing by the gate of their farm to see him pass. He at once commanded to the coachman to stop, and alighting from the carriage, inquired of the two bystanders if they were not members of the Society of Friends. When they replied in the affirmative, the Emperor asked if he and his sister who was with him might go into the house for a little time and hold some converse with them. The Emperor and Her Imperial Highness were gladly admitted by the Quaker family. After a short visit, the Emperor left for Portsmouth to imbark for Russia.

The next Quaker who played a great part in introducing Quakerism to the Russians was Daniel Wheeler (1771-1840). He was essentially a Quietist, who sought to regulate his daily activities entirely by his sense of Divine leading.

In the early months of 1817 he was confronted with a difficult and momentous decision. Some years before the conviction had been born upon him that he would at some time be called to serve abroad – in what capacity he had no idea. Then one day as he was pacing up and down his parlor, wrestling with his problem, his eye fell on a puzzle which his little son was piecing together on the table – a dissected map. The name St. Petersburg sprang into his vision with the flash of revelation. Henceforth he knew that his field would be Russia. A little time after this first insight, as he was returning home one evening, the thought came unbidden into his consciousness: "What if the Emperor of Russia should want a person for the superintendence of agriculture?"

Meanwhile, Alexander I, in the midst of his plans for re-shaping international relationships and the affairs of his own dominions, had not forgotten the Quakers. For long he had nursed a project to reclaim the desolate marshes around St. Petersburg and had even made one attempt at this, which proved abortive through the instability of the man entrusted with the work. In 1817 the Emperor determined to renew the scheme. Starting entirely afresh, he remembered the high level of English husbandry which he had seen, the neat Quaker farmstead where he had called on impulse, his talks with William Allen, Stephen Grellet and John Wilkinson.

In the request which he sent to England for a competent agriculturalist to take in hand the task of reclamation, he stipulated that the man chosen should be a member of the Society of Friends. The invitation and the requirements of the Emperor were sent on to the Society and circulated among its meetings. When Daniel Wheeler heard about the invitation, he made his way into Sheffield to offer himself for this service. In June 1817 Mr. Wheeler sailed for St. Petersburg to explore the position and to make arrangements for the transfer of his family. Soon after his arrival, he met Alexander's chief Minister, Prince Golitsyn, when he had made a first cursory survey of the land. The Prince asked question after question about the state of the land and the course Mr. Wheeler proposed to follow.

At the conclusion of the meeting, they all rose from their seats, and Wheeler felt that the time had come to proclaim his message – the basis of his faith. When he finally came to an end, both men stood like statues for a time. Then the astonished Prince took him by the hand, saying, "Although our languages are different, the language of the Spirit is the same."

Mr. Wheeler spent a month examining the crown lands and marshes in the vicinity of the capital, carefully observing the soil, which he found better than he had expected. The Emperor had declared his willingness to take on his own account all the expenses of the preliminary journey and of the support of the Wheeler family and their assistance during their sojourn in Russia. At length he was summoned to Alexander's presence with whom he would deal for many years ahead. During his audience with the Emperor, he handed the Emperor a paper which he had prepared upon the principles of the Society of

Friends. Mr. Wheeler soon left for England and returned in June 1818 with his family.

Mr. Wheeler started with a pioneer scheme, covering about a thousand acres, at Ochta, a few miles outside of the city. The methods which he pursued in attaching this first stretch of land were adopted in his successive ventures. As a preliminary, the ground was cleared of the thick, white moss which covered it to a depth of about 16 inches and which held water like a sponge.

The project excited a great deal of curiosity in St. Petersburg. Distinguished visitors began to arrive daily to see the progress of the work. Even the Empress arrived one afternoon to see the work. Finally, the Emperor came himself to visit the area and spent about two hours going over the land with Daniel Wheeler, who used the opportunity to proclaim his doctrines to the Sovereign of the Russian Empire.

On Sundays and Thursdays throughout his years in Russia, Mr. Wheeler gathered his household in a meeting for worship, which was attended also in the earlier years of his sojourn by some of the English and other foreign merchants in the city. Sometimes there were about 18 or 20 people in the meeting. Occasionally there were visitors from England who attended the worship services. During his first winter in Russia in 1818-1819, the presence of William Allen and Stephen Grellet in St. Petersburg brought much consolation and courage to Wheeler.[3]

## The Influence of Allen and Grellet Upon the Imperial Family

Mr. William Allen and Stephen Grellet had an audience with the Sovereign of Russia in 1819, which was a most pleasant one. The Friends encouraged and strengthened the Emperor in faith, who made many inquiries of religious character. The influence of the Holy Spirit was a subject on which he appeared to delight to dwell, being as the Emperor called it, one of the cornerstones of the Christian religion. For if a man has not the Spirit of Christ, he is none of His. And if the things of God could only be known by the Spirit of the Lord, then what hope of salvation can a man have who disregards the Spirit of Christ.

The Quakers then gave the conversation a practical turn, telling His Majesty of the abuses and misery they had found in the prisons.

3.Ibid., pp. 46-67.

They showed him a sketch they had made of a man who had been loaded with fetters for 18 years. The Emperor was much affected, and said: "These things ought not to be; they shall not continue so." The Friends then spoke of their little book, the "Scripture Lesson," and gave Alexander a brief outline of the contents. The Emperor remained a few moments absorbed in deep thoughtfulness, and then said: "You have done the very thing I was anxious should be done." He had for a long time been contemplating how that mighty machine, public education, could be used for the promotion of the kingdom of Christ. His Majesty requested to send him immediately what the Quakers had prepared.

The Emperor spoke very favorably of Mr. Daniel Wheeler. It was not actually the cultivation of the morasses, nor any outward object that led the Emperor to wish to have Quakers in Russia, but a desire that by their genuine piety and uprightness in life and conversation, an example might be set before his people for them to imitate, and he found that Mr. Wheeler set such an example.

Before they separated, the Emperor requested a period of religious devotion; and these three men, of such striking difference in origin, experience and rank, settled down into the solemn silence of spiritual worship together. Soon Stephen Grellet kneeled down in prayer, and then the Emperor knelt beside him as a humble suppliant to their common Heavenly Father. After another short time of silent communion, they separated, having been together for about two hours.

Shortly after this, the Empress-Mother (1759-1828) – formerly Duchess of Wurttemberg – received them in the private apartment of her palace. The attendants stood at a respectful distance while the Friends conversed with Her Majesty in French. They soon opened the subject of the excellent character of the special schools which were under Her Majesty's patronage, but expressed their regret that no schools for girls were to be found among the masses of the people of the Empire.

### The Quaker Relief Work in Russia

The relief work undertaken by the Quakers at moments of disaster, brought by war or famine, opens a new era in the history of Quaker relationships with Russia. During the early months of the Crimean War, the British fleet, which had been dispatched to the Baltic, was unable to inflict any damage to the Russian shipping nor destroy the Russian naval bases; so it launched an attack upon the unfortified coast of Finland. Landing parties systematically pillaged and burned the villages and townships near the coast, drove off the cattle, destroyed any ships or boats on which they could lay hands, and burned stores, timber and fishing nets on which the people depended for their trade and livelihood.

As soon as the way was open after the war, Joseph Sturge (1793-1860) and Thomas Harvey (1812-1884) set out for Finland to see for themselves what damage had been done and to contrive measures of relief for the suffering population. Mr. Sturge pointed out that many people in Britain had been gravely critical of the action of the fleet and that the relief fund he planned to raise was intended, not as an act of bounty or of mercy, but of mere justice. In the old Finnish capital of Abo (Turku) the Friends helped to gather together a committee of merchants who were prepared to administer any relief funds raised in Great Britain.

On their way back to England, they made a brief stay in St. Petersburg and drew up a letter and an appeal to the new Emperor, Alexander II (1855-1881). They told the Emperor that they had been led to visit his dominion by motives springing from that Christian love which is not limited by geographical boundaries, nor interrupted by international contests, but which embraces the whole human family. The Emperor was incouraged to pursue the principle of arbitration in settling international disputes, to permit the free circulation of the Bible in the Russian language, and to emancipate the serfs.

A report was made to a small group of Friends when the two returned to England, and a committee was formed to raise funds privately from members of the Society which was to be used to restore the fishing nets, boats and other equipment to the poorest of those who had suffered from the navy's attack. Mr. Sturge and his brother headed the subscription list with a sum of 1,000 pounds. The Quaker Committee seized the opportunity to send out a general appeal for assistance for Finland, which met with a liberal response. The Committee's intent of restitution to the war victims was merged in the effort to supply food immediately to the starving people at large. The relief fund raised in Great Britain amounted to 8,930 pounds all told, of which 7,345 pounds was allotted for the immediate relief of the starving, while the balance was invested for a term of eight years with the Agricultural and Farming Association in Turku.

A second call on the initiative of Friends came in 1891 when a series of bad harvests produced a great famine in the Volga provinces in 1891. The Quaker Committee sent relief to the starving in the Volga provinces.

In the German and Austrian drive of 1915 great numbers of Poles and Russians were driven out of Bessarabia and White Russia, many of whom settled in the lower Volga Valley. Quakers began relief work among these refugees in Russia in 1916. During the years 1921-1922, a terrible drought ruined the harvest in the Volga basin which produced accute famine. The war had seriously impaired the railroad system of Russia so that it was very difficult to get food stuffs into the region even where they were available. Friends undertook relief work among the refugees in Samara province and afterwards opened a center in Moscow which also had suffered from a serious food shortage. In 1921-1922 the Quakers fed 260,000 people daily in the Soviet Union. When the American Relief Administration was organized under the direction of Herbert C. Hoover (1874-1964), Friends' workers in Russia assisted it in the distribution of food. But in spite of the utmost endeavors of this and other relief organizations in England and of the League of Nations, it was estimated that at least 2 million people died of starvation and diseases of undernourishment in the Volga basin. Here again many of the workers contracted typhus fever from which two of them died. Anti-malaria work extended under the Quakers' care into Siberia as late as 1923. Friends continued to work in Russia with Moscow as a center, especially for the restocking of the peasants' farms and the care of orphan children until the Soviet government relieved them of further opportunities.[4]

### The Molokans

Because so many of the Molokans were converted to the Baptist ranks, it is necessary to know who they were. Simeon Uklein, a son-in-law of N. Pobirohkin, early Dukhobor leader, became dissatisfied with his father-in-law's contempt for the Bible and his claims to be "Christ" and judge of the universe and left the Dukhobors to form his own sect. Selecting 70 apostles among his peasant disciples, Uklein entered with them in a solemn procession into the city of Tambov, the residence of a bishop and of the governor of Tambov province. Acting with extreme boldness and self-assurance, Uklein began to preach his

4. Ibid., pp. 127-130.

gospel in the streets of the city. The authorities arrested Uklein and imprisoned him and his companions. After being thrown into prison, Uklein's disciples returned one after another to the Orthodox Church, and at last Uklein himself denounced his errors and was reconciled to the State Church.

Uklein, however, submitted only superficially; and after he was free again, he began to preach his doctrines again but far more discreetly. He achieved a remarkable success.

He proclaimed that the Bible was for him the sole authority of faith. The Old Testament was for him a guide to Christianity; and the New, its foundation. Christ, Uklein preached, founded one true Church, which visibly existed until the fourth century when the Fathers and the General Councils diluted the pure Word of God with pagan philosophy. Nevertheless, the Church did not disappear but survived in small scattered and persecuted communities of true Christians, among whom Uklein's followers take an honorable place.

However, Uklein was unable to overcome his strong unitarian tendency of the Russian sectarians. He considered Jesus Christ and the Holy Spirit inferior to the Father, although of the same substance. Christ, according to Uklein, was clothed with angelic flesh, and not human – that Christ used the same peculiar flesh which the archangel Raphael had used previously as related in the book of Tobit. Admitting the resurrection of the dead, Uklein believed that men will receive new bodies, different from those they now possess.

The social teaching of Uklein was one of equality of men. There must be neither rich nor poor, neither noble nor simple, neither masters nor servants. Uklein categorically rejected war and military service and approved of those who deserted. Like most of the Russian sectarians, Uklein was a strong anti-ritualist and denied any need of sacraments and rites.

Uklein's liturgy consisted of reading from the Bible, commenting on it, and singing hymns. The Orthodox called Uklein's followers Molokans, or Milk Drinkers, because they, rejecting fasts, drank milk during Lent, when it is forbidden in the Orthodox Church.

While Uklein abolished Christian fasts, he introduced among his disciples the observance of the Mosaic dietary law on the advice of Simeon Dalmatov, a convert minister of the Judaizers.[5]

[5] Bolshakoff, op. cit., pp. 105-107.

## CHAPTER III

# THE BEGINNING OF A GREAT REVIVAL IN THE RUSSIAN EMPIRE

### Spiritual Awakening in South Russia

The powerful revival movement in the middle of the 19th century, which by the turn of the century spread rapidly in the Russian Empire, was the result of a great spiritual hunger in the hearts of the Russian people and the activities of the German and Swedish missionaries.[1]

In the Russian Empire the revival movement arose almost simultaneously in three areas. In the Caucasus, the Christians received the name of Baptists. In the Ukraine, the Evangelicals were called Stundists; and the believers in St. Petersburg, known first as Pashkovites, were later identified as Evangelical Christians.

In reality, this was a single movement of a Russian religious reformation, confirmed by their nearly identical doctrine and their subsequent unity in one mighty Evangelical Baptist revival. The movement in Russia did not emerge from a religious vacuum. Rather it appealed to dissatisfied, open-hearted people among the Orthodox and the Molokans, who were seeking a faith that could fill their hearts with joy and peace. Many of the Molokans (Spiritual Christians) such as Voronin, Ivanoff and Pavlov searched the Scriptures for further truth. Nikita I. Voronin (1840-1905), a wealthy merchant and former Molokan leader, experienced his conversion by means of personal prayerful study of the Russian Bible.

In 1862 Martin Kalvet, a German artisan of the Baptist faith from Lithuania, had settled in Tiflis, Caucasus, and became an active propagandist of evangelical truth. He and Voronin were brought together by a Syrian evangelist Kasha Iagub, who preached for 30 years in Russia. Kalvet shared his evangelical beliefs with the merchant, including his understanding on the mode of water baptism. On August

[1] Chas. T. Byford, **Peasants and Prophets** (3d. ed.; London: The Kingsgate Press, 1914), pp. 76-84.

20, 1867, the latter was baptized by Martin Kalvet in the Kur River, Tiflis, and became the first Russian Evangelical believer to be baptized by immersion.[2]

This merchant baptized a young convert V. G. Pavlov (1854-1924) by name. These two, together with Ivanoff, began to preach the gospel among the Molokans; and in many villages churches were established. In 1875, Pavlov enrolled at the Hamburg Baptist Seminary in Germany and later was ordained to the ministry by John G. Oncken. The first Russian Baptist congregation was founded by Nikita Voronin in 1868 in Tiflis.[3]

The numerous German colonies in the south Ukraine provided the source of a new religious movement among the Russian peasants. Attracted by the better working conditions and standard of living in the German colonies, many Russian peasants and workers arrived annually at the colonies from many parts of Russia. Regardless of the government restrictions against the proselytizing of any Russian by the colonists, the laborers were invited to the "Stunde," the German term for Bible hours. In the homes of godly Germans they heard preaching in the Russian language and learned to read in order to study the Bible. Many were called Stundists in jest by the Orthodox as they visited the "Stunde." German Pastors Jacob Spener and the Bonekempers encouraged the godly to devote certain hours, especially on Sunday, to reading the Scriptures.

Conversions followed, and the number of Christians increased. Bible reading and study continued in peasant homes for six years before Efim Tsimbal was baptized in the Sugakle River by Abraham Unger in 1869, becoming the first Stundist to be immersed in water. In the same year, Tsimbal baptized Ivan G. Riaboshapka, who in 1871 baptized Mikhail Ratushnyi. The three Stundists spearheaded the new movement and were successful in gaining many converts among the Orthodox, the dissatisfied Molokans, and the Khlysty.

Most of the Stundists accepted infant baptism and maintained relationship with the old religion. However, their outward conformity to the State Church was mixed with inward contempt. At this point of spiritual conflict, the visiting Baptist ministers from Germany encouraged many Stundists to take a definite stand. The transference to the Baptist ranks was so common that they were called Stundobaptists

2. Durasoff, op. cit., pp. 36-37.

3. Byford, op. cit., p. 80.

by the Orthodox. By 1877 about 10 provinces between the Austrian border and the Volga River contained about 250,000 Stundists, with the province of Kiev in the lead, numbering 80,000. Thus the new revival movement in the Ukraine became the religion of Russian peasants.[4]

**The palace square and the monument of Alexander I. At the left is the former Royal Palace.**

### Pavlov, the Great Pioneer

One of the greatest workers in the pioneer days of the Baptist movement was V. G. Pavlov. Shortly after his conversion in 1870, he began to preach the gospel and frequently visited the villages around Tiflis, with the result that quite a few churches were started. For 10 years he regularly preached the gospel in and around the city. At that time no obstacles were placed in his way, and the work grew amazingly; many hundreds of people were saved and baptized. From Tiflis the work spread throughout Transcaucausia to the Transcaspian States.

In the beginning of Pavlov's work, V.V. Ivanoff-Klishnikoff (1846-1919) was a great help to Pavlov in spreading the gospel. When

[4] Durasoff, op. cit., pp. 39-41.

Pavlov started out, Ivanoff-Klishnikoff was 25. Ivanoff travelled as a missionary, and during the years of 1871 to 1876 founded many Baptist churches in Transcaucausia.

From 1901 to 1907 Pavlov served as the general missionary of the Baptist Union, an appointment made at the congress of 1884 but rarely discharged because of successive terms in exile. During this period he concentrated his activity in Transcaucausia and the region of the lower Don. In 1907 the Baptist Union organized a Mission Society and named Pavlov its chairman. To discharge these new responsibilities more effectively, Pavlov moved the base of his operations from Tiflis to Odessa. Each of the three years that it functioned, the Society engaged from 20 to 26 missionaries who traveled and preached the gospel and spent for this purpose more than $4,000. In 1910, unable to obtain permission from the authorities to legally exist, the Mission Society ceased its operations. Freed from this responsibility, Pavlov took over the editorship of "The Baptist" (Baptist), the weekly organ of the Baptist Union.

In addition to the broader tasks of missionary administrator and religious editor, Pavlov served as the Pastor of a Baptist church in Odessa. He preached in a large hired prayer hall that seated 760 persons. The gatherings were always crowded, especially Sunday evenings. During his activity in Odessa, in the space of three years there were added to the church 185 souls through baptism. In 1910 there were established many mission stations in the vicinity of Odessa as in Nikolayev, Tiraspol, Bendery, and Kishinev. Three of those stations were Russian, one German, and one Jewish-Christian congregation of baptized members.

The work of Pavlov in South Russia was ably supported by D.I. Mazaiev (1852?-1922) and F.P. Balikhin (1854-1920?). Mr. Mazaiev was born of Molokan parents in Rostov-on-Don. He was converted in 1887, and two years later he became Chairman of the Baptist Union. Mazaiev was re-elected to this post, with but few exceptions, at every Baptist congress up to the year 1920. He had great organizing ability. He succeeded in convening Baptist congresses in the extremely difficult years of 1889, 1890, and 1898. He was the chief inspirer of the annual congress held between 1902 and 1915.

Led by Mr. Mazaiev, the Baptists wove their various ideological strands together by adopting "Articles of Faith," launched a missionary drive by appointing itinerant evangelists, and strengthened their indoctrination work by inaugurating a weekly publication. "The

Baptist," which was first edited by Mazaiev, appeared in 1907. Later the four Mazaiev brothers, of which two were Baptists and two Molokans, moved from the Lower Don region to Siberia. These men in the new lands founded and developed an agricultural enterprise that brought them great wealth.

In 1908, D.I. Mazaiev organized the Siberian Baptist Union as a federated division of the Russian Baptist Union. In the same year, with means provided by the Mazaiev brothers, the Siberian Baptists constructed and dedicated a tabernacle with a seating capacity of 8,000 in the city of Omsk. D.I. Mazaiev was elected as a member of one of the Russian Dumas.

Mr. F. B. Balikhin was born of Molokan parents in 1854 and was converted in 1882. Two years later he was appointed one of the 33 delegates to the first Russian Baptist Congress. From 1904 to 1908 Mr. Balakhin travelled on missionary duty for the Baptist Union in 35 provinces of the Russian Empire. During this period he organized 40

**The Neva River in Leningrad. The former Royal Palace in the background.**

Baptist churches, baptized over 1,300 persons, and ordained 58 presbyters, deacons and preachers. In 1908 Balikhin attended the international congress in Berlin, Germany, as a representative of the Russian Baptist Union.

The New Mennonites and the German Baptist colonists formed

the nucleus of the German Baptist Union in Russia, which by 1911 claimed about 27,000 adherents.[5]

### Revival in Rohrback in the Ukraine

God's chosen tool in Rohrback was Pastor Johannes Bonekemper (1795-1857). He was born in Numbrecht in the Oberbergischer Kreis of the Rhineland. After his military service, he became a member of Pastor Doring's young men's association where he heard about the German emigrants to the Ukraine. It was at this place that he heard his Lord's call to the ministry. In October 1821 he went to Basle mission school where he studied for two and a half years, one of his subjects being the English language. He was ordained in 1824 and left for Rohrback, north of Odessa on the Black Sea.

His parish included some 2,500 community members. Besides the village of Rohrback, there were settlements of Worms, Johannesthal, Friedrichsthal, Waterloo, Stuttgart and Julienfeld – all between one and a half and two and a half hours' journey away. There were also a few scattered German Protestants in the three nearest towns: Voznesensk, Nikolayev, and the provincial capital of Kherson, which was 150 kilometers away. Johannes Bonekemper labored here for 24 years, until 1848.

The condition of the community was very bad – alcoholism and immorality were widespread, and the school was in a state of neglect. He began with the young people and soon introduced community Bible studies in hope of bringing a revival, which reached its peak in the years 1835-1846.

Pastor Johannes Bonekemper was a key figure in the stundist revival, and for a decade Rohrback was cited by the authorities and by the Orthodox Church as the place where it started. It was here that the spiritually awakened Ukrainians gained their first teaching, and also advice in their early needs and difficulties.

When Pastor Bonekemper started in Rohrback in 1824 with great fervor and hope to change the pathetic spiritual and moral condition, to his surprise 10 years later, the picture had not changed very much. In the fifth year of his ministry, the Spirit of God began to move a little. In March 1829 the attendance at the normal Sunday and festival

[5] Ibid., pp. 48-52.

services had been unusually observant and numerous. The weekly catechismal sermons, which had been introduced there over this time, had been listened to by many with reverence. In great demand were the private gatherings in the homes for edification.

The people began to visit the Pastor either by day, or by night like Nicodemus for fear of the Jews. During those visits, people told the Pastor about their fear, their need, and the danger in which their souls stood, and begged the Pastor to tell them how to get saved.

During a funeral service, a woman heard the words from Isaiah 26:2, "Open the gates, that the righteous nation which keepeth faith may enter in." Terror struck, she recognized that she did not belong to the righteous nation because she had not kept the faith. The next day came her husband, saying that he could no longer endure the disturbance of his soul! He had already been on his way to the Pastor several times, but had always turned back again. Soon after this came a man who had been earnestly reading the Bible with another who had been a soldier for 8 years – a rough, godless man. He had heard the sermon about the four-fold field and was afraid that he belonged to the bad ground. Soon after that came his companion and confessed that he had been struggling for years with the flesh, the world and the devil, but now along with other visitors, was singing and praying with them. The doors of the Pastor's house were open both day and night to those seeking salvation.

In his pastoral ministry, Bonekemper always pointed to a right relationship with Jesus Christ and the necessity of the new birth. Even those who only passed through his home as guests heard about the one thing that was necessary – salvation of one's soul.

In order to protect the growing movement from the sects that were widespread in southern Russia, he moved the meetings into the schoolhouse, chose a council of eight brethren, and together with them worked out an ordinance for the stunden. Three men were elected as leaders. After a message to a large audience on Hebrews 10:19-25, the ordinance was read out and within a week it was signed by the participants. There were about a hundred members. The Pastor found great support in a Christian teacher, Eberhard, from the settlement of Worms, who led the Stunde there.

In the winter of 1837-1838 the wave of revival rose once again. In the colony of Waterloo sometimes half of the whole community attended the Stunde. The young people were particularly gripped by the Spirit of God in those days. In 1846 there were turbulent revivals, but they were all directed into the structured meetings. Thus any splits were avoided.

Pastor Bonekemper was invited to preach in the surrounding communities also. In 1838 he accompanied his provost on a tour of visitation through Bessarabia. Both in Tarutino and in Sarata, Ignaz Lindl's former congregation, he was asked to remain as Pastor. But Bonekemper remained faithful to Rohrback until 1848. It was only then that he was forced through gossip originating from Odessa to take a congregation in Dobrudja, which at that time still belonged to Turkey.

When Pastor Bonekemper ministered in Rohrback, his oldest son Karl held the Stunde in Russian for the Russian harvesters. These Stunden were undoubtedly the basis for the awakening of several men who later became leaders in the Russian stundism. It was as a result of the profound revival in Rohrback, which God granted during his ministry, that some 10 years after his departure from Rohrback the spark of revival spread to the Ukrainian peasants. Johannes Bonekemper ministered for a few more years until 1853 in the German settlement of Atmagea. At the outbreak of the Crimean War, the Turks left the Dobrudja region. Bonekemper then returned to his native Germany. He was laid to rest in his native Numbrecht in the Oberbergischer Kreis. On his tombstone is inscribed the name "father of stundism."

The Stunde in Rohrback remained intact until the Bolshevik era.[6]

**German Baptist Influence in Poland**

The history on the Baptist movement in Poland is not easily written. The various sections of the country were, in earlier years, politically separated under alien rule. Owing to this separation and to linguistic differences, the denomination movement appears in a number of isolated beginnings.

It was among the German colonists of Poland then under Russian rule that the Baptist movement appeared. On Sunday, November 28, 1858, at Adamow, nine persons, converted through the ministry of the German Baptists, were baptized. Among these was the young teacher Gottfried Alf (1831-1898), who became the pioneer in this region of a vigorous evangelistic work which within 10 years had won about a

6. Brandenburg, op. cit., pp. 48-55.

thousand converts. The State Church tried to stop the Baptist movement by imposing heavy penalties, arrests and imprisonments. Trials were made the occasion of preaching to judges; imprisonments furnished opportunities of winning converts.

The first Baptist church in Poland was founded in Adamow, as well as the first mission school where a number of young men were trained as preachers. In July 1860 Alf visited Kicin which became another Baptist center. The first convert of that place was Mr. Ewert, a Mennonite, who lent Alf his house as a preaching place. The rooms proved too small; after the first meeting, a barn had to be secured. Several people were converted including Ewert, who became a Baptist preacher, and a church was established which became the most influential center in Poland. Rev. Mr. Gottfried Alf transferred his residence to Kicin, and there for many years directed the Baptist movement.

In process of time the denomination steadily advanced, and from the year 1859 a Baptist church in Edinburg, Scotland, supported Mr. Alf.

In the beginning, the spiritual movement was almost exclusively confined to the German minority in the land. Of the 4,162 Baptists in 1900, not more than 200 were Slavs, and these were mainly Bohemian settlers. The German colonists, who had welcomed the gospel message, were, unlike the Polish nationals, loyal subjects of the Russian Emperor. For the Polish language and tradition they cared little, and as a rule their children were educated in German and Russian; but no pains were taken to teach them the language of the mass of the people. It was difficult for such people to win Polish converts, especially in view of the widespread idea that national loyalty and Roman Catholicism belonged together, and that to become a Protestant was to cease to be a good Pole.

The few Poles who became Baptists found themselves forming insignificant minorities in foreign-speaking churches, while in daily life they were exposed to the hatred or contempt of their fellow-Slavs. As a result, most of them lapsed or emigrated to the United States.

About 1908 Mr. Truderung from Warsaw began to preach in Polish and won a few young people. His successor, the Rev. Mr. F. Brauer, followed up the work. About the same time, the Rev. Mr. J. Petraz began preaching in Posen as a Polish missionary.

In 1872 a Bohemian (Czechish) church was organized in the

village of Zelow under the leadership of K. Jersak, a Bohemian who had been converted in 1869.[7]

## The Baptist Movement in Lithuania

The Lithuanians are racially and linguistically akin to the Letts. In 1841, a Baptist church was founded in Memel by the Rev. Mr. Oncken, the famous German preacher. It attracted Lithuanians living on the German side of the frontier; and of these several were converted, baptized and received into fellowship in 1860. After the conversion of a gifted Lithuanian named Albrecht, efforts were made to extend the work for his race to the other side of the frontier. Those efforts were largely frustrated by the Roman Catholic clergy, with the help of the Russian government, which placed every possible difficulty in the way of the evangelical movement.

In the capital city of Kowno (Lithuanian Kaunas) a German-speaking church existed. Mission work commenced there in 1879, and for 10 years was carried on under the control of the church at Eydtkuhnen, East Prussia. The growing difficulties in communicating with the mother church across the border led to the organization of an independent church in 1889. Its most effective minister was the Rev. Mr. Otto Lenz, who after World War I moved to Poland. During his pastorate from 1900 to 1911, the church founded stations in Vilna and Bialystok, cities which after the war were ceded to Poland. Before 1914 the church in Kowno had 230 members. Mission work in the Russian language was carried on by the Kowno church, and a few Russians were converted. At that time there was not yet any preaching in the Lithuanian language to the masses.

The Baptist activities were greatly enhanced by the Rev. Mr. Theodour Gerikas (1890-1945?), who was converted in a Lettish Baptist church in 1906, and at once the longing awoke to preach the gospel to his own people. From 1908 he assisted Mr. J.A. Frey of Riga as a colporteur. Soon he became a translator of tracts and pamphlets into Lithuanian, and Frey's press printed some of his work.

Because there were no theological institutions in the Russian Empire, he entered the Hamburg Seminar in 1912. In the next year he was recalled to serve in the medical corps of the Russian army. During World War I several of the soldiers who had been captured and placed in

7. Byford, op. cit., pp. 81-82.

the German and Austrian prison camps were saved and returned to Lithuania to witness to their own people.

In 1910 there was a spiritual movement among the few thousand Calvinists in Lithuania, but owing to lack of leadership, this degenerated into disorderly fanaticism.

After the war, Mr. Gerikas continued with his successful work in Lithuania.[8]

**The Baptist Movement in Latwia**

The Baptist churches in the Czarist Latwia did not result from foreign missionary activities, but from a religious movement in the nation. From 1847 to 1879 in a village school of Ziras on the seashore of Kurzeme a pious Lutheran, a Mr. Hamburger, was working as a teacher.

He did not ask his pupils to recite their prayers learned from a prayer book, but taught them to kneel down and tell God about their needs. In such devotions also the pupils' parents participated, and eventually a group of believers came into existence who occasionally came together to appraise their own lives and convictions as well as that of the State Church in the light of the Bible. The leader of this group was one of Mr. Hamburger's pupils, Ernests Eglitis (1830-1919) who later became their Pastor. In 1857, Mr. Adams Gertners (1829-1875) joined this group.

In 1855, under the leadership of a salesman, Mr. Kanaiss, a group of people in Liepaja began to search for the divine truth as it is revealed in the Bible. Around 1859 a group of spiritually awakened people began to gather together in Ventspils under the leadership of Janis Vikstrems (1829-1913).

In 1857 a German Baptist family moved from Memel (now Klaipeda) to Grobina. In 1859 Mr. Gertners had several encounters with this family. Those talks made it evident that the seekers for the truth were identical with the Baptists. In the course of one of the conversations, Mr. Gertners, having already understood the meaning of the biblical immersion, exclaimed: "Now I know upon what I am standing. Now I know what I must do."

Convinced of the truth of water baptism by immersion, the trailblazers of the Latwian Baptist movement took a daring step and

8. Ibid., pp. 83-84.

went to Memel to be baptized by immersion. On September 2, 1860, about nine Latwians were baptized in Memel, among them also Adams Gertners. This event is considered by the Baptists of Latwia as the beginning of their history. In June 1861, two more groups made their way to Memel to be baptized. For this decisive step, many of them were severely persecuted.

The first act of water baptism in Latwia by immersion was performed by Mr. A. Gertners on September 22, 1861, in Ziras river, baptizing about 72 converts. A month later, another group of believers were baptized by immersion.

The first Baptist churches in Latwia were organized in 1861 in Sakas, Uzava and in Ventspils. In 1863 several more churches were established in Piltene, Skatre and in Liepaja. The Baptist church, Sakuma (the beginning) in Riga, was founded in 1867. Mr. Adams Gertners carried upon his shoulders the greatest responsibility of the young Latwian Baptist movement. He was severely punished for his faith.

The first school of general education belonging to the Latwian Baptist Church was founded in 1870 in Gramzda. The same year the first Young People's Society was organized in Riga's Sakuma church. The first Sunday School in Riga, Latwia, began its work under the leadership of the Rev. Mr. J. Zirnicks and professor V. Ritters in 1870.

Mixed choir singing in the Baptist churches began in 1870 in Riga, in Ventspils and in Liepaja. Over 2,000 songs were published by the choir leader Jekabs Simanis (1865-1941). At present (1980) there are about 900 choir singers in the Baptist churches in the Soviet Latwia.

The literary work began in 1875. The first Baptist paper, "Evangelist," was published and edited by Mr. J. Rumbergs (1846-1923) from 1881 to 1887. Later several more Christian papers appeared. The "Avots" (The Spring), "Kristigs Draugs," (The Christian Friend), "Kristigs Vestnesis," (The Christian Messenger), and others. The first hymnal in Latwia was published in 1880 by Mr. Rumbergs, and in 1909 by Mr. J. Inkis (1875-1958). In the Soviet Latwia, the hymnal was published in Riga by Mr. M. Dakne in 1978.

The publishing of Christian calendars began in 1888. Since 1979 the calendars are published by the Brotherhood of Latwian Baptist churches in Riga. In 1882 an organized women's work began in the church to help in the Lord's work. At the present, the women give their time and abilities to the loving service of others in the local churches.

The ministers and workers in the early days had no theological training. They studied and majored in the ministry. The first Pastors who received some education were Mr. Rumbergs and Mr. M. Riss, who had completed a few theological courses in Humburg, Germany. Since 1876, there were held three- to four-week-long Bible courses in the Latwian Baptist churches to improve the qualification of religious workers.

From the beginning of the Baptist movement, a wonderful unity prevailed in the local churches. From 1866 to 1874 Mr. Adams Gertners was Bishop of the Baptist churches in Kurzeme, who from the beginning united the Latwian Baptist churches for common thought and work. In the district of Liepaja, Pastor Skuja Dingse (1820-1874), leader of the churches in that area, was a good educator of young workers. In 1875, at the Convention of the Baptist churches, a Committee of Missions was elected to head the team work of which Pastor J. Rumbergs was the leader until 1884.

From 1885 to 1891 the churches were troubled by the spirit of dissention during which time Pastor Janis Kulbergs (1848-1895) was a wise leader. He restored the unity and later the united work was headed by Pastor Janis Inkis.

**Riga, the Capital of Latwia**

In the Soviet Latwia, since 1977 the Latwian Baptist Brotherhood is headed by Bishop J. Tervits (born 1936). At the celebration of the

120th anniversary (1980) there were about 61 Baptist churches with 5,500 members, including 700 Russian believers. At the present, about 46 ministers serve in the local churches, and 16 retired ministers also minister in the churches. The Baptist churches of Latwia are in connection with the Baptist World Alliance.[9]

Another noteworthy worker and administrator in those days was Rev. Mr. John A. Frey (1863-1935?). His parents were poor, but his mother was a well educated Christian woman who was able to speak in five languages, encouraged the passion for knowledge which the young boy early displayed. By hard study in Riga, an important seaport in those days in the Russian Empire, he qualified as a teacher.

He was converted in 1876 and promptly began to preach the gospel while following his profession. The youthful preacher's success in Riga and the district was extraordinary. Soon his great unusual administrative abilities and talents were manifested. He had unusual organizing and executive powers. He took hold of a church with a crushing debt and a depleted congregation. Within four years its mortgage was cleared and substantial sums of money were afterwards raised for missions and for a new building.

At the same time realizing the appalling lack of Christian literature in Latwia, he set up a small publishing business. His knowledge of German and English enabled him to select the best books, especially those written by Spurgeon and Moody. He translated many tracts into the Latwian language, which were published and distributed by his colporteurs.

In 25 years the output reached 728 books and over 2.7 million tracts. The enterprise was financially successful, and the publishing house came to possess the finest printing plant in Latwia.

Mr. Frey was an author as well as a publisher. His best known work was, "The Land Where Jesus Walked." It was published in five languages. As an educationist, he had always been deeply conscious of the need of a trained ministry. In the Russian Empire, no theological institution could operate; but he formed the ingenious plan of a "traveling seminary," providing a month of study for preachers every winter. He himself taught Lettish grammar, history, pastoral theology and biblical exegesis. Espionage and police raids seriously hampered the "traveling seminary."

An exceptional feature of an evangelical pioneer in Russia was active participation in public life. John A. Frey, however, in spite of his own identification with the despised and harassed Baptists, secured the confidence of the leading men in the great commercial city of Riga, and for 11 years served on the Board of Aldermen of Riga.

When World War I began in 1914, the Lettish Baptists appointed him their delegate to convey gifts and relief to the Russian army in the war zone. However, in 1915 he was exiled to Siberia as a dissenting preacher. In 1917 he returned home to find the Germans occupying Riga. After their departure, the communists secured the upper hand and Mr. Frey was arrested as a member of the "bourgeoisie." He spent several months in prison under hard conditions; but his Christian serenity, ready wit, and manifest detachment from political intrigues secured his liberation. After the war when Latwia became an independent republic, Mr. Frey continued with his activity until his death.[10]

### The Baptist Movement in Estonia

It was after a long period of formal Christianity that revival began in the last quarter of the 19th century. The year 1877 witnessed a great outburst of religious feeling in the country of Estonia, and first of all among the Swedish-speaking inhabitants of the islands of Worms and Esterholm, initiated by the Swedish missionaries. After the Swedish missionaries were expelled by the Russian authorities, the converts, which probably numbered in the thousands, were left on their own. Two years after the departure of the missionaries, a credulous and fanatical spirit took possession of some of the more enthusiastic of these. Visions, revelations and tongues, and similar phenomena became common, and even gross sins of the flesh.

The remnant of faithful persons, who received the nickname of "holy vagabonds," refused to be swept into fanaticism, or to relapse into conventionalism. They steadily maintained evangelical preaching and were responsible for a daring innovation which brought them into sharp collision with the religious traditions of their neighbors. They ceased to observe the Lord's Supper in the familiar forms and adopted practices suggested to them through direct study of the New Testament. They avowed their intention to realize, as far as possible in every respect, the primitive and apostolic ideal of the Church.

It was noteworthy that ill-educated men and women, some of them comparatively young but speaking from a real experience, were

[10] Byford, op. cit., pp. 85-86.

able gospel preachers. In the midst of this mental and spiritual upheaval came the recognition that baptism should be associated with personal faith. The time of preparation, during which infant baptism was rejected, and the character of the New Testament Church came slowly to be understood, may be dated from about 1877; and it lasted until 1884. The evangelical groups knew nothing of Baptists; it was by the reading of the New Testament, interpreted by the Holy Spirit of God, that they had reached their position.

Realizing that faith should preceed baptism, they first sprinkled one of their number, and he in turn sprinkled the others upon personal confession. Further study of the New Testament brought to light the idea of baptism as a "burial." It was after long search for fruth that they heard for the first time of the existence of churches in St. Petersburg and Riga, which were communities of believers, and whose baptism, celebration of the Lord's Supper, and discipline were modeled on New Testament practice. They sought instruction from the church in St. Petersburg, and A.R. Schiewe, a German Pastor in that city, was sent to them. It was on February 11, 1884, that the first baptism by immersion of nine believers took place at the city of Hapsal (Haapsalu) on the Baltic Sea. On the following day, Pastor Schiewe baptized 15 more in ice-cold water, 13 degress below the freezing point. Thousands of spectators had assembled for this second occasion. In a certain sense, this German Pastor may be regarded as having definitely founded the Baptist community in Estonia.

About the same time as the Hapsal baptisms took place, Juljus Herrmann, Pastor of the German Baptist church in Riga, baptized seven persons near the city of Pernau (Parnu), in a neighborhood on which the revival already had taken a firm hold. The brethren suffered much persecution, and some of the preachers and believers were deported to Siberia.

The Estonian Baptist Association was founded in 1896, but was suppressed by the Russian authorities. It resumed its activities at the conclusion of World War I when Estonia became an independent republic.[11]

One of the great pioneers of the Baptist movement was Rev. Mr. Peter Kaups (1856-1926). He was saved in 1881 and baptized in 1885. This great preacher established six Baptist churches and baptized about

[11] J.H. Rushbrooke, **Some Chapters of European Baptist History**, (London: The Kingsgate Press, 1929) pp. 39-44.

2,000 persons. He was incarcerated 14 times for the preaching of the gospel of Jesus Christ.

The revival movement also touched some of the aristocratic families in Estonia. Baron Manfred von Ghlen (1867-1924) was saved in 1889 and was called by the Lord into the ministry. He founded two Baptist churches. Another aristocratic preacher was Baron Woldemar von Uxkull, who was saved in 1890, baptized the following year, and began to preach the gospel. He founded a Baptist church in 1898.

By 1916 there were about 37 Baptist churches in Estonia.[12]

### Podin – The Apostle of Mercy

The Rev. Mr. Adam K. Podin (1862-1935?) was born in Lithuania. He received a good education and was able to speak in seven languages and preach in five. He was in his native country as a school master under the Russian government. When he was converted in 1889, he was promptly dismissed from his office. Following his dismissal, he went to England in the same year to visit friends in London; and after a few months in Great Britian he returned home and was baptized by Baron Stackelberg, Pastor of the church in Kegel. Later he returned to London and spent some time in the Missionary Training Home at Drayton Park, N. At the conclusion of his studies, he returned to Kegel, where he succeeded Baron Stackelberg in the pastorate in 1900.

A highly placed official in St. Petersburg, a Bapist, approached him with a request that he should visit the prisons throughout the northern part of the Russian Empire, including the exile settlements in Siberia. Thus Mr. Podin was destined to become the Russian prisoner's friend, the God-equipped man for the work. The necessary papers were obtained, granting him permission to hold gospel services in the prisons, exile settlements, and etapes – the latter on the great Siberian road.

In addition to his services as preacher, he was well supplied with a thousand copies of the New Testament for free distribution among the prisoners and convicts he met on his journeys.

On one journey in the spring of 1911, he distributed 3,400 New Testaments in seven different languages. At Perm, the great exile-forwarding station from whence the convict convoys started almost daily on their way to Siberia, the Prison Inspector, after examining his papers, promised to help him and invited the preacher to

12. **Viiskummend Aastat Apostlite Radadel,** (Tallinn: Eesti Baptisti Liit, 1934), p.127. Translated from Estonian by Albert W. Olema.

be his houseguest during his stay in the town. Altogether there were more than 6,000 prisoners awaiting their turn for the road. The Inspector impressed upon his visitor that in speaking to the convicts he would be addressing men who probably would never see Russia proper again. The Governor assembled the men in groups, and the first day was spent with 180 men, all manacled and fettered, sentenced to life transportation, destined for the gold mines beyond the Urals. As he spoke to them of the risen Christ, tears streamed down the cheeks of many; and the Word, preached in such strange surroundings and with great simplicity, reached the hearts of men about to commence their long tramp along the way to their destination.

The second day was devoted to 800 men, all manacled, sentenced to 20 years exile, who were leaving the following day for the Amur, there to help build a branch railway as forced laborers. The Governor related to Mr. Podin that those men would never return; the majority of them would die before they completed the first five years of their service. They were to travel thousands of kilometers, through forests and across deserts where there was no human habitation.

The third day was devoted to the women convicts, of whom more than 200 were gathered together in one group. Many of them were quite young, some fresh from their classes in the university – young women going into exile for the crime of loving their fellow beings too

**The former Holy Synod in Leningrad**

well and seeking their material welfare in a manner contrary to the regulations of the central government.

So the days passed by until more than 6,000 men and women had been reached, the majority of them gladly accepting the gift of a New Testament. On that same journey, Mr. Podin visited a prison high up in the Ural Mountains. The Governor was very courteous and assisted the preacher all that he possibly could. On Sunday, a thousand men were assembled, and after service leave was given for personal interviews with those impressed during the service.

One service was always vividly in Mr. Podin's memory. Before meeting a group of men, the Governor informed him that 15 of his hearers were to be shot on the following morning. Their identity was hidden from the preacher, and the men themselves were unaware of the fate awaiting them with the rising of the morrow's sun.

In 1900 Mr. Podin settled down in Keila, Estonia, which at that time was a province of Russia. He founded a vigorous Baptist church in Keila with many outlying stations, and a spacious chapel was built and maintained in Keila. In 1905 Mr. Podin began another distinctive enterprise by devoting himself to the spiritual welfare of the numerous lepers in Estonia at that time. Between 10 percent and 15 percent of the lepers in Estonia were baptized by him and were accepted as members of his church in Keila. He was a very busy man in the service of the Lord. His trips to the prisons in the Russian Empire, his responsibility for the church in Keila and evangelistic trip in Estonia made him a distinguished minister of the gospel of Jesus Christ. When Estonia became independent, he became the first Rector of the Theological Seminary in Keila, which was founded in 1922.[13]

### A Mighty Revival in Tallinn in Czarist Estonia

In 1895 Tallinn was blessed by a mighty visitation of God. John Rubanovitsch (1864-1941), a converted Jew from Lithuania who had moved to Tallinn, was baptized in the Estonia State Church according to the Lutheran rites. The Spirit of the living God at once began to move in the life of this young convert.

In 1895 Mr. Rubanovitsch began with his first revival at the Evangelistic Center (Brethren) on Liivalaia Street, which accommodated about 500 people. The move of the Holy Spirit was of

[13] Byford, op. cit., pp. 128-133.

an extraordinary magnitude, and the revival meetings continued for two years. Very often more people were standing in the yard than in the crowded church. Most of the outsiders even did not hear the message, but in great agony called on the name of the Lord for mercy, like those inside.

During the next two years, meetings were held twice every day, sometimes with three meetings a day, producing remarkable results. According to the information available, it can be concluded that some 2,000 people were saved.

The new converts were more openminded than the major established Christians and spoke openly of God's work in an atmosphere of continuous revival, being led and controlled by the Holy Spirit rather than by leaders of any denomination. However, the conditions were not favorable.

In 1905 thousands of red-minded and restless workers in Tallinn joined the revolutionary movement. Because of the ill outcome of the Russo-Japanese War of 1905 when Russia was totally defeated by Japan, tension ran very high. However, Christians during that time were praying for another revival. Mr. J. Rubanovitsch, who had moved to Hamburg, Germany, returned to Tallinn in 1905 to visit his mother and to help the local brethren.

However, Mr. Rubanovitsch was not welcome to hold meetings anymore at the Liivalaia church. However, Allika Street Baptist church opened the doors for him. This church had only 250 seats, which were filled and about a thousand people were standing outside. In June 1905 a wealthy Christian merchant, James Liljendahl (1871-1952), allowed the evangelist to hold meetings on his property which was about three kilometers from the city. The merchant had a big cottage which was to serve as a meeting place. However, about a thousand people had come to hear the evangelist, who had to speak to the crowd from an open window on the second floor. This date is considered as the beginning of the Estonian Free Church. The people of Tallinn, hearing about the revival in the cottage, thronged the building the next night – with about 5,000 people circling the cottage. Mr. Rubanovitsch had to climb up on the roof where he could speak to the whole multitude. The Spirit moved so mightily on the hearts of the people that almost everywhere in the crowd one could hear the same question, "What shall we do?"

The meetings lasted for two months. Several thousand people were saved and Christians revived and edified. Because of the great revival, opposition grew strong, which forced the Brethren to move back into the city where they were able to rent a church for meetings.

The Russian government did not give the believers permission to build a church of their own, but in 1912 Mr. Liljendahl got permission to erect a warehouse for the storage of merchandise, which was to be converted later on into a church building. The church had about 1,200 seats.

Taking into consideration the fact that Tallinn in 1895 had a population of only 65,000, the nightly crowd of 5,000 can be considered as an unusual manifestation of great spiritual hunger and of the move of the Holy Spirit.[14]

**Tallinn, Capital city of Estonia**

## Estonian Baptist Church in Siberia

In 1894 a Baptist sister, Madli Miller of Narva, moved to the Estonian village in Siberia. In that Estonian community there was not even one Christian. Sister Miller prayed five years that the Lord would send a revival to the Estonian village. She invited preachers from other locations to visit the Estonians and preach the gospel.

The first preacher who visited the Estonian community in Siberia was Brother Tonurist from Simveropol. He preached for a while and

[14]. John Laks, **Arkamistuuled Kodumaal,** (Toronto: Ortoprint, 1966), pp. 16-22. Translated from Estonian by Albert W. Olema.

several people got saved. As the revival spread in the village, they invited Brother J. Brantmann and P. Ane from Narva, Estonia, to establish a Baptist congregation. In 1904 they baptized about 20 people. The Brethren stayed about one year in the Estonian village in Siberia with good blessings of God bestowed upon their ministry.

Brother Juri Miller was elected as their Pastor. After his death his son, Alexander Miller, was elected as his successor.

Because of the forceful preaching of the Estonian Brethren in the surrounding area, several large Russian churches were established. The Estonian Baptist church in Siberia was a thriving church until the Communists closed it down.

### Pastor Raud's Evangelical Activities in Estonia

Pertel Raud (1834-1918) was saved in 1860 in his native Estonia through reading a Bible which someone had given to him as a gift. Upon his conversion, he dedicated his life to the service of the Lord. He read the Word of God continually, which strengthened his faith and made him a man of prayer. Mr. Raud had only one purpose in life – to reach souls for Christ. This zealous man of God went to various towns and villages together with other believers, gathering the people together as many as possible in the farmhouses for evangelistic services, and preached Jesus Christ to them which always produced good results. The spiritual need was very great among the peasants, and Mr. Raud with his faithful wife, did their best to meet that need.

Around 1868 Mr. Pertel Raud founded a church in Kadrina, Northern Estonia, which he pastored for 50 years. He had much opposition from the police, which sometimes threatened him with heavy penalties. Regardless of the persecution, he managed to establish many gatherings or Christian groups in Estonia. Some of these groups had members in the congregation who were gifted by the Lord to preach. These men would branch out from their groups to reach the surrounding areas. This faithful servant often traveled on sleigh with his two sons, Wil and Gans, from place to place in the winters, winning hundreds of souls to Christ.[15]

[15]. Doris Salter, **The Story of the Bible Christian Union,** (New York: Bible Christian Union, 1968), pp. 16-21

## CHAPTER IV

# THE GREAT 19th CENTURY REVIVAL PENETRATES INTO THE 20th CENTURY

### Swedish Missionary Activity in the Province of Estonia

The third contributing factor to the revival was the activities of a Swedish Missionary Society, concerned for the welfare of Swedes living in Estonia. Two Lutheran Pastors, Thoren and Osterblom, were sent. The Rev. Mr. Ture E. Thoren (1843-1930) was a member of a Swedish aristocratic family and was converted at the age of 20. The Rev. Mr. Lars J. Osterblom (1837-1932) was the son of a Swedish mason, converted in his late twenties. These two young men studied four years at the Johannelund Mission's Institute in Stockholm, preparing for missionary work.[1]

In 1873, after graduating from the Institute, they volunteered to go to Estonia in response to the request of Pastor Lars Mozell from Tallinn, who asked a Swedish Missionary Society to send some teachers to this Baltic province to teach the people to read. In August the same year, Thoren and Osterblom arrived in Tallinn, Estonia.

Thoren settled in the village of Paslepa – a Swedish settlement – on the Baltic Sea Coast. He opened a seminary in 1873 in the same community to train teachers for the Swedish people on the coastal regions. Twelve young men enrolled in the fall semester. Most of them were Swedes, but a few were Estonians. The teaching was performed in the Swedish language, but they also studied Estonian, German and Russian. The Bible was one of the main text books which brought revival to the seminary, resulting in the conversion of eight young men. Prayer meetings were held in the evenings where the Christians sang and testified. Young people from the surrounding area came to hear the new songs, learned them and brought these spiritual songs back to their own homes, singing the songs to their families.

Soon the people were interested in the new teaching and in the songs. Thoren was invited by the people to their villages to preach the

[1] Byford, op. cit., pp. 81-82.

gospel. The students also arranged prayer meetings in the communities, and the revival spread from village to village. New life in Christ made the people happy. Places of amusement were in trouble. Because of the lack of customers, seven taverns were forced to close down. The seminary was closed down by the authorities in 1886, and Mr. Thoren returned to Sweden.

Osterblom settled down on the island of Vormsi, populated by the Swedes. He too opened a school to teach children. He had about 144 children, 84 boys and 60 girls, in his school. Mr. Osterblom arranged meetings to preach to the people forgiveness through faith in Christ. A real revival broke out in the spring of 1876.

The second revival brok out in 1878, and the third in 1879. During the summer of 1881 many of the converts who were working at various places were deprived of the privilege of hearing the Word of God and grew cold. A spiritual indolence settled over the flock. In the fall of the same year, Osterblom spoke from Matthew 3:10, "And even

**Missionary T.E. Thoren with his pupils in Estonia in 1873.**

now the axe lieth at the root of the trees: every tree therefore that bringeth not forth good fruit is hewn down, and cast into the fire." After the message, Osterblom fell on the ground and confessed the sins of the people and his own sins. A mighty revival broke out for the fourth time in the fall of 1881.

Thus far the missionaries had preached to the Swedes, but Andrew Braus (1854?-1920?), who got saved at Thoren's seminary, began to preach to the Estonians in 1876. Soon revival broke out among the Estonians and spread mightily into many areas. It is believed that several thousand people were converted during those 11 years in Estonia. The Rev. Mr. Lars J. Osterblom was deported from Estonia in 1887 for preaching the gospel.

The revival was not limited to the peasants, but the gospel was also preached to the Estonian aristocracy, producing good results. In 1886-1887, a Swedish gentleman, Pastor Fjader, preached in Tallinn at the residence of Mrs. von Uxkull, mother of Baron Woldemar von Uxkull. This noble family got saved along with several other aristocratic families. Some of them became preachers and pastors.

### The Spreading of Revival in Estonia

In 1874, the same Swedish missionary society sent Mr. Peetrus Bergsten to the island of Naissaar, a little ways off the northern seacoast of Estonia, to teach children in the local public school. The island was populated by Swedes and by Estonians; 90 percent of the population spoke both languages, and 10 percent spoke Estonian only. The people were members either of St. Mihkli or Jaani Lutheran churches of Tallinn. Most of the people worshipped at the local Lutheran church built in 1553. On Sundays at the local church, a Mr. Rosen held church services in the Estonian language and read a sermon from a book.

When Bergsten arrived in Naissar, he began to preach God's Word in the Swedish language in the Lutheran church, after the Estonian service was concluded. He preached on the subject of conversion and the new birth with great anointing. Revival broke out at first among the school children and then among the adults. He taught faith in Christ and salvation by faith in the name of the Lord Jesus Christ.

Because he was also a minister, he had to baptize infants in the island communities, through which he got acquainted with the way of the people, their customs and dancing. Soon after he arrived in Naissaar, he was invited to a home to baptize an infant by sprinkling. After the ceremony, a great meal was served, and then began dancing. This worldly manifestation hit the missionary so hard that he began to weep, saying that he had made a vow before 300 people that he would never partake of such worldly practice, and left.

Mr. Bergsten proclaimed the gospel faithfully, and it produced results. Dancing and other sinful festivities ceased. People began to celebrate Sunday as the Lord's Day, and the spiritual life grew.

Mr. Bergsten read good Christian literature and learned that born-again believers shall not take Communion together with the ungodly in a State church. He began to break bread secretly with believers in 1876, and by 1881 he had over 10 believers who partook the Communion. At the time of his departure, he appointed a local brother, Franz Berg, to break bread.

Because of his rough handling of the children, he ran into a controversy. People complained to the Swedish Missionary Society about his harsh attitude at the school. He was recalled in 1881, but the seed he had sown grew and produced fruit.

In the fall of 1881, Mr. Gustav H. Matson (1855-1930) was converted. Soon after his salvation experience, he began to hold revival meetings in his own home in Tagakula, and in the home of Mr. Ambrosen in Eeskula. He also traveled in the mainland where he met Baptists and people from the Free Chruch. He was baptized by preacher A. Tetermann (1854-1925) and returned to Naissaar. It is an astounding fact how these unlearned young converts were able to preach and to hold great successful revivals. The work in Naissaar grew, and in 1900 a Baptist church was established.

A great revival broke out in 1876 in Osterby on the mainland. Mr. Kristian Engbusk (1855-1931), who studied at Thoren's seminary, was converted. After the graduation, he became a school teacher in Osterby, a large Swedish community. Besides his regular work as a teacher, he also held revival meetings, which produced a revival of unprecedented magnitude. People flocked together from the community and from other communities from a longer distance. Sometimes the Swedish missionaries, Mr. Thoren and Osterblom, helped the local brethren in the revival. At first the preaching was in Swedish only, but later in Swedish and in Estonian.

People walked many miles to attend the meetings, and many came in horse-drawn buggies. The crowd was so great that most of the people stood outside of the school building listening through the open windows. Sometimes the entire audience fell on their knees in great agony and cried out to God for mercy. After much prayer and agony, the Lord saved them in multitudes. Very often people, while singing, began to clap hands and to wave back and forth, praising God in loud voices; and some began to dance in the Spirit. Great powerful singing lasted until late at night.

Some ridiculed the meetings, saying that the movement was a fake; but the Lord converted them as well. To the Pastors of the Lutheran Church, the marvelous revival caused much anxiety, and they began to preach against it. The revival movement lasted for several years until Mr. Engbusk was releaved from his responsibilities as a teacher.

At first the revival spread among the Swedish-speaking people. When the Estonians began to attend the revival meetings in Osterby, many of them got saved and the revival wave spread among the Estonians in the province of Laanemaa. The Estonians came to the meetings for two main reasons:

1. They came because of an inward desire to have peace with God.
2. They came because of curiosity. Many of the people just wanted to see what was going on in those revival meetings and to ridicule the humble gospel preachers. The Holy Spirit touched them all. People got saved by the multitudes. Those that got saved ran quickly to the other villages to tell their friends what the Lord had done for them. Such joyful testimony led many to Christ, but some of them also were annoyed by the gospel news. Those who were saved, especially the brethren, began to hold revival meetings; and thus the revival spread from village to village, and even into the next province.

Nobody knows the exact number of the converts, but it can be estimated that thousands were saved. Many of those converts became Baptists and some became members of the Free Church.

At this time, God raised up a fiery preacher named William Roomus (1849-1923), who was converted in 1879. He proclaimed God's Word with unusual success to the Estonians in the mainland. At his meetings people cried out to God for mercy. At one place after reading his text, a mighty anointing fell upon Brother Roomus. He said with a loud voice, "Oo!" and the people fell on their knees on the floor, resulting in numerous conversions. He preached the gospel for over 40 years. By 1916 there were about 37 Baptist churches in Estonia.

In 1862-1865 a Brother John Schwan worked in Saaremaa as a land surveyor. He had studied in St. Petersburg and was baptized by the visiting German preacher, John G. Oncken, in 1864 in the Russian capital. Through the preaching of this godly man in Saaremaa, a revival was kindled. People were stirred and some accepted the Baptist views of baptism by immersion.[2]

### Lord Radstock's Preaching to the Russian Aristocracy

In the aristocratic circles of St. Petersburg there had always been men and women with a hunger for God. The German Protestants, who formed a relatively high proportion of the capital's population, did not play a large role in the awakening at the time of Alexander I, because the Protestant Church in the capital was then gripped by an arid rationalism. But this had changed in the course of the century. Like the Lutheran Church in Germany, the Russian Lutherans had moved on to confessional theology. Teaching at the theological faculty in Tartu, Estonia, were converted men who represented a positive and vital Lutheranism.

Theodosius Harnack taught applied theology there. He was in Tartu from 1844 to 1875, apart from his time in Erlangen from 1833 to 1866, and came from Gossner's congregation in St. Petersburg. His colleagues in the faculty were the Lutheran-Orthodox Philippi, a baptized Jew, who was in Tartu 1842 to 1851; Old Testament scholar Keil, 1833 to 1858; later, von Oettingen, 1853 to 1890; and von Engelhardt, 1853 to 1881. All these men influenced more than one generation of German Pastors who went on to serve in the Baltic and throughout Russia.

Court society in St. Petersburg had considerable contact with Protestants because the Emperors always invited many members of the Baltic nobility to come to the capital. There were also many marriages between Baltic and Russian nobility. An intellectual and spiritual exchange could not be avoided, although Protestant sermons in the Russian language were still forbidden.

The Lieven Princes, who were Protestant, were considered one of the oldest noble families of the Baltic, since according to tradition they were descended from Kaupo, from the Cremon region, the first Livonian chief to be baptized after 1200. From the time of Catherine II and particularly from that of Alexander I, members of the Lieven family were being summoned to positions of responsibility in the court of St. Petersburg. Thus they became a kind of traditional link for Protestant influence in the capital city of Russia.

2. R. Kaups, **Hea Sonum ja Eesti Baptisti Kogudused,** (Santa Barbara: California, 1974), pp. 11-35, 53, 39, 91, 103. Translated from Estonian by Albert W. Olema.

Up to that time Bible distribution among the Russian people in the vast Russian Empire was carried on by numerous Bible couriers. For example, Baron Hendrik Wrede (1854-1929) from Finland, brother of the famous Baroness Mathilde Wrede (1864-1928), who was famous for her work among prisoners, was active in Bible distribution in Siberia. Even before that, Count Korf (1842-1933), later Master of the Ceremonies at the imperial court, had distributed Russian Gospels in St. Petersburg on behalf of the British and Foreign Bible Society. This took place in 1870 at the first trade exhibition, where about 62,000 Gospels were distributed free of charge at the Bible kiosk erected at the expense of the Holy Synod. On each Gospel was printed the words of Acts 16:31, "Believe in the Lord Jesus, and you will be saved, you and your household." Count Korf later became a very active member of the St. Petersburg revival.[3]

The great revival which started in the Russian capital among the Russian aristocracy was occasioned by a British nobleman, Lord Grenville Radstock (1833-1913). He was converted in 1856 in the

**On the front seat is Pastor Malof. Opposite of him is Lord Radstock and Countess Tcherkoff.**

Crimean War and began to pray that the gospel might find its way into Russia.[4]

[3] Brandenburg, op. cit., pp. 103-104.

[4] Byford, op. cit., p. 83.

For ten years he prayed that God would open the door for him to go to Russia. At the end of those ten years he was in Paris again for testimony meetings. Since high-class Russian society liked to visit the French capital on the Seine, it was here that he met the first Russians. Here, too, he met a Russian Grand Princess. This unexpected meeting allayed her misgivings and in the end she invited him to St. Petersburg, promising to put her palace at his disposal. The other Russians who were present agreed enthusiastically, and this was the answer to Radstock's prayer.[5]

Later, when preaching in Switzerland, a Russian aristocratic lady, Madame Tcherkoff, was introduced to him. In his address, she recognized the same message which her son, Misha, at home during the last days of his life, had tried to tell her. The boy was converted through his Christian tutor, who now witnessed to his mother about his Savior. Madame Tcherkoff acknowledged her need and accepted Jesus Christ as her Savior and Lord. This became Lord Radstock's first opportunity to win a Russian to his Lord.[6]

He travelled to St. Petersburg in the winter of 1874 and stayed for about six months in the Russian capital. Despite his aristocratic origins, Radstock had an unfeigned modesty and humility, and it was certainly these qualities which gave him such an opening among the Russians in the capital city, for he had no gift for oratory. But the Russians are particularly sensitive to genuineness, and they had long held humility to be the chief Christian virtue. Radstock did not seek respect and did not promote his own personality among his listeners. He had a simple way of developing the main Christian concepts by using the Bible, to which he constantly referred his hearers. He belonged to the so-called Open Brethren, as did two men of German origin: George Muller (1805-1898), the father of orphans in Bristol, England; and Dr. Baedecker, who later followed Radstock's footsteps to Russia.

Radstock began in the little English-American church on Post Office Street in St. Petersburg. Many of his hearers came with a desire for clarity and certainty, for the Holy Spirit had already been at work, preparing their hearts. Count Korf distributed Bibles. Princess Lieven, who was still young, had already had a glimpse of the life of a spiritually awakened English lord in the home of the former Transport Minister, Blackwood, and had found assurance of forgiveness.

5. Brandenburg, op. cit., p. 105.

6. Astakhoff, op. cit., pp. 90-91.

A surprise to all of the people involved was the conversion of Colonel Vasili Alexandrovich Pashkoff (1831-1902), head of the imperial guards. He had a deep mistrust for Radstock and tried to avoid him. But when he met the English lord unexpectedly at a coffee gathering and the two men finally had a private talk, the conversation ended with them kneeling in prayer. This fabulously rich Russian surrendered his life and wealth to the Lord Jesus Christ. Pashkoff then became the leading personality in the movement. His palace became the meeting place for the believers. Count Bobrinsky, then Minister of Transport, also became a willing and outspoken member of this circle. At first he emphatically rejected Radstock's message, particularly since the latter never referred to anything but the Bible. The Count undertook to prove to Radstock that the Bible was full of contradictions. He took great pains to write out the relevant passages. But in conversation with Radstock (as he is supposed to have said later), all the Bible references which he had cited were turned into sharp darts against him.

Princess Lieven's sister, Countess Gagarin, whose palace was next to that of the Lievens, joined herself to them very decisively. The Countess, too, happily married and a charming personality, heard Lord Radstock's exposition of the Creator's question to Adam: "Where are you?" It opened her eyes to the condition of her heart. When Radstock asked at the conclusion of the message those who wanted to give their life to Jesus Christ, Countess Gagarin stood up and declared that she had grasped the saving hand of Christ in faith.

After Lord Radstock's first visit, which only lasted six months, he returned to St. Petersburg in 1877, bringing his family with him. At this time he remained for one and a half years in the Russian capital. His second visit was of particular importance, for his meetings virtually represented a Bible school. Knowledge of the Bible was a distinguishing feature here in the North. Because of the higher intellectual level of the core members of the community, there developed a thorough general Bible training which was to prove a great support in face of the reaction from the State Church later. Deep grounding in the Bible strengthened understanding, and tireless labor strengthened love.[7]

[7]. Brandenburg, op. cit., pp. 105-109.

## Self-Sacrifice of the Evangelical Christians for the Furtherance of the Gospel

The success and the advance of the gospel in St. Petersburg and other parts of the Russian Empire was a result of the faithful witness and self-sacrifice on the part of the Evangelical Christians.

Many of the aristocratic families opened their places for gospel meetings and contributed large sums for the support of the Lord's work. The new converts, whether aristocrat or plebian, in their new-found joy testified enthusiastically to the unconverted. Some of the most prominent workers were Colonel Pashkoff, Count Korf, and Duchess Tcherkoff.

Colonel Pashkoff, a very gifted and energetic man, besides possessing great wealth, occupied also an important and influential position in the highest circles of society. The Colonel owned a magnificent palace in St. Petersburg which had several auditoriums. These he made at once available for the revival meetings. At first only a few people attended the services, but later on so many people came that sometimes there was no room for all the people and hundreds were turned away.

There were usually 1,300 to 1,400 persons in each meeting. Prior to the banishment of the Colonel from Russia, so many people gathered in his house every night that another meeting was held in the lower auditorium which held about 700 people. The audience represented all strata of society. There were horse drivers, peasants, army generals, people of the high aristocracy, university students, and sometimes even some Orthodox priests. On his estate the message of salvation was preached and many of the people were saved, who in turn carried the gospel to their fellow countrymen.

The State Church became greatly alarmed and resorted to every possible measure to terminate this new evangelical movement; but the clergy were not too successful in their efforts against those who were so close to the ruling circle, and the movement started by Lord Radstock spread rapidly among both upper and lower classes.

The proclamation of the gospel by Colonel Pashkoff reached an ever wider circle. Groups of believers were organized in St. Petersburg, in Moscow, and in many other cities. The people began to call the Christians, Pashkovtsy, after the name of their chief pioneer leader. The leader of this movement and his friends realized the importance of the written Word of God in the hands of the young converts to read and to learn about the Christian life, and made it their aim to supply the people with the Word of God.

New Testaments, portions of the Scriptures, and spiritual literature were printed in great quantities. Colonel Pashkoff dedicated his large fortune to the cause of Christ and for the furtherance of the gospel. Colporteurs were sent out, and tens of thousands of copies of the Scriptures, tracts, and leaflets were distributed all over Russia. These colporteurs were zealous Christians and testified for Christ wherever opportunity arose.

The Colonel opened homes in St. Petersburg for orphans, workshops of various kinds, and restaurants which became favorite eating places for the working people, where they could get abundant and good food for low prices.

With the material help given to the workers, the good news of salvation was also preached to them and many of the people accepted the Lord Jesus Christ as their Savior. Those who were converted, carried the truth of eternal salvation to their homes, and also to the factories where they were working. Thus the gospel began to triumph in Russia, winning thousands of converts.

Colonel Pashkoff and his friends started a strong gospel work which could not be stopped by the Orthodox Church because the Colonel was a friend of the Imperial Court. However, in 1884 the government banished him from Russia for his evangelical activities. He died in Paris in 1902. The work which he had begun continued to grow, and the gospel triumphed. Following the Colonel's exile, Ivan V. Kargel (1846-1933) zealously led the work in St. Petersburg.[8]

The Colonel, prior to his banishment, had purchased a plot of land in the northeastern suburb of St. Petersburg and built a kind of temperance cafe. Above were rooms for a working women's club, and mission work on social and industrial lines was carried on under the direction of Madame Pashkoff and her daughters before World War I, as in the days of the Colonel.[9]

Another zealous worker for the Lord was Madame Tcherkoff (1832-1922). After her conversion, she dedicated her life fully to the service of God. She sold most of her jewels and with one part of the money built the first Evangelical Church in St. Petersburg. It was in this church that the famous Russian preacher Pastor Fetler preached his first sermon in the Russian capital in 1907.

8. Ibid., pp. 91-93, 55.

9. Latimer, op. cit., p. 37.

Madame Tcherkoff was engaged in philanthropic work through which she won many of her fellow countrymen to the Lord. Her methods were simple. Once in her buggy she went to the slum areas of St. Petersburg and invited about 200 poor women to her church building. There the kind lady had several large tables on which were 200 brand new Singer sewing machines. After talking to these women on the love of God and forgiveness through faith in Christ, she encouraged them to accept the Lord as their Savior and Lord.

Madame Tcherkoff taught them how to use a machine and gave one to every poor woman. In this way this wealthy but humble lady of the Russian aristocracy preached the gospel to her fellow citizens. Thousands of souls have been saved in her church.[10]

Another active member of this small household community in the Lieven palace was Baroness Alexandra von Peucker, who had been converted through the famous American Evangelist Dwight L. Moody (1837-1899) on a visit to England. She was German by origin, but like many Germans in St. Petersburg, she was accustomed to speaking Russian. She originally wanted to train for the opera, but now she placed her beautiful voice at the service of the gospel. At the same time she displayed a great energy for organization in the believers social work. Together with a number of young girls, she formed a women's choir, including Princess Lieven's daughters, Colonel Pashkoff's daughters, three daughters of Konstantin von der Pahlen, the Minister of Justice, two Golitsyn Princesses, Countess Shuvalov and two Koslyaninov sisters.

Old Prince Lieven, who died in 1881, was a Lutheran; but he was not the only Lutheran among the people of the revival. When a committee was formed for the welfare work, its secretary and treasurer was Dr. Mayer, head of the Lutheran hospital, which had an excellent reputation in the city. His daughter, Jenny de Mayer, worked in the Midnight Mission in Moscow, later among the convicts on Sakhalin Island, and finally found her life's work in the Bible Mission among the Muslims of Turkestan. Whereas Jenny's parents had been persecuted by the Emperors, she was hounded by the Bolsheviks. She spent many years in Soviet prisons.[11]

Regardless of severe opposition, the St. Petersburg evangelical

10. Basil A. Malof, **100% For Kristus** (Orebro: Evangeliipress, 1955), pp. 134-135. Translated from Swedish by Albert W. Olema.

11. Brandenburg, **op. cit.**, pp. 108-109.

group was put firmly on its feet. A Christian magazine, "Khristianin," made its appearance in 1907; and in 1908 a local evangelical organization was established in St. Petersburg; and in 1909 a national organization was founded. The Baptists were mostly Ukrainians; the Evangelical Christians predominantly Great Russians.[12]

In 1900 there were about 40 groups of believers in the Russian capital.[13]

## The First United Evangelical Conference in 1884

### The Purpose of the Conference

The four streams of Evangelicals which started between 1867 and 1874 in the Ukraine, in the Caucasus, and in St. Petersburg and the Baltic countries were independent of each other, with little knowledge of other Evangelicals in the vast Russian Empire.

The doctrinal and theological standard was very limited and different views were held in regard to the sacraments, especially water baptism by immersion. These questions could only be resolved by a general conference in St. Petersburg. The chief purpose of the 1884 conference in St. Petersburg was:

1. To unify all the Russian Protestants into a single centralized and dynamic movement.
2. To discuss the essence of faith.[14]
3. To discuss water baptism by immersion.
4. To discuss common participation in the Lord's Supper.[15]

Colonel Pashkov had travelled widely in Russia, was acquainted with many Stundists and Baptists, and invited the leaders of various parts of the country to attend the United Evangelical Conference in St. Petersburg. The Colonel accommodated them at a hotel, having paid the fares of those too poor to defray their own expenses.[16]

12. Kolarz, **op. cit.**, p. 285.

13. Robert P. Casey, **Religion in Russia** (New York: Harper Brothers, 1946), p. 42.

14. Serge Bolshakoff, **Russian Nonconformity** (Philadelphia: The Westminster Press, 1949), p. 116.

15. Durasoff, **op. cit.**, p. 41

16. J.C. Pollock, **The Faith of the Russian Evangelicals**, (New York and Toronto: McGraw-Hill Company, 1964), p. 69.

More than 70 arrived from all corners of Russia. The first session was held in Pashkov's large dining hall, where they discussed key questions on the essence of their faith, including the ordinance of baptism by immersion.

The mode of baptism became a painful issue, although all present acknowledged the sacrament as one ordained of God. The Baptists insisted on the validity of immersion alone as taught in the Bible, whereas others maintained that the ordinance was to be fulfilled according to one's conscience, consistent with his understanding of the Holy Scriptures.

The following day the discussion continued in the mansion of Princess Lieven with 400 in attendance. The problems of the previous day were compounded when the question of common participation in the Lord's Supper was proposed. The Baptist delegates absolutely refused to partake in the Holy Communion with the pedobaptists.

During a heated exchange of opinion on the debatable issue, Lord Radstock suddenly entered, and with Pashkov as his interpreter said: "Brethren, on your knees! Our unity is in Christ; He is our peace and life. Let us give Him praise and honor." All the delegates knelt at once and repented in fervent prayer. Arising from their knees, they perceived the unity of the body of Christ, and these debates on baptism were terminated.[17]

When the denominational representatives returned to their hotel, they found the police waiting to arrest them. When the next day no provincial delegate appeared, their aristocratic allies were puzzled by the absence of the delegates far from their homes. Colonel Pashkov, with other Christian friends, investigated the matter and found that the hotel was empty. Two days later, one of the delegates secretly slipped into the palace. He told how they had been arrested shortly after leaving the conference. Police had escorted them to railway stations and sent them home at government expense.

The surprise action abruptly terminated the conference of 1884, but the failure of a merger of the denominations present was caused by the intransigency of the delegates.

It was followed by an intense and violent persecution in which the Church and State cooperated to suppress the Evangelicals.[18]

17. Durasoff, op. cit., pp. 45-46.

18. Pollock, op. cit., pp. 69-70.

## The Results of the Conference

The 1884 Conference in the capital city produced three negative results.

1. Banishment of the delegates from St. Petersburg.
2. Failure to unify the evangelical denominations.
3. An intense persecution of the Evangelicals.

## The Union of Russian Baptists Founded in 1884

Another conference was held (April 30 – May 1, 1884) in the Ukrainian village of Novo-Vasilevka, in the Zaporoshe Province where the Union of Russian Baptists was founded. John Willer, a Mennonite preacher, was elected the first president of the Russian Baptist Union.[19] The Union was illegal until 1905, when religious toleration was proclaimed. After the edict of 1905, the Baptists held their first open congress in Kiev attended by a hundred delegates; and its effective work began. The Russian Baptists kept in close touch with the Baptist World Alliance, which was founded in 1905.[20]

## Prokhanov – a Gifted Christian Leader

Ivan S. Prokhanov (1869-1935) was born in Vladikavkaz, Caucasia, and experienced conversion at home. In 1888 he came to St. Petersburg to study in the Technological Institute of the Emperor Nicholas I.[21] In the capital he met well-educated Evangelical Christians and soon took a leading part in the activities of the St. Petersburg evangelical community and helped to found the first Russian Baptist periodical, "Beseda." The magazine was quickly suppressed by the imperial government, but the "Beseda" which had to be printed in Stockholm, Sweden, and smuggled in, helped the Baptists in Russia.[22]

In March 1895, Mr. Prokhanov secretly left Russia via Finland to inform the European community of the religious persecutions which

19. Durasoff, op. cit., pp. 47-48.

20. Kolarz, op. cit., p. 285.

21. Durasoff, op. cit., p. 50

22. Pollock, op. cit., p. 74.

were in progress in his country. During his three and one-half years in Western Europe, he attended the theological colleges in Bristol, London, Berlin, and Paris, where he received some theological training and a comprehensive view of the Protestant denominations in Western Europe. From 1899 to 1901 he served as an assistant professor at the Riga Polytechnic Institute. In 1901 he returned to St. Petersburg where he accepted employment at the Westinghouse plant as an engineer, but he utilized every free moment for the work of evangelism. He edited and published Christian magazines, such as "Discourse," later "The Christian," and printed a paper under the name "Morning Star," and a magazine called "Evangelical Faith." By God's help in 1901, Prokhanov succeeded in printing 20,000 hymnals with censor approval, despite the prohibitory laws.[23]

In 1908 he founded the Union of the Evangelical Christians, of which he was the first president. In 1909 Mr. Prokhanov predicted by faith that 500 missionaries would be ministering across the Russian Empire. The basic unit was the entirely autonomous local congregation. After five or more local groups were found, a sectional association was formed to expand missionary work and religious work in the area. By 1928 over 600 missionaries were dispatched over the Soviet Union.[24]

Mr. Prokhanov did not like to work in the Russian Baptist Union because he believed that the very name, Baptist, was alien to Russian people and the views of the Russian Baptists were too rigid to him.

In 1914, the Russian Baptist Union had 97,000 baptized members, while the Evangelical Christians numbered only 8,472; but it was rapidly increasing. In 1913, Prokhanov founded in St. Petersburg a Theological College, which was closed in 1914 because of the war. At the conclusion of the war he was able to open the Theological College again, which operated until 1930 when the Communists closed the college. It produced about 420 graduates, who entered the ministry.

Mr. Prokhanov founded the Evangelical Publishing House, Raduga, and published the weekly magazine "Morning Star," calendars, pamphlets, and books. He presided at the all-Russian evangelical conference in 1909, 1910, 1911, and in 1911 was elected the vice president of the World Baptist Alliance.[25]

23. Durasoff, op. cit., p. 51

24. Ibid., p. 56.

25. Bolshakoff, op. cit., p. 118

The tremendous growth of the Evangelical Christians under the leadership of Prokhanov surpasses the achievements of any other evangelical leader of Russia. By 1922 the Evangelical Christians numbered 250,000. The ever-active Prokhanov visited the United States in 1926 and raised $100,000 among churches and colleges for the publication of Christian literature. He printed 60,000 Bibles, 15,000 Bible concordances, and 60,000 hymnals.[26] The great Russian evangelical leader also wrote about 600 hymns and adapted others.[27]

In 1928, when it was obvious that Ivan Prokhanov could not reenter the Soviet Union without being arrested, I.I. Zhidkov (1885-1966), his assistant in the thriving St. Petersburg church since 1903, succeeded him as the leader of the Evangelical Christians. There is no record of Zhidkov's activities from 1938 to 1943, but in 1944 he became the first president of the All-Union Council of Evangelical Christians and Baptists.[28]

The Rev. Mr. Ivan S. Prokhanov died in Berlin, Germany, on October 6, 1935.[29]

**General Secretary A. A. Karev (left) and T. T. Zhidkov**

[26] Durasoff, **op. cit.**, p. 57

[27] Pollock, **op. cit.**, p. 74.

[28] Durasoff, **op. cit.**, pp. 104-106.

[29] Astakhoff, **op. cit.**, p. 129.

## The October Manifesto of 1905
## Tolerates Freedom of Conscience

On April 17, 1905, Emperor Nicholas II (1896-1917) of Russia proclaimed an act of toleration, followed by a manifesto on October 17, 1905, giving freedom of conscience, freedom of press and liberty of political activities. Having published the new general laws which brought about these freedoms, the government, however, omitted the issuance of special decrees to liberate religious exiles. On the behalf of the deported Christians, Prokhanov petitioned Count S.J. Witte (1849-1915), the President of the Council of Ministers. As a result of the petition, Count Witte liberated those who were imprisoned and exiled for religious reasons by the means of a special circular.[30]

Freedom proved conditional and somewhat precarious, beset by nagging police and exasperated priests. Regardless of the Toleration Act, religious liberty was still limited, and meetings at prayer houses were often police controlled. After the toleration manifesto, the Baptist Union was re-established, and in 1906 the Union was able to send out about 50 evangelists throughout the empire.

In October 1910, Mr. Pyotr A. Stolypin (1862-1911), Prime Minister of Russia, approved the rules to be observed at the religious meetings of the non-orthodox people. Sectarian worship meetings were held without hindrance in temples or rooms or other premises constructed by permission. However, the police had to be notified in advance. Nevertheless, from 1905 to the outbreak of World War I, many new prayer houses were built in many cities and villages, and religious magazines began to appear in St. Petersburg.[31]

## The Russian Bible

The spread of Russian evangelical movements was considerably enhanced by the publication of the complete Russian Bible by the Holy Synod in 1876. At last the Russian people had the Bible in the vernacular rather than in the old Church Slavonic.

In 1499, Saint Gennadius of Novgorod edited the first complete Slavonic Bible in Russia, which included all the canonical books as well as the Apocrypha.

30. Durasoff, op. cit., p. 51.

31. Byford, op. cit., pp. 150-151.

In 1580-1581, the Saint Gennadius Bible was published in the Ukraine by Prince Constantin Ostrzhsky, who improved the text.

In 1663, the Slavonic Bible was printed in Moscow, which excelled the Ukrainian edition of 1580. It followed the Septuagint's order and not that of the Latin Vulgate, on the pattern of which the first two Russian Bibles were modeled.

Revised by several Greek and Slavonic scholars, the Slavonic Bible was reprinted in 1751 in Moscow, and in 1756 a new revised edition made its appearance. Since that time only reprints had been available. The Slavonic Bible did not entirely satisfy the Russian need. The spoken language came to vary seriously from the Slavonic, and poorly educated persons failed to understand it properly. Unpardonable mistakes and outright heresies frequently followed efforts of simple monks and peasants to interpret the Scriptures.

The publication of the Bible in Russian vernacular was chiefly due to the efforts of the British and Foreign Bible Society, which in 1810 began to operate in Russia.

The Bible Society, finding ready support from several provincial governors, published in succession the Bible in Slavonic, modern Russian, and many other languages. All translations were supervised by the Christian clergy of many denominations, including the Orthodox and Roman Catholic prelates.

At last it was decided to publish the Russian Bible, and the translation of the original into Russian began in 1816. The Old Testament was taken from the Septuagint, and the translation supervised by several prelates and scholars proceeded slowly. Then the work was stopped and the Society itself dissolved. This happened because the Russian Bible Society had become a convenient center for Russian Freemasons, mystics and sectarians, inspired by Bohme, Swedenborg, Jung-Stilling and Eckartshausen. These enthusiasts even succeeded in strongly influencing several Russian prelates.

Count Alexis Arakcheev (1769-1834) was minister and favorite of Alexander I, disliked Prince Golitsyn and his mystics, whom he considered heretics corrupting the Church of the State. He acted accordingly. In 1824 Prince Golitsyn was dismissed from his ministry and deprived of the presidency of the Bible Society. In the year of 1826 the Society itself was dissolved and its assets handed over to the Holy Synod.

Although the slow printing of the Russian Bible went on, in 1836 it was again stopped by Count Protasov, the high procurator of the

Holy Synod from 1836 to 1855. This pupil of the Jesuits looked upon the Slavonic Bible in the same way as the Latins do on the Vulgate. The Slavonic text was for Protasov a sacred inheritance from the ancestors, the common treasure of the Slavs. He considered it quite adequate for the Church services and private reading by educated persons. Protasov considered the Russian Bible not merely useless but positively harmful in a country full of sects and almost illiterate.

To distribute the Russian Bible among the illiterate peasants would accomplish nothing, according to Count Protasov, but the spreading of sects. The future largely justified Protasov, who, unsatisfied by merely stopping the printing of the Bible, ordered the books already printed to be destroyed.

Only in 1858, after Count Protasov retired, did Archpriest Pavsky and Archimandrite Macarious succeed in securing permission to resume the publication of the Russian Bible. In 1876 the complete Russian Bible was on sale, and the Russian Protestants received their Bible from the Holy Synod. The translation was accurate and clear, and the language refined and solemn. Since then, the British and Foreign Bible Society has reprinted this Bible regularly.

In 1948, G. Bessonov, anxious to convert the masses in the Soviet Union, suggested to the Society that it prepare a new, more up-to-date translation; but the Society took the position that another version was unnecessary since both the Orthodox and the Protestants were quite satisfied with Pavsky's translation and do not want another.[32]

### The Joint Conference of 1920 Fails

Separate conferences were held by both the Baptists and the Evangelical Christians, but the first of three joint conferences was held in St. Petersburg January 15–22, 1907, to form a commission to advance the work of unity. The third joint conference of 1919 produced an agreement on a project for the uniting of the two unions, to be effected in the 1920 conference.

In January 1920 a preliminary gathering of five executives from both unions met in St. Petersburg, resulting in two important advances:

1. To publish a magazine called "The Fraternal Union."

2. To agree on a common seal depicting the image of two staffs in one hand.

[32] Bolshakoff, op. cit., pp. 129-132.

In June, 1920, the most important congress since that of 1884, assembled in Moscow to work on the behalf of the Union. After a lengthy discussion, a reciprocal concurrence was produced on the merger name of "Union of Evangelical Christians and Baptists." The Evangelical Christians were very cautious to interpret unity as one based upon freedom and equality, unity in which neither side was to be subjugated to the other, nor strain laid upon anyone's liberty.

The decision of the selection between St. Petersburg and Moscow as the headquarters of the united evangelical body was left unresolved. However, questions on dogma needed to be resolved, such as the laying on of hands, the conducting of baptism, and the breaking of bread. Regardless of the concurrence reached in all organizational matters and dogmatic differences, the unification of the two evangelical bodies was not effected. Zhidkov in retrospect made the comment that the merger did not take place because the administration of the Baptists was in Moscow and the one of Evangelical Christians in St. Petersburg. It was almost impossible to decide where to have the headquarters of the united fellowship.[33]

**Leningrad lighthouses at the right**

33. Durasoff, **op. cit.**, pp. 61-63.

The historic merger of the two unions did not take place until October 26-29, 1944, at the Council in Moscow. It resulted in the creation of the All-Union of Evangelical Christians and Baptists, and the Evangelical Christians and Baptists merged.[34]

## Missionary Work Among the Wild Tribes in Siberia and Caucasus

The Theological College which was opened up in Leningrad after World War I was training young workers for the ministry. It was not only their own people the young workers had in mind, but also the heathen in Siberia who had never heard the gospel. On the other hand there were already small evangelical congregations among many peoples of the Empire, like the work among the Mordvinians, the Cheremiss, and the Chuvash on this side of the Urals, among Armenians, Georgians in the Caucasus.

A young Christian girl about 20 years of age came to Prokhanov and said she felt the call to Siberia to the Yakuts, whose capital Yakutsk lay 1,500 kilometers north of the Siberian railway. Although many sensible people tried to talk the girl out of her plan, Prokhanov gave her his blessing for this missionary work.

The young girl set off through the taiga (primeval forest) and the tundra, the northern marshes of Siberia. Nothing was heard of her for several years. Then she wrote to say that the number of those who had believed and who were spiritually touched had become so large that she did not feel herself capable of carrying out the number of baptisms that were necessary. She asked for a minister to come so that a proper congregation could be formed. Because of her exemplary life and her selfless work of love which did not shun the meanest service in the Yakut huts, she had soon won the love of the people. Her request was answered and a church was formed.

A few missionary brothers were working among the Ostyaks, a wild Samoyed tribe in the far north of Siberia. They attempted with some success to make the nomadic tribes settle. These faithful workers had gone out in 1913 and worked for 14 years, cut off from all culture. When they came back to Tomsk, the Siberian railroad station, for the first time (in 1927), they had heard nothing about the war nor the

34. Ibid., p. 106.

revolution of 1917. However, their work had produced a number of converts among the wild Ostyaks.

In Wernigerode the workers got to know a noble representative of the Osetian people, a mountain tribe in the Caucasus, part Muslim and part Orthodox, who offered strong resistance to the Russian conquest in the 19th century. This man, Kapo Bayev, a cultured Osetian who had been mayor of the large town of Vladikavkaz, had been driven out of his country by the revolution. On his departure he had promised to representatives of his people to send them the Word of God. Now he sat in the Harz mountains, like Luther on the Wartburg, translating the Bible into his mother tongue. Up to that time there had only been the four gospels in Osetian.[35]

Leningrad

[35] Brandenburg, *op. cit.*, pp. 179-180.

## CHAPTER V

# RELENTLESS PERSECUTIONS OF THE EVANGELICAL CHRISTIANS UNDER THE EMPERORS

### Reasons for the Persecutions

The Russian Church in her history relative to her internal government has passed through three stages:

1. From 988 to 1589, the Church was ruled by the Metropolitans.
2. From 1589 to 1720, the Patriarch ruled supreme.
3. From 1720 to the Communist Revolution in 1917, the Church was governed by the Holy Synod established by Emperor Peter the Great. The Holy Synod was a replica of the administrative colleges presided over by the High Procurator. His function was to insure that business was conducted regularly and efficiently, including the interests of the Emperor. The High Procurator received reports of the diocesan inspectors on conditions in the different dioceses and presented those to the Synod to be acted upon. The Procurator was subject to the Emperor only.[1]

Through these changes the internal organization of the Church did not suffer because they did not bring any fundamental reforms to her. It brought a change only in the role the Church had in the secular government. Under the ecclesiastical scepter of the Metropolitans and the Patriarch, the high clergy had a great influence over the Russian government. From Peter the Great, the Holy Synod governed the Church, and the State and the Church were considered as one organism of which the Emperor was the head.

Russian history reveals that sometimes during an interregnum and disturbance, the Patriarch intervened as the highest authority in State and Church. In the early 17th century on the imperial decrees, the patriarchal signature was next to that of the Emperor.

The State Church, having unlimited power, absolutely forbade the preaching of the gospel among the people. Every attempt in this

[1] Casey, op. cit., p. 17.

direction was severely opposed in its very beginning. Because of this fact, for many centuries the Greek Orthodox Church remained the only church organization in Russia.

Although the Western protestants in Russia enjoyed full freedom to arrange their own church policy, they were not allowed to proselytize. The State Church allowed no introduction of other religions to her members. An Orthodox Church member was born in the Church and had to die in the same. Any appearance or preaching of a new faith to the Russian Church members was considered a crime and provoked severe persecutions. The existing conditions recorded in Russian Church history reveal at least three reasons for this powerful opposition to proselytizing.

### The Orthodox Conception of a Supreme Religion

During the Mongol occupation (1240-1480), the Church was comparatively free to arrange her own matters at will. This in due time created a feeling of superiority over the heathen oppressors, which feeling later on was fostered toward all other nations. The clergy assured the people that God had chosen Orthodox Russia to be the bearer of the only true faith, while all the Westerners were heretics and their culture and civilization were instigations of Satan. Thus, the Russians had the only true and superior religion, which no one could forsake, and was to be brought to all the peoples.

### Fear of the Clergy to Lose Supreme Governmental Power

The clergy had gained supreme governmental power which they wanted to keep at any cost. Prompted by the fear of losing this power, they used every possible means available to suppress every awakening, any religious movement, and all aspirations for progress – and kept the people in gross darkness and ignorance.

Every new religious movement was destroyed because it brought new ideas and light to the people which could undermine the clerical authority over state affairs. With all their might they hindered the Russian people and their ruling princes from any association with the West.

## Religious Movements in Czarist Russia Considered Revolutionary

In the Russian Empire, proselytizing among the Orthodox Church members or people was a punishable offense involving, according to Article 189 of the Criminal Code, imprisonment of up to four years and deportation to Siberia, with the loss of nearly all civil rights. The imperial government decided to suppress the Russian Baptist movement. The government, led by Constantine Pobedonostsev (1827-1907), high procurator to the Holy Synod, became convinced that the imperial regime had been undermined by revolutionary propaganda and could be saved only by the strict application of the Uvarov's formula: Orthodoxy, Autocracy, Nationalism. It was a widely held belief that in order to remain a great power, Russia must preserve intact its unifying spiritual force – the State Church – its centralized autocratic government and the predominant position of the Great Russians and their language among all others.[2]

From this point of view, all religious movements among the Russian Orthodox people were dangerous and all religious separatists were destroyers of their spiritual and cultural unity and were potential traitors. The Russian Baptists and Catholics, being closely connected with the West, were most obnoxious to the Orthodox and to the Emperor. They were considered as revolutionists who must be removed.

## Devastating Malevolence Against the Evangelicals

The revival which started in the Ukraine and in the Caucasus was not ignored by the Orthodox clergy. Severe and bitter persecutions broke out against the early converts.

The first three converts in the Ukraine were incarcerated and brought before the Russian tribunal. They would not desist from preaching the new message and were sentenced to exile. The Russian Orthodox Church had no mercy on the believers who were called "heretics." With all her might, the Church persecuted the Christians and thousands were deported to Siberia.

The remote corners of the Empire, Siberia, and Transcaucasia, were filled with the banished Christians who, even in exile, preached

2. Ibid., pp. 36, 116-117.

the Lord Jesus and had the joy of seeing the dwellers in strange lands being brought to the feet of the Christ. Two cases will be presented in this chapter to show the sufferings of the Evangelicals in Russia under the emperors.[3]

Gate of Novgorod

### Ivanoff and Erstratenko Exiled to Siberia

Vasili J. Ivanoff (1848-1908?) was converted at the age of 22 and was baptized in 1870 in the Tiflis River. His great love for his Lord encouraged him to witness wherever opportunity arose. He was bitterly persecuted by the police. For many months he was arrested upon various pretexts every Saturday and kept in the prison until Monday noon, with the purpose of preventing him from meeting with the Baptist people on Sundays.

During the weekend imprisonments, Ivanoff spoke boldly to his fellow prisoners, and scores of them got saved. The year of 1884 will be long remembered by the Baptists in South Russia. Homes were broken up, prisons were crowded, children were taken from their parents and

[3] Byford, op. cit., p. 81.

placed in monasteries. The exile convoys had their quota of believers on the way to Siberia and Transcaucasia. Ivanoff was banished to Caucasia for four years, and at the expiration of his sentence was deprived of all civil rights. Returning to Tiflis, he was without passport; and at great risk, he travelled through the villages comforting the women whose husbands were in prison or exile. He continued this itinerant ministry until 1895 when he was again arrested and imprisoned for six months without trial, and then sent to Transcaucasia. Half of his head and beard were shaven, and chains were rivoted to wrists and ankles. For four months he was treated little better than a beast of burden: With 15 other men, Ivanoff was chained to a treadmill and for eight hours every day, he had to grind corn for his fellow-convicts.[4]

When he was released from the Transcaucasia imprisonment, he went to Baku and began a great work in the "oil city." He baptized about 1,500 people in Baku.

Andreas Erstratenko (1863-1925) was born at Balashov, in the province of Saratov Russia. He persecuted the believers with his gang. In the spring of 1890 he was converted, and the following year he was baptized and received into the Baptist church. Shortly after his baptism, six families out of the 11 in the church were banished to Siberia; and young Erstratenko became leader of those still at liberty.

In 1893, Erstratenko was banished to Siberia for 12 years for preaching the Baptist message; but even at that remote part of the Empire, he continued to witness faithfully for his Lord. His ministry was so successful that thousands of political and criminal exiles were converted through his ministry alone. He travelled widely in Siberia south of the Baikal Lake.

He baptized many political exiles, and during his ministry in Siberia immersed more than 2,500 men and women and was the Pastor of many scattered churches embracing more than 6,000 members. So successful was the ministry of Erstratenko and his brother exiles, that as many as half the villagers in that great district around Omsk became members of the Baptist churches. The Baptist church in Omsk seated 2,000 worshippers. Through the faithfulness of the exiled Baptist believers, the gospel light shined in the darkest place of the Russian Empire, and the villages and communities in Siberia were privileged to turn to the living and true God.[5]

4. Ibid., pp. 108-109.

5. Ibid., pp. 126-128.

## Christian Communities in Siberia, the Land of Exile

Siberia is a vast area in North Asia, comprising the Asiatic portion of the Russian Empire. It has an area of about 6,086,681 square miles. In the 16th century, Tatars immigrating from Turkestan subjugated the tribes of the southwest Siberian plains and organized a khanate, with its capital at Sibir, on the Irtish River, thus giving the region its eventual name. Russian expansion eastward into Siberia was begun in the 16th century under Emperor Ivan the Terrible. In 1579, a Russian expedition captured Sibir and destroyed it and built, in 1587, the Russian city Tobolsk at its location. Little attention was given by the Russian emperors to development of their Siberian possessions. Because of extreme climate and rigor of living conditions, Siberia became around 1600, a place of exile for political, religious and criminal offenders. A few settlements were established and in 1891, the imperial government began to build the Trans-Siberian Railway. In 1891 the population of Siberia was about 5 million; but in 1910, about 9 million.

When the Baptist movement increased and spread in the Russian Empire, thousands of the Christians were deported to Siberia. In the exile settlements, there were tens of thousands of political prisoners as well as multitudes of criminal offenders. The exiled Baptists were deported to those settlements in Siberia. Many of the Baptists were preachers who preached to their fellow prisoners and made numerous converts. New converts won others to the Lord; and thus, the numerous conversions in Siberia increased the number of the Baptists, and Christian communities resulted in many places.[6]

[6] Byford, op. cit., p. 128.

## CHAPTER VI

# WILLIAM A. FETLER BUILDS THE FIRST RUSSIAN BAPTIST CHURCH IN ST. PETERSBURG

### His Conversion and Early Activities in Latvia

William Andrew Fetler (1883-1957) was the son of one of the early Baptist pioneers in the Baltic countries. He was born in Talsi, Latwia and was converted at the age of 15. He and his father were opposed by the Lutheran clergy for preaching the gospel. At the age of 15, young Fetler began to arrange meetings where the young people sang and prayed. He was used of God to the conversion of many of the young people.

At the age of 16 he went to Riga as a bookkeeper in a business house. Here he continued his religious activities and gradually the purpose formed in his heart to become a missionary to China. This decision led him in 1903 to England to attend the Metropolitan College in London, where he spent four years in preparing himself for his life's work.[1]

### Fetler's Successful Ministry in St. Petersburg

In the summer of 1907, Fetler arrived in St. Petersburg where he pastored a Lettish Baptist church with considerable success. During that time he came into contact with Princess Sophie Lieven (1880-1964) and made his home in her mansion. Other influential people were brought within the sphere of his influence. Several halls were hired and even the use of the Twon Hall was granted by the Duma, and the young preacher had started a promising work. Thus, the Lord led him to Russia instead of China.[2]

Mr. R. Latimer, who visited Fetler in the imperial capital, says that the Russian Christians themselves compared him to Spurgeon. This

1. Byford, op. cit., pp. 147-148.

2. Ibid., p. 148.

young preacher, only 27 years of age at that time, soon gained the public ear in St. Petersburg. There seemed to be no limit to the willingness of the people to come and listen to the preaching of this young man. The men would stand patiently in long rows in the narrow aisles of his meeting places for hours, in their earnest enjoyment of the message of grace proclaimed to them by the young Pastor.[3]

**Pastor Malof in his office in St. Petersburg in 1914.**

[3] Latimer, op. cit., pp. 25-26.

For nearly two years the Pastor with his supporters succeeded in hiring a schoolhouse for his Sunday services, which was available only for Sundays. And even for those meetings, the auditorium was too small and inconvenient. Regardless of all the difficulties and inconveniences, a solid work was established.

Mr. Fetler translated several popular songs into the Russian language, including the "Glory Song." There was also a simple Russian hymn by the Grand Duke Constantine, "I Am Standing at the Door and Knocking," which was a favorite song at the meetings.[4]

Under the leadership of Pastor Fetler, the production of evangelical literature in the Russian language considerably increased. Translations of some of the more popular elementary expository and devotional works of Great Britain and of the United States into the Russian tongue found a ready acceptance by the people. Evangelistic tracts, gospel hymns, and other religious literature was also sold in large quantities. An illustrated religious magazine too was in circulation, which had attained a circulation of 3,000 to 4,000 and proved most useful. Everything of a political character was carefully avoided, as well as all attacks on the State Church. The people were exhorted to read the Bible, to repent of sin and forsake it, accepting the Lord Jesus as Savior and Master, to be devout, prayerful and reverent, to seek the divine grace to live a holy life in the sight of God.

There was also the Tuesday night Bible School, which was very useful and interesting to the people. Originally it was held in the palace of Princess Lieven, where about 300 adults studied God's Word. Pastor Fetler used the blackboard, and the audience followed the lesson with close attention. This grounding in the scriptures was of great value to the young converts.[5]

Pastor Fetler was able to open many places for preaching and establishing Sunday Schools in the capital city. The young Pastor opened about 12 preaching halls, formed Sunday Schools, inspired the building of the House of the Gospel in St. Petersburg, and the opening of the church in Moscow which is now famous as the Baptist/Evangelical Christian Center.[6]

[4] Ibid., pp. 25-31.

[5] Ibid., pp. 203-204, 33.

[6] Pollock, op. cit., p. 74.

**The Baptist church in Moscow**

## The Erection of the First Baptist Church in the Imperial Capital

The work grew so rapidly that, at last, it was necessary to acquire property and build a permanent church home where the people could worship. Plans were drawn; and in October 1910, the foundation was laid. The church was opened for worship Christmas 1912.[7]

The church was called Dom Evangelia and accommodated some 2,000 people.[8] Pastor Fetler started a new Baptist work in Moscow also and baptized converts that were saved through his ministry.[9] In 1914, Pastor Fetler was arrested and sentenced to Siberia; but two days later, by special decision of the Cabinet of Ministers in answer to the Pastor's appeal, the sentence to Siberian exile was commuted to banishment abroad.[10]

7. Byford, **op. cit.**, p. 149.

8. Oswald J. Smith, **Tales of the Mission Field** (London and Edinburgh: Marshall Morgan & Scott, 1966), p. 103.

9. Latimer, **op. cit.**, pp. 107-112.

10. Smith, **op. cit.**, p. 111.

Dom Evangelia erected by Pastor Malof in St. Petersburg.

## Fetler Starts Work Among Russian War Prisoners in Europe in 1916

From Russia, Pastor Fetler went to Scandinavia. In Sweden he met one of his former associates, Ivan Y. Urlab, who had recently returned from Germany and told the Pastor about the great numbers of Russian soldiers captured by the Germans. In one battle alone in Eastern Prussia, the Germans had taken about 100,000 Russian prisoners.

As soon as Pastor Fetler heard that, he proposed to start work among 2 million Russian war prisoners in Germany and Austria. Up to 1914, he had been privileged to preach only in some of the important cities in Russia, but now through the persons of the converted war prisoners, he could reach the whole Russian Empire.

Burdened by the plight of the Russian war prisoners, he decided to go to the United States to organize a committee for the evangelization of the unfortunate Russians in Germany and Austria.

On February 1, 1915, Pastor Fetler, by the help of the "American Christian Herald" and a number of prominent Americans, founded the Gospel Commission for Work Among Russian War Prisoners in Europe.

Some of the most prominent members of this organization of the Baptists were Charles A. Brooks, L.A. Crandall and others. From the Methodists, Bishop William Burt (1852-1936) and J.C. Hartzell (1842-1928). From the Presbyterians, J.H. Jowett and J. Ross

Stevenson. From the Lutherans, Pastor William B. Schoenfeld and Pastor J.B. Remensnyder, and many others who participated in this work in one way or another.

Large quantities of Bible portions and other Christian literature were printed and shipped to Germany via Sweden.

The work of Mr. J.G. Lehmann, Director of the Christian literature distribution work in Kassel, Germany, became a great work. He was in constant communion with the prison camps and got the support of several hundred war prisoners who were willing to partake in the distribution work of the Christian literature among the war prisoners.

The prisoners were very thankful that such friendliness was manifested towards them, and Mr. Lehmann received thousands of letters, thanking him for the Christian kindness and for the literature. One prisoner, who was a co-worker, wrote: "I have distributed literature among the prisoners who have expressed their gratitude in saying that Mr. Lehmann had showed them the way and was bringing them up in a new life. Men who before played cards have turned their backs to the cards and are reading the literature in their free time."

One of the men who was a German Baptist missionary, Mr. H. Reimer, just returned from Kamerun, spoke Russian. He was accepted as an interpreter in one of the prison camps. He gathered together the converts among the war prisoners and preached to them on the Christian topics. As a result, several Baptist congregations were established in the prison camps.

The gospel tracts which were translated by Mrs. Fetler into Russian were printed in Kassel, and distributed to the Russian war prisoners in Germany. Several other Christian organizations took part in the work started by Pastor Fetler.

At the committee meeting in Berlin on November 28, 1917, Mr. Lehmann revealed that up to that time already 4,079 Bibles, 2,649 New Testaments and 87,237 Scripture portions had been distributed in 24 languages in the prison camps. By the funds raised by Pastor Fetler in America, a great quantity of gospel tracts had been printed, whereof 1,652,754 were distributed up to date. About 900 prisoners partook in the gospel work in the prison camps. The printed gospel messages led great numbers of the Russians to Christ. In one camp, there were about 10,000 Russian prisoners, of whom about 18 had been converted in Russia. They received Christian literature and began to distribute the tracts and sermons in the prison camp. By the permission of the camp commandant, a special barrack was set aside for prayer meetings. More and more war prisoners began to attend the meetings, which produced conversions; and by the end of six months, the number had grown from 18 to 628 who, upon the confession of their faith, were baptized in a nearby river. It was estimated that at least 20,000 Russian war prisoners were converted in the 36 prison camps which were visited by the evangelists in Germany and Austria.

**Pastor Basil A. Malof with his wife Barbara, 1929.**

By the end of 1920 more than 500 Russian converted prisoners had completed a Bible course provided by the Missionary Alliance.

By the end of the war, all these converted Russians returned to their native villages and towns, scattered all over Russia. They were all supplied with New Testaments and Bibles, some hymn books and tracts. Satan banished one missionary from Russia in 1914, but now Fetler sent 20,000 missionaries back to his country to preach the message of salvation. News soon reached the Committee that evangelical churches were growing all over Russia. In one province alone some 800 evangelical churches had been organized in the space of one year.

In an article (Dein Reich komme, No. 1-3, 1927) Mr. Fritz Lieb, Basel, wrote that at least 8,000 churches had been organized. Especially in Siberia, South Russia and Caucasus. The evangelical movement spread fast like a mighty stream. At one place in Siberia about 3,000 converts were baptized in one day and about 1,500 congregations were organized on both sides of the Siberian railroad.

A Russian, Professor V. Belotikov, spoke about this mighty spiritual move that spread from village to village like a great burning stream. In the Ukraine, in Odessa area, in many places, entire communities were saved and baptized. Villages with a population of about 2,400 to 4,000 were completely won by the gospel message.

At the conclusion of World War I, Pastor Fetler established a Bible School in Philadelphia, Pennsylvania, U.S.A., to which were accepted about 50 Russian students. In 1925 the Russian Missionary Society, headed by Pastor Fetler, supported about 85 missionaries and evangelists in the Soviet Union.[11]

[11] Oswald A. Blumit, **Sentenced to Siberia** (12th ed.: Washington: Mayflower Publishers, 1946), pp. 119-128.

**This ornate sanctuary, formerly a Russian Orthodox Church, is the home of Evangelical Christians—Baptists in Leningrad, U.S.S.R. Isolated on the northern outskirts of the city, with no transportation available to serve the people, this church was placed at the disposal of the believers when their centrally-located property with sanctuary built in 1910-12 was confiscated by the city to send this congregation to oblivion. (1970)**

# CHAPTER VII

## THE BIBLE SOCIETIES IN RUSSIA

### Publication of Lettish and Estonian Bibles

An aspect of Lutheran mission endeavor in Russia deserving of at least some attention was the work pursued in the field of Bible dissemination. In its broader aspects, this task encompassed all Christian denominations in the Empire, Lutherans included, and it would be difficult to discuss the distribution of religious literature by the Evangelical-Lutheran Church without placing it into the broad context of which it was an integral part. The Lutheran Church in Russia had already from its beginnings in Russian history played an active role in the field of Bible translation and dissemination. During the period 1689 to 1825 the Lettish Bible, in three separate editions, had been printed in 11,000 copies. The first edition probably never reached the homes of free Letts, and of the subsequent editions, 3,000 copies remained unsold as late as 1816. A restrictive factor in their sale was undoubtedly their relatively high cost, although the later editions were somewhat reduced in price. In 1730 some 15,000 copies of the New Testament alone were printed, but lack of a market consigned a good part of this edition to little more than waste paper. No further edition of the Lettish New Testament was therefore published until 1815. A traveller in 1810 reported the fact that no Lettish Bibles were to be found among Lettish families in the vicinity of Riga, and Superintendent-General Sonntag of Livonia in 1813 commented on the small use made of the Bible in the Baltic region. The New Testament in the North Estonian dialect was printed on five different occasions in small editions between 1729 and 1790, and the Bible in its entirety in this dialect was issued in only 4,000 copies between 1739 and 1773. More depressing yet was the status of Bible publishing in the South Estonian dialect. The Bible was never printed in full in South Estonian during this period, and the New Testament published in this dialect in 1727 was so scarce that in 1813 less than 200 copies were to be found among 106,000 inhabitants of the district. Even some of the clergy who preached in the dialect had no copies.

Copies of the Bible in other languages and dialects were equally scarce. In Finland the Bible printed in 1642 in Finnish was very rare and expensive. An investigation in 1815 revealed that although in the past 234 years the Slavonic Bible in Russia had been published in 22 editions, scarcely 60,000 copies had been issued. The old-Armenian Bible was so scarce in 1813 that even the Bible Society could find no complete copy and at first had to be satisfied with printing only the New Testament. And only with a great deal of trouble was it possible to obtain a copy of the 1771 edition of the Polish Bible. In the Russian, new-Armenian, new-Greek, and the Samogitian languages, the Holy Scriptures did not exist, and in Georgian it had completely disappeared.

Such then was the status of Bible publication and dissemination in Russia in the year 1812 on the eve of Napoleon's invasion of the Empire.

### The British and Foreign Bible Society in Russia

Emperor Alexander I, by nature a mystic, was much influenced in this perilous period by his Director-General Prince Alexander Golitsyn, later Minister for Ecclesiastical Affairs and Public Enlightenment. The way was prepared, therefore, for the arrival in 1810 of an agent of the British and Foreign Bible Society, the Rev. Mr. John Paterson (1776-1855). His purpose was to establish a Bible society for Finland at Turku, a project supported by a generous contribution from the Emperor. The French still occupied Moscow when a Bible society was also founded in St. Petersburg. The project not only received the Emperor's approval but was given added stimulus by a royal grant of 25,000 rubles plus an annual subsidy of 10,000 rubles; and other leaders of the Empire soon followed suit. The final statutes of the society were signed by Alexander on December 6, 1812. Evangelization of the Moslems and other non-Christians in the Russian Empire as well as promotion of Bible study among Christians were declared to be the principal objectives of the new organization; and Orthodox and Roman Catholic prelates, as well as Protestant clergy, were invited to join in sponsoring it.

With the preliminaries concluded, spiritual and secular dignitaries of the Empire together with the members of the British and Foreign Bible Society, Rev. Mr. Paterson and Rev. Mr. Robert Pinkerton (1784-1857), met on January 11, 1813, with Prince Golitsyn; and at this meeting the St. Petersburg Bible Society was constituted. Golitsyn was elected president, and as a vice president and director, the Lutheran Superintendent-General Thomas Rheinbott was chosen.

In June 1813 Paterson travelled to the Baltic provinces where he was well received. He was, however, appalled by the lack of Bibles there. After stopping over in Riga, where he held discussions with Superintendent-General Sonntag and the head of the city council Bergmann, he continued on to Mitau, where the director of the St. Petersburg Bible Society Lieutenant-General Count (later Prince) Carl Lieven (1767-1844) had prepared the way. Here plans were carried out for establishment of a Courland Bible Society. Lieven proposed Baron Medem, president of the Courland Consistory, as vice president.

On June 10 Privy Councillor Baron von Vietinghof, director of the St. Petersburg Bible Society, arrived from Tartu, where he had instituted a society earlier; and on June 23 a meeting with the Rev. Mr. Paterson in attendance was assembled to form one also in Riga. The president of the Livonian Consistory, Count Mellin, and Superintendent-General Sonntag were named vice presidents and Dr. Bergmann and Baron Comphausen directors.

On July 4, 1813, the Reval, later Estonian, Bible Society was formed with the consistorial president District Councillor von Loewenstern and Provost Holz as vice presidents. On the same day, a Bible Society was also established in Moscow, where Pinkerton had arrived with letters from Golitsyn for the Metropolitan-Vicar Augustin and the Archives Director of the Collegium of Foreign Affairs Bantysh-Kamenskiy. This was only 10 months after the burning of Moscow by French forces.

Evangelical colonists on both sides of the Volga, in Saratov and Samara guberniyas, also formed their own Bible Society organization. The society on the Hillside of the Volga joined the main Bible Society in St. Petersburg as a section committee. Its counterpart on the Meadowside at the time of its establishment, which had occurred somewhat earlier, joined the section committee in Moscow as an aid committee. Many thousands of copies of the Bible were sold in the colonies at a minimal cost, while many others were given away free, some to Siberian deportees. The local Volga groups also contributed money to the central organization. A Bible Society was organized also in Odessa to serve the requirements of the South Russian colonists.

In September 1814, at Emperor Alexander's request, the St. Petersburg Bible Society was renamed the Russian Bible Society and under this new name held its first annual meeting on September 16.

Present were the dignitaries of the Greek Orthodox, Armenian, Roman Catholic, and Georgian churches and leading men and women of the Empire, both civil and military. The grand dukes Nikolay and Michael, following the example of their brother the Emperor, also joined the society.

Establishment of the new Russian Bible Society and the subsequent founding of its branches were a manifestation of the period of rationalism and represented an attempt to combat its influences. The new society's aim was a Bible or at least a New Testament for every family in the country. The first Bibles issued were distributed to the destitute, prisoners-of-war, civil prisoners, hospitals and poor houses. All faiths of Russia were affected.

Emperor Alexander followed the society's activities with interest and at his request a translation of the Bible from Old Slavonic into popular Russian was undertaken. By the end of 1823 the Russian Bible Society, consisting by then of 57 section societies which were in turn broken down into 232 aid societies, had printed 804,881 copies of the Bible in 45 languages and dialects and had undertaken new translations in 16 languages and dialects. The society, in addition, received 48,700 Bibles from abroad from the British and North American Bible societies. The total distributed during its first 10 years of existence amounted to 861,106 copies. During the period 1812 to 1822 the British and Foreign Bible Society, exclusive of texts, expended 354,000 rubles in the Empire. The effort, however, was to come on bad times.

### Strong Opposition to the Bible Societies

Near the end of Alexander's reign, the earlier enthusiasm and support from the highest quarters of the Russian government gave way to doubt and mistrust. The translations undertaken by the society were regarded as tendentious and the whole project itself by reason of its support from abroad, was regarded in Russia with some suspicion. Furthermore, the ecclesiastical authorities in Russia were alarmed by the Society's open encouragement of Evangelical Christianity and its covert relationship with dissenting sects in the Empire. The result was a growing lack of confidence in the Society's leadership. Thus, by a decree of May 17, 1824, Prince Golitsyn was released as president of the Society and Seraphim, Metropolitan of Novgorod and St. Petersburg, was installed as his successor. Alexander I's early support and encouragement of the Society left apparently no lasting impression upon his successor and on April 12, 1826, Nicholas I issued a decree ordering discontinuance of the Russian Bible Society's activities and dissolution of all its subordinate organizations.

This setback, at least from the standpoint of the Lutherans, proved only temporary. Five years later the provincial authorities of the Baltic Evangelical Church petitioned for permission to retain their local Bible societies which had remained in existence until now, and on the basis of new statutes issued on March 14, 1831, the Evangelical Bible Society was created with a purpose similar if somewhat more limited than its predecessor. Of the great Russian Bible Society the Evangelical branch thus remained the only in existence. It was founded in order to provide Bibles to all Protestants in the Empire. The society's central committee under the presidency of Count Lieven, the Minister of Public Enlightenment, had its seat in St. Petersburg, while 20 sections and 277 branch committees in various parts of the Empire aided in the work of dissemination. From the time of its inception until the end of the century, the Evangelical Bible Society in Russia distributed 322,177 Bibles, 775,725 New Testaments, and 25,081 psalters.

A short-lived effort to carry on the work which the defunct Russian Bible Society had in supplementing the activity of the Evangelical Bible Society, was undertaken in 1869 with the establishment on May 2 of the Society for Dissemination of the Holy Scriptures in Russia – an organization based on a small group assembled in 1863 and led by the Lutheran bookseller Forchhammer. Forchhammer's group distributed Bibles at low cost, mainly around St. Petersburg, but also on the Volga from Perm to Astrakhan, in Moscow, and in the Caucasus.

On October 20, 1866, a ministerial decree abolished all societies not having prior government sanction, but Forchhammer's group submitted an appeal for such sanction on January 27, 1867; and when this was approved, the group was reorganized as the Society for Dissemination of the Holy Scriptures in Russia, and continued its work. Lack of funds to carry on the work, however, forced the society to give up its independent existence, and it eventually merged with the British Bible Society.

Still another organization created as an instrument for disseminating religious literature was the Christian Literature Agency for the Evangelical Communities of Russia, established in 1860 with headquarters in Riga. The literature produced by this agency was sold very cheaply. It was in effect the publishing house of the Lutheran Church in Russia.[1]

### The Bible Distribution Paved the Way for the Stundist Movement

The distribution of the Word of God and the brief life of the Russian Bible Society helped to prepare the way for the Stundist movement in the Ukraine.[2]

In the middle of the 19th century in the Caucasus, the preparatory evangelical work was greatly aided by William Melville (1806-1886), agent of the British and Foreign Bible Society, who devoted 60 years of his life to the circulation of Scripture portions during the reign of four Emperors.

The Scotsman Mellville, known in Russia as Vasili Ivanovich, was a leader and example to a host of colporteurs as he devoted his life to the circulation of Scripture portions in the Russian Empire. Kasha Iagub, born in Umrii, Persia, continued the work of Mellville. A graduate of Moody Bible Institute in Chicago, Iagub evangelized among the poor throughout Russia and Siberia under the name of Iakov Deliakovich Deliakov for almost 30 years with great success. The widow he married was the grandmother of Iakov I. Zhidkov, the first president of the All-Union Council of Evangelical Christians-Baptists.

In 1862, the complete Bible in the Russian language became a reality. Colporteurs of the Bible Society covered the Russian Empire, trying to reach everyone – rich and poor, simple and wise, educated and ignorant. Thus did the Bible become available to all the Russian people. In the Molokan, Stundist, and Evangelical-Baptist homes it became the book of the family, zealously studied and reverently observed.[3]

The Word of God was also studied among the Old Believers in the Cacasus, and one Old Believer priest (unidentified), who read the works of Martin Luther (1483-1546), experienced conversion and contributed to the start of the evangelical movement, which in the middle of the

1. Edgar C. Duin, **Lutheranism Under the Tsars and the Soviets, Vol. I**, (Ann Arbor, 1975), pp. 372-379.

2. Pollock, **op. cit.**, p. 59.

3. Durasoff, **op. cit.**, pp. 35-36.

19th century began in the Caucasus. Between 1869 and 1892 70,000 Bibles a year were sold.[4]

In 1907, at the request of the British and Foreign Bible Society, the Holy Synod agreed to print the Old Testament without the Apocrypha. The society, which received its supplies from the Holy Synod, could not circulate the Apocrypha. The society ordered an edition of 25,000 copies, which was quickly bought by the public. Further requests by the society for Bibles without the Apocrypha were rejected by the Holy Synod.[5]

In 1910 the Bible Society had an excellent representative in Russia in the Rev. Dr. William Kean (1870?-1918). He purchased all the Slavonic and Russian scriptures from the Holy Synod, and circulated the Word of God throughout the Russian Empire. By the means of its many colporteurs, the Scriptures were distributed in about 60 languages and dialects.[6]

The imperial government encouraged the distribution of the Holy Scriptures in prisons, accompanied by preaching of the gospel by the representatives of the Bible Society.[7]

**St. Basil's Cathedral in Red Square, Moscow, has been transformed into a museum.**

4. Pollock, **op. cit.**, p. 59.

5. Latimer, **op. cit.**, p. 123.

6. **Ibid.**, p. 204.

7. Pollock, **op. cit.**, p. 71.

## CHAPTER VIII

# THE 19th CENTURY EVANGELICAL MOVEMENTS IN FINLAND

### The First Methodists in the Russian Empire

The first Methodist in Finland was Miss Maria C. Hyden (1805-1885) in Tampere. She had been a member of George Scott's Methodist congregation in Stockholm, Sweden, about 1840. But the cradle of Finnish Methodism was the Bethel ship (a missionary boat) "John Wesley" in New York harbor, U.S.A. In it, seamen and immigrants were converted; and returning to their homeland, brought with them the message of a personal Savior. In the 1860s, Gustaf Barlund (1837-1889) and his brother Wilhelm from Kristiina, gathered a group of friends in an early Methodist society, gave their own house to be the first Methodist chapel in Finland, and asked both America and Sweden for ordained ministers.

A local Swedish preacher, Karl J. Lindborg (1854-1926), went on his personal initiative in 1880 to western Finland and preached in Vasa, Kokkola, and several other places. He published a church magazine and then was called before the Archbishop's Council in Turku and denied the right to preach. In 1883 Gustaf Wagnsson (1857-1929) got the first formal appointment in the Sweden Conference to go to Finland. He worked in many places and organized several congregations. In 1884 Bengt A. Carlson (1833-1920) was sent to Helsinki. There he worked for several years, formed a society, started a Methodist magazine, "Nya Budbararen" (New Messenger), travelled in many parts, even to St. Petersburg, Russia.

Another Swede, Gustaf A. Hiden (1864-1937) tried to learn Finnish in order to reach the vast majority of the people. In Pori he met Jonas W. Haggman (1864-1946), a chemist, who became the recognized leader of the Finnish-speaking Methodism. Hiden, however, started the Finnish Methodist periodical "Rauhan Sanomia" (The Message of Peace) and a Sunday School periodical, "Lasten Ystava" (Children's Friend). He also arranged for the translation of the Discipline and a Finnish hymnal.

Until 1892 the work in Finland was organized as a district of the Sweden Conference, but that year the Finland and St. Petersburg Mission was formed, with Johannes Roth (1850-1909) as its superintendent. In 1907 George A. Simons (1874-1952) from the United States was sent to take care of the work in the Russian capital, and at the same time he was named superintendent for both Finland and Russia. In 1904, Karl J. Hurtig (1870-1947) came from Sweden to take care of the Swedish-speaking work in Helsinki, and he stayed there for the rest of his life.

The Finland Annual Conference was organized in 1911, with the work in Russia being made a separate mission. A preachers' seminary was started in Tempere in 1897, with J.W. Haggman for many years its leader. It moved to Helsinki in 1907, where it still is. Social work has had an important part in Methodism in Finland. Already in 1886 a Swedish-speaking Methodist woman in Kristiina, Christina Svanstrom, started a home for destitute children. A Finnish-speaking home was instituted in 1909 at Epila, near Tampere. In 1912 Karl Hurtig in Helsinki started a children's home in nearby Kauniainen, still in operation, where over a thousand children have been brought up. An international seamen's mission, established in Kotka in 1881, was entrusted to the Methodist Church in 1901, and the work was carried on until 1964. A.K. Aulanko (1883-1960) was its leader for many years.

In the Swedish conference in session in Stockholm in 1874, the presiding Bishop, William L. Harris (1817-1887), brought to the attention of the conference the need of evangelizing Finland and Russia. Ten years later, Bengt A. Carlson was appointed to Helsinki, the capital of Finland. As soon as possible, he visited St. Petersburg to study the possibility of starting a Methodist work in the Russian capital. After the annual conference in 1889, Bishop Charles H. Fowler (1837-1908) and Carlson visited St. Petersburg and rented a house at Vasili Ostroff. In November 1889 the first Methodist congregation was organized with seven members in the Russian capital.

The work was carried on by preachers and laymen from Finland – one of them, Hjalmar Salmi, mastered three languages: Finnish, Russian, and Swedish. He became the best helper to Mr. Simons. Rev. Mr. George A. Simons was appointed superintendent of Finland and Russia, with special direction to carry on and develop the work among the Russians and throughout the whole Russian Empire.

During the first 10 years, however, the Methodist work in Russia was concentrated in St. Petersburg in the district of Ingria (Ingermanland) west of the city, where the people were Finnish-speaking, and in the Baltic States – besides two congregations in far-off Siberia. When the work in Finland was organized as an annual conference in 1911, Russia became a "mission," and so was the work in the Baltic provinces until the Baltic and Slavic Missions Conference was organized in 1924. In 1911 there were 19 places mentioned in the appointments; eight, however, "to be supplied." In 1920 there were only six Pastors in the Russian Mission. World War I had claimed its victims, and so did the Russian Revolution, which began in 1917. In October 1918, Rev. Mr. Simons was compelled to leave Russia.

In 1922 and 1923 Bishop John L. Nuelsen (1867-1946) paid short visits to Russia. His presence caused some sensation and great expectations. As a consequence, some of the bishops and leading men were invited to Moscow by a reform movement within the Russian Orthodox Church, asking them to help in organizing a democratic living church. Out of it, however, came nothing. After many difficulties, Raymond J. Wade (1875-1970) in 1928 had been assigned as Bishop of Northern Europe, got a visa to Russia, and there held the last annual conference of the Russian Mission. He baptized four children and married two couples. The situation was such that the Bishop advised the few remaining Methodists to join the Baptists or other evangelical groups. This they did, so Methodism ended as a denomination in Russia.

The only Methodist who stayed in Russia to 1931 was Anna Eklund (1867-1949). She prepared for her future work as a deaconess at the Methodist Deaconess Institute in Hamburg, Germany. In 1907, when Mr. Simons was named superintendent for Finland and Russia, she was called to join him in his work in St. Petersburg. Sister Eklund started a deaconess institute, and several of her young pupils have continued her work in Estonia, the other Baltic States, and Germany. When Mr. Simons was compelled to leave Russia in October 1918, she stayed and took care of church property, the pastor's home, and the congregation. The good lady acted as Pastor and Sunday School teacher, and leader of a steadily growing social work. In the 1920s she was leader of the great relief work carried on by the Methodist Episcopal Church in the United States. Ultimately she had to leave Russia, fleeing to Estonia and thence returning to Finland in 1931.

The Methodist work in Estonia was started by Rev. Kaarel Kuum (1867-1932) in June 1907. He visited St. Petersburg and met Bishop

Simons of the United States and accepted the Methodist doctrine. The Methodist churches were established between 1910-1913 in Tallinn, in Tartu, and in Kuresaare in Saaremaa. By 1914 there were 500 Methodists in Estonia.

The first Methodist church in Lithuania was founded in 1904. The Rev. Mr. George R. Dundis worked in Kaunas.[1] (In 1900 there were about 317 Methodists in Finland, and in 1980 there were about 1,300 Methodists in Soviet Estonia.)

The front of the Palace of Peter the Great

## The Baptist Movement in Finland

The Baptist doctrine entered Finland about 1854. A noble man of Sweden, Carl J.M. Mollersvard (1832-1901) arrived in the United States of America in the early 1850s and was converted and baptized in 1853 at the New York Baptist Marines' Church. Upon his return to Sweden, he began with the evangelistic activities as an independent evangelist. A priest of the Ahvenamaa Islands in the Botnis Bay belonging to Finland (but populated by Swedes) wrote to the Evangelical Alliance in Stockholm, Sweden, requesting the organization to send an evangelist

1. Nolan B. Harmon (Editor), **The Encyclopedia of World Methodism**, Copyright © by the United Methodist Publishing House, (Nashville: 1974), Vol. I. pp. 843-844, 759-760. Vol. II. p. 2057.

to Ahvenamaa to rejuvenate the spiritual life on the islands. The organization knew that Mollersvard was a Baptist, but they extracted a promise from the evangelist not to mention anything about the baptism by immersion in his messages, nor about church affiliation.

He began with his evangelistic work in Foglo in 1854. The beginning was very promising because so many people attended the meetings and were converted. However, when the State Church realized that there was "another spirit" in the Swedish preacher, the opposition began to intensify. The opposition forced him to abandon his work, and he fled secretly to Sweden. But the fire had been kindled which the Holy Spirit kept burning. The believers gathered together to sing and to pray. Mollersvard never spoke about baptism publicly, but privately he explained it to the people, and they knew that the evangelist was a Baptist preacher.

Some of the Christian fishermen visited Stockholm and brought with them some of the Baptist literature, which the Christians studied in the light of the Bible. Thus the teaching of the baptism by immersion and the New Testament assembly became clear to them. Three people went to Stockholm where they were baptized and three were baptized in Ahvenamaa. These six people established the first Swedish-speaking Baptist church in Ahvenamaa, Finland, in 1856.

The Baptists were severely persecuted, especially because they refused to baptize infants. The State Church summoned the Baptists to Turku to give an account to the Archbishop. The humble Baptists had to travel twice to Turku to give an account of their faith. However, on the second time the Lord intervened on the behalf of His people and touched the hearts of some of the members of the Church Council. A priest, Henrik Heikel (1808-1867) of the State Church, invited the Baptists to his parsonage where the conversation continued until early morning hours. Two of the priest's daughters and two of his sons were converted, baptized and joined the Baptist ranks. Later, Heikel was transferred to Pietarsaar to oversee the Lutheran work there. The Baptist congregation in Pietarsaar was established in 1870, and in 1871 the first Baptist church was built in the same community as the first evangelical church in Finland.

The Baptist work among the Finnish-speaking people was started in Luvia, close to the city of Pori, in 1867, by a seaman, J. Henriksson (1820?-1969). In 1870 the Baptist congregation in Luvia was established. At the same time, the second Baptist church in the Karelia was founded. In 1872 a Lutheran minister, John Hymander

(1803-1877) was baptized in Stockholm, Sweden, and upon his return to Finland he baptized his wife and some people of his church who had been converted. He separated himself from the State Church and established a Baptist church. By 1879 four Finnish-speaking Baptist congregations had been established in Finland. In 1880 the Baptists had a real breakthrough, and the movement began to spread in the country. In 1881, Erik Jansson (1848-1921?) joined the Baptist ranks and in 1882 established a Baptist church in Amos, which he pastored for 19 years. By 1901 his congregation had about 400 members.

In 1883 there were about 10 Baptist congregations in Finland. By 1889, with the help of other evangelistic associations, the Baptists established their own organization; and in 1891 the Baptists had their first Baptist conference in Finland. In the same year the Baptist magazine was published and was printed in Finnish in 1896. In 1892 a Baptist Bible School was established and young men were trained for the ministry. By the late 1890s, a great revival blessed the Baptist work. In 1900 there were about 2,800 Baptists in Finland – 300 of them Finnish-speaking. The Baptist movement spread rapidly among the Swedish and Finnish-speaking people in Finland, having about 5,000 members in 1914.[2]

**The Free Church in Finland**

The Free Church (Covenant) work as such was established in Finland about 1880. It entered the country in two ways: the Swedish Missionary Organization (Fosterlandet's Mission's Forbundet) and the British Missionary Alliance. The movement began slowly in several places.

In the city of Oulu, close to the Swedish border in the north, the Swedish Free Church had left its marks already in 1860, and in Tampere in 1871. In the same city, a businessman C.J. Hilden (1817-1891) was saved in Sweden in 1869. In Oulu, Hjalmar Braxen (1854-1934) was saved in 1876 and became a great preacher for the Free Church. Another great worker was Baron Constantin A.L. Boije (1854-1934) who was saved at the age of 16, terminated his education at the age of 19, and went to Sweden in 1873 to study at the Swedish Mission's School for the ministry. While studying in Sweden, he met people of evangelical movements and adopted their views.

2. Kuosmanen, **op. cit.**, pp. 227-231.

He returned to Finland in 1877 and began revival meetings with a teacher, James Forsberg (1852-1938), in Sipoo near Porvoo. This revival spread in a mighty way, producing numerous conversions; and in 1877 the first Free Church house of prayer was built it Vehkakoskee. At the same time, another good preacher, Edvard Bjorkenheim (1856-1934), began with his evangelistic work in Pohjanmaa, which was helped by a Swedish preacher A.F. Tiselius (1837-1907). He was Baptist in belief but travelled and preached for the Free Church as well. He ministered in Pietarsaar in the spring of 1879.

The Baptist congregation started by the Heikel sisters in Pietarsaar joined the Free Church. The Hellman sisters, who at first had Baptist views, joined the Free Church and played a great part in the growth of the work. Miss Alba Hellman (1845-1894) was baptized in 1870, and together with her sister Hilda began the temperance work in 1877.

The revival fires for the Free Church in Helsinki, the capital city of Finland, was started by Lord Radstock's visit to Helsinki in October 1879. This revival started among the educated class of the Swedish-speaking people. The work was carried on by Baron Boije and Tiselius. In 1881 Baron Boije established a Free Church congregation of the Swedish-speaking people with membership cards. At once, 180 people joined the church and the work grew quickly.

One of the most outstanding preachers and Bible teachers of that time was Antti Makinen (1857-1936). He joined the movement in 1881 and for 20 years led the Free Church work in Finland. A great revival swept Turku in 1884 when Edvard Bjorkkenheim preached there. Every day 30 to 40 people visited him to ask about the way of salvation.

Baron Boije held revivals in the city of Loviisa, Braxen in Tammisaar and later in Tampere. In the latter city, a businessman, Hilden, built a house of prayer in 1884. The work at that place was started by Antti Makinen and Mr. Boije. Mr. Braxen began with his revival in Tampere in February 1885 and established a choir, which became a great attraction. The people were hungry for the Word of God in those days. In the evenings, one hour before the service, the people lined up on the street to wait for the doors to open. By the end of the same year, the Free Church had in Tampere about 100 members. The work in Finland was greatly helped by visiting British preachers, especially Reginald Radcliffe (1825-1895). The years of 1875-1889 have been called the years of first revival.

A new wave of revival blessed the work in the years of 1890-1893.

In 1891 Fredrik Nyren (1859-1908) from Sweden had many great revivals in Finland. The most notable is the one in Jyvaskyla which lasted for seven weeks, resulting in the conversion of about 300 people. One of the converts was Sulo S. Salmensaari (1874-1966), who in the 1900s was the leader of the Free Church for several years.

In the beginning of 1890, the Free Church was riddled badly by heretical doctrines. The teaching of sanctification came from Sweden, which was twisted by some of the Finnish Bible teachers – teaching "sinlessness." The believers divided into two groups: the "sinless" and the "sinful." This damaged the work badly, but the majority stayed faithful to the Free Church. The leader of the "sinless" group was Dr. Erik Hertz. The teachers of the "sinless" taught that a Christian is so dedicated that his flesh is dead and does not bother him anymore. They believed that they had already entered the "Sabbath of rest." This heresy split the Free Church Home Mission (founded in 1889), called Free Mission, into four sections, the "sinless" and the "sinful" and the "old" and the "young." Of course, there were still old and young people on both sides. The most difficult year was 1894 because at that time the young people connected with the Free Mission had to separate themselves from the Mission. However, some shocking occurrences began to open eyes of many of the deluded people.

Around 1902 or 1903 one more heretical doctrine invaded Finland. At that time an eloquent preacher, Akseli Skutnabb (1875-1929) accepted a new teaching from Sweden. According to this doctrine (salvation of the whole world), all the people who came to God as a prodical son would be converted, and thus the whole world would be saved. A group of the "sinless" joined Mr. Skutnabb, but this group had no success and never had any revivals worth mentioning. These storms hurt the movement badly in many places throughout the country. In 1902 the Free Mission became as a foreign Mission.

There was a great need of Finnish-speaking preachers, so the Free Mission established a Bible School in Tampere in 1905. Regardless of all the storms, the Free Mission had to face, its membership doubled from 1900 to 1911. The largest congregation was in Tampere where in 1904 they had 145 members.

New life was infused into the movement by Eeli Jokinen (1888-1963) and his brother William (1889-1958). These men were capable preachers and had great revivals. From 1907 to 1911 Pohjanmaa had successful revivals that resulted in many conversions. In 1911 there was a 12-week revival in Helsinki and about 150 converts joined the movement. In 1912 in Lahti, about 150 converts were accepted as members of the church, and in Jyvaskyla in one night, 108 joined the church. There was a 10-week revival in Turku in 1914 that resulted in the conversion of about 300 people. In Tampere in 1914, there was a 10-week revival and about 400 joined the church. The Young People's Conference was started in 1915, followed by the publication of the "Nuorten Todistus" (Young People's Testimony) in 1916. Their first missionary, Agnes Meyer (1861-1897), was sent to China by the Free Mission in 1890. By 1898 they had about 16 missionaries in the Far East.[3]

## The Salvation Army in Finland

Baron Constantin A.L. Boije had contacted the Salvation Army in Sweden in 1883 and had liked its way of operations. Baron Boije was a member of one of the noble families in Finland, which was then an autonomous grand duchy within the Russian Empire. He was sent by his government in 1888 to inspect night refuges for the poor in different countries and had seen the Salvation Army at work in Stockholm, Berlin, and London. Already influenced by revival meetings conducted by Lord Radstock in Helsinki in 1879, Baron Boije formed the converts into what became known as the Free Church, but when he saw the Army at work he was greatly impressed and desired to organize the Free Church like the Salvation Army. However, the majority of the congregation did not like this, and Baron Boije separated himself from the Free Church and joined the Army. He began another mission in a small room with a group of enthusiastic evangelists, which included Mrs. Louise af Forselles, (1850-1920?), wife of a military colonel and sister of Princess Ouchtomsky.

Mrs. af Forselles was saved in France in 1875 and became an enthusiastic witness for the Lord Jesus Christ. In 1888 she visited Switzerland where her sister joined the Salvation Army. From Switzerland, Mrs. af Forselles went to London to see the Army operations there and to visit the Army Headquarters, especially General Booth. In one of the officer's meetings, General Booth asked her: "Would this be acceptable in Finland?" "Oh, yes," replied af Forselles, "come and visit us."

Upon her return to Finland, she began with meetings on the Army

3. Ibid., pp. 232-273, 312.

line on Metsastajankadu (now Jaakarinkatu). She herself never became an officer in the Army, but she worked for the Army until her death and helped the Army work get started in Finland.

The third person who helped to get the Army work started was Hedvig von Haartman (1862-1902), who was saved in a crusade in Turku contacted by E. Bjorkenheim in 1884. She helped Baron Boije in Helsinki and later was with Mrs. af Forselles on Metsastajankadu. Baron Boije and af Forselles got her interested in the Army work. In 1889 three people, Baron Boije, Haartman, and Alva Forsius (born in 1866) were encouraged by Mrs. af Forselles to go to London to study at the Army Cadet School. After half a year of studies, they returned to Finland the same year. Six months later, Baron Boije separated from the Army and returned to the Free Church and became a Pastor.

The Salvation Army operations began in Finland on November 8, 1889. The whole staff of officers consisted of only Captain and Mrs. Boije and Lieutenants von Haartman and Forsius. The inauguration took place in Broholm's Riding School, Helsinki, and attracted a great many kinds of people – from the impressive general in his gold-trimmed uniform to the lowly workman, from the fashionable lady to the poor shop assistant. Also present was one of the outstanding figures of Finland's public and intellectual life, Professor Zacharias Topelius.

Soon after its beginning, the Army submitted its statutes to the Imperial Senate for approval. They were rejected and Salvationists were now then confronted with many difficulties. They were forbidden to open their halls, to advertise, to take up collections, to sell their papers, to wear uniforms – they were even brought before the police authorities and their insignia removed.

Captain Boije had been a personal friend of the Governor-General, General von Heyden, since military academy days, and being well acquainted with the Russian authorities' fear of all international movements, stressed the importance of the work being put on a national basis. This proposal was laid before William Booth, who contrary to his usual attitude in such circumstances, gave his consent in the hope that the national Army would join the international Army at a later date. But the majority of Finland's Salvationists did not subscribe to Boije's idea. They desired to profit from the international link and requested that it should be maintained, whereupon Boije withdrew and at the beginning of May 1890, Lieutenant von Haartman took over the responsibility for the work provisionally. She was appointed leader in

September with the rank of Adjutant. She possessed an indominable spirit and soon had organized everything well.

The Army's work attracted the attention of the Russian government, and having fears regarding the future, von Haartman sent the Governor-General a copy of William Booth's "In Darkest England and the Way Out," and then sought an interview with him. The Governor-General was greatly impressed by the Adjutant's calm, modest dignity, her common sense and her message; and gave his consent for the continuation of the activities of the Salvationists.

Souls were converted despite the opposition. Within four months the names of 80 soldiers and recruits had been placed on the roll, and the average Sunday night congregation numbered 900. The first meeting in Finnish was conducted in May 1890 by Lieutenant von Haartman, who had considerable difficulty in speaking the language of which she, in common with most members of the Swedish-speaking "upper class" of those days, had very little knowledge.

The second opening took place on August 18, 1890, at Borgo, a town of some 4,000 inhabitants. The third opened five weeks later at Hameenlinna, a military town with a garrison of 1,000 Russian soldiers. This was the first Finnish corps. A Swedish corps at Abo, a seaport of 25,000 at that time, one half speaking Finnish and the other half Swedish, was opened in October by women officers. At Pori, another seaport, the first two lad-lieutenants were "making the salvation fire blaze." Here the officer was arrested, taken by prison-sleigh to Abo (Turku) and then to Helsinki, but was soon afterwards set free by the Governor.

By November, five corps with 19 officers and about 200 soldiers had been established, and an auxiliary league (non-Salvationist friends) met in the home of Baroness von Kothen.

In June 1892 Captain Glad of Helsinki IV, was imprisoned for 14 days as she was unable to pay the fines imposed upon her in Turku for defying the ban on the holding of public meetings.

Twelve corps had been opened by the spring of 1893, besides four slum corps and several outposts – the officers numbering 41.

Opposition was still very much alive in official circles, and expulsion from the country of all foreigners belonging to the Army was insisted upon by the Governor-General. It was while attending a congress in Copenhagen in 1893 that Major von Haartman received a telegram announcing the date when the first batch of alien officers under her command would be expelled. Work among children had been started, printed regulations issued, junior soldier local officers appointed, and a Christmas feast held in Helsinki. The Helsinki Temple was built in 1895. In 1897 there were 32 corps in Finland with 104 officers and 1,300 adherants.[4]

### Prison Work in Finland and in Siberia

The evangelization of prisoners in Finland was begun by the Hellman sisters in Vasa in 1860. They visited the prison houses voluntarily as Christian workers in the kingdom of God. Three of the Hellman sisters were school teachers and all four sisters worked for the Lord whenever opportunity arose. Because of sickness, Alba Hellman terminated her prison work in 1869. Her work in the prison was carried on by her sister, Hilda Hellman (1839-1901). Alba suffered because of heart disease and for nearly seven years she slept in a sitting position. However, in 1883 she was able to encourage Baron Henrik Wrede to engage in the prison work which he also accepted. His sister, Baroness Mathilde Wrede, became famous in this kind of work. She was able to win the confidence of the prisoners who used to say, "God in heaven and Miss Wrede on earth." She began with this work in 1883 and continued until 1921 when she resigned because of old age.

Alba Hellman was very much concerned with the poor spiritual condition of the prisoners in Siberia, but her health and lack of funds did not make it possible for her to visit distant Siberia. However, in 1876 a British preacher Henry Lansdell visited Vasa, Finland, and visited the city hospital. A lady who had come with the same boat to Sava encouraged him to see Alba Hellman. Alba had studied a little English and was able to understand some of the conversation. When she learned that the English Pastor had been to Russia before and that he was interested in the prison work, Alba asked him if he could do something for the prisoners in Siberia. Later she wrote to him and asked if they had a Morrison or a Moffat for Siberia who could lead some of the prisoners to Christ. Pastor Lansdell was so impressed that he visited many prisons in Russia in 1878, and in April 1879 he went to Siberia. He met also some Finns in that land and their Pastor, Roschierin. Pastor Lansdell travelled through Siberia and distributed much of God's Word in that land of horror.

[4] Arch Wiggins, **The History of the Salvation Army,** Vol. IV: 1886—1904. (Edinburg: T.A. Constable Ltd., Hopetown St. Printers to the University of Edinburg, 1964), pp. 46—51.

The British and Foreign Bible Society had been looking for a suitable person whom whey could send to Siberia to open a Bible bookstore, but had not had any success. The Society requested Baron Wrede if he were willing to go to Siberia. In the fall of 1883 Baron Wrede left for Irkutsk and established a bookstore and was its manager for two years. During this time he travelled through Siberia, even to the Chinese border.

When Mr. Wrede returned to Finland, he established on his own property in Anjala a home for the freed prisoners, which he managed for 10 years.[5]

**The Pentecostal Movement in the Russian Empire**

Since 1797 the baptism of the Holy Spirit with the evidence of speaking in tongues has never ceased in Finland. Around 1900 there were groups of believers who spoke in tongues. The best known speaker in tongues was Hilda Sarlin (1850?-1921). There was an outpouring of the Holy Spirit among the followers of the Swedish revivalist Lars L. Laestadius (1800-1861) in Narva, Estonia, in the late 1890s. They were simply called the people of Narva. Some of the Narva people had come to Helsinki, where they had prayer meetings in a small room, called the "Catacomb." There were others who joined the Narva people, and prayer meetings were held every day before noon in the homes and in the evenings at the "Catacomb." These meetings continued for about six weeks. The people were expecting an outpouring of the Holy Spirit.

The Pentecostal movement began in Finland among the Swedish-speaking people in 1911. The years of 1906-1911 were years of preparation for the new Pentecostal revival, because news of the new revival from America had reached Finland. A Methodist preacher of England, Thomas P. Barrat (1862-1940), who lived and preached in Norway, had received the infilling of the Holy Spirit. In 1906 Pastor J. Haggman told the students at the Methodist Theological Seminary in Tampere, that Pastor Barrat had had the Pentecostal experience – speaking in tongues. After that experience, he ministered with great blessings in Norway, and the gifts of the Spirit were also manifested in his meetings. This sparked a great interest in the hearts of the students to study the Bible to find out what the Word of God said about the Holy Spirit, the baptism with the Spirit, and the gifts of the Spirit.

5. Antti Makinen, **Vapaakirkollinen Liike Suomessa** (Helsinki: Mercator'in Kirjapaino, 1910) pp. 155-160.

The other channel through which the people were informed about the new movement was the "Kotimaa lehti," a Christian paper. Later also some of Barrat's papers in the Norwegian language arrived in Finland, and also some from America. All this information of the new movement created a great expectancy in the hearts of many hungry souls. In 1907 when the Methodist Seminar was moved to Helsinki, the students began to pray for the outpouring of the Holy Spirit.

In 1911 Pastor Barrat visited Finland and held meetings in Turku, in Helsinki, in Kuopio, in Viipuri and in Tampere. At his first visit, only one woman, a follower of Laestadius, was baptized with the Holy Spirit. However, his messages strengthened the faith in the hearts of the believers and increased their desire to pray more earnestly for the baptism of the Holy Spirit. His visit did not produce any Pentecostal movement in Finland, but a group of determined people were left behind to pray for an outpouring of the Spirit. Prayer meetings continued in the home of a school teacher, Hanna Castren; and more and more people began to experience the Pentecostal blessing of speaking in tongues. Emil Danielsson and Pekka Brofeldt (1864-1945) were leaders in these meetings.

In 1912 Gerhard O. Smidt arrived in Finland from Norway, and became known as the Pentecostal Apostle of Finland. He was an officer of the Salvation Army but had been filled with the Holy Spirit in the United States. In 1912 he began a great Pentecostal revival which lasted for three years, and Smidt was the undisputed leader in 1912-1914 and 1919-1925. People of all faiths joined the Pentecostal ranks as well as multitudes of converted people. In 1912 there began a real outpouring of the Holy Spirit, and people were filled with the power of God. From which faith the first Pentecostals came is difficult to determine. The new revival moved among all of the different faiths. In Helsinki the Spirit-filled people were primarily Methodists, followers of Laestadius, and from a Foreign Mission's Society. After this, people came from the Salvation Army and from the Baptist ranks. In the city of Turku people came also from the Free Church, and small groups of people came from every group of believers.

At first the brethren had no intention to establish a new denomination, but the Pentecostals were so strongly opposed and often asked to separate themselves from the churches, that they were forced to establish their own denomination. Also, Smidt encouraged people to separate themselves from all other groups and have their own Pentecostal movement.

From the beginning, many of the Pentecostals believed that believers should be baptized by immersion, because all the saints of this new revival studied the Bible and sought the deep truths. After Smidt sanctioned water baptism, they began to baptize believers in the summer of 1912 (July 1) in Lempaala where 7 people were baptized. The next two baptismal services were held in Helsinki on July 7 the same year, when about 63 people were baptized. Another factor that helped the Pentecostal revival to become a separate movement was the appearance of the Pentecostal magazine "Ristin Voittu." In 1912 Pastor Barrat's magazine in Norway "Korsets Seier" (Victory of the Cross) was translated by Pekka Brofeldt into the Finnish language, printed in Norway and sent to Finland. The next year the translation and publication of the magazine moved to Finland where the paper was translated by Arno Fellman (1882-1954) and edited by H.V. Sjoblom.

On July 6, 1912, the first Foreign Missions worker was ordained. Smidt and the visitng Rev. Mr. King (1869-1946), Overseer of the Pentecostal Holiness Church of the U.S., officiated. The first missionary dedicated on that date was Emil Danielsson, who went to Africa and worked in Kenya until 1919.

Pastor Barrat visited Finland annually during the early years of the Pentecostal revival. Through his magazine he was an unofficial leader of the movement, while Smidt was a local leader. In the spring of 1912, Pastor Barrat preached in Helsinki and in Tampere. In Tampere great crowds of people attended the meetings with a number receiving the Pentecostal experience and many being healed of diseases. In 1913 the new Pentecostal revival spread throughout the country, and in the city of Kuopio about 100 people took Communion as members of the local body; and in Helsinki during Barrat's meetings, several hundred people partook. In the city of Oulu, a Methodist Pastor, Akseli Puhakainen (1879-1949), had to separate himself from the church and a part of the congregation went with him. He became a Pentecostal Pastor. In Viipuri, the Pentecostal revival began among the Methodists and spread in 1913 to the Russian Baptists.

In June 1913 the first Pentecostal Conference was held in Lahti, which was of great importance to the new revival. The same year there was also a conference in Tampere. It was there that for the first time they began to call the new revival "the Pentecostal revival." In January and February of 1914 in Turku, the Pentecostal revival attracted great crowds – from 600 to 1,000 people. At the end of 1914, G. Smidt had to leave Finland for Norway because of war. In 1915 in Helsinki, the Pentecostal-Baptists established their own church known as Siloam. That was the first Pentecostal church in Finland. In 1914 Pekka Hakkarainen brought from Leningrad the "Jesus Only" teaching, but the Finns did not accept it. World War I hampered greatly the new revival, but after the war it began to gain momentum again.

Before World War I the new revival had to contest with some heretical doctrines. The first had to do with the doctrine of sanctification and the gift of prophecy. This was promulgated in 1914 by a missionary, Oskari Puutula, and a teacher, Lyydi Tapio. This was rejected and later Puutula himself with others joined the Pentecostal revival. In 1914 Pekka Hakkara brought from St. Petersburg the "Jesus Only" doctrine, but this was rejected and it never gained ground among the Finns. The third wave of trouble was the teaching about the washing of feet at the Communion services, and Saturday as the day of rest. Finally in 1919 at the Pentecostal Conference, this teaching was excluded. However, the question about this teaching produced a discrepancy; and Pekka Mikkonen separated himself from the Pentecostals and established his own group, known under the name of "God's People."

The Pentecostal revival entered Russia proper in three ways: It spread from Finland to St. Petersburg, from the United States to the Ukraine, and from the province of Estonia to various parts. In 1911 Pastor Barrat visited St. Petersburg and proclaimed the Pentecostal doctrines. The same year the Russian Baptist congregation in Helsinki joined the Pentecostal revival. A missionary, Urshan, had returned from the United States and through his influence, this congregation accepted "Jesus Only" teachings and joined the Pentecostals. In Finland this teaching was called the Smorodin doctrine. Mr. N. P. Smorodin and Mr. N. I. Ivanov, former leaders of the Helsinki Russian Baptist church, moved to St. Petersburg and began the Pentecostal work in the Russian capital city.[6]

The American Assemblies of God work was started after the revolution in the Ukraine by Ivan Voronaev. (See Chapter XI)

[6] Kuosmanen, **op. cit.**, pp. 334-342.

## CHAPTER IX

# OTHER EVANGELICAL MOVEMENTS IN THE RUSSIAN EMPIRE

### The First Attempt to Evangelize in St. Petersburg in 1820 to 1824 Fails

During his short reign, Emperor Paul I had invited the Catholic Order of the Knights of Malta, which Napoleon (1769-1821) had expelled from Malta, to come to the Russian capital and had built a church for them – one of the whims of this strange ruler. When Emperor Alexander I, his son and successor, was faced with the necessity of calling a Catholic priest to this church, he wanted to find a man who, despite his affiliation to the Catholic Church, preached an evangelical gospel.

During those years there was a healthy wave of revival running through the ranks of the young chaplains in Bavaria. It had been set in motion by Professor Johann M. Sailer (1751-1832) and by the influence of the priest Martin Boos (1762-1825), who himself had been brought to faith in justification through the blood of Jesus Christ by the means of the testimony of a dying woman. From the circle of these awakened Catholic priests, Alexander in 1818 called Ignaz Lindl (1774-1845) to the Maltese church in St. Petersburg. Two years later he migrated back to Germany. It was he who recommended Johannes E. Gossner (1773-1858) as his successor at the Maltese church, who like Lindl had been saved through the testimony of Martin Boos.

Gossner was son of a Swabian farmer from the vicinity of Augsburg, studied theology under Sailer and prepared for the ministry in the Catholic Church. As a young chaplain, he read Martin Boos' letters from the ecclesiastical prison in Goggingen. He experienced a deep awakening and from then on he became a reformed preacher and Pastor in a Catholic cassock.

In 1819 came a letter from the Russian ambassador in Berlin announcing his summons to the Maltese church in the Russian capital. On July 30, 1820, Gossner gave his first sermon. Some 500 people filled the little church. Those who sincerely wanted to become Christians he gathered in his apartment.

Soon the apartment was too small, and his friends rented him a palace where more than a thousand people could be seated in the banquet hall. Here Gossner held his weekly Bible study. It is said that the Emperor himself contributed to the rent of this house. Twice a week he taught religious classes for young people. Each Monday was devoted to the German almshouse, which up to then had been neglected spiritually. He had good success and quite a few converts as a result of his preaching in St. Petersburg. His audience even included some of the ministers of Emperor Alexander I.

This time of rich blessing did not last long. Among Gossner's opponents were Dominican monks then allowed in Russia. The opposition of the State Church was growing stronger. The Metropolitan Serafim begged the Emperor to dismiss Prince Golitsyn, to suspend the ministry for religious affairs, and to put controls on the harmful books. With the fall of this fine Christian man, Gossner's position too was undermined. On April 19, 1824, he gave his last message, lasting one and a half hours. He sensed the end of his work in St. Petersburg and gave one powerful testimony to Jesus and His saving blood. He closed with the words of Luther in Worms: "Here I stand, God help me, I can do no other. Amen."

Although befriended by Metropolitan Mikhail, who translated some of his religious tracts into the Russian langauge, Gossner was pictured by Count Arakcheev as an enemy of the Orthodox Church.

The following Saturday he was forbidden to preach. On Sunday came the Governor-General's order that he must leave the country within a few days. His work which lasted only four years, kindled a revival spirit which survived for several decades. His followers had meetings in the homes. The fruit of this revival even reached Estonia. The Baltic painter Baron Ludwig von Maydell from Tartu, Estonia, and a famous theologian Brehm, was a fruit of Gossner's work.[1]

### Conversion of Count Zaremba and His Missionary Work in Russia

One of the most unusual men of this circle was Count Felician Zaremba (1794-1874) of Poland. After finishing his studies, he came to

[1] Brandenburg, **op. cit.**, pp. 34-38.

St. Petersburg as a child of enlightenment full of religious questions. Here the reformed nobleman became acquainted with the Bible through his Baltic friend from student days, Baron von Trompowsky, and the Count experienced a thorough conversion. He gave up his diplomatic career and became a missionary, working for the Basle Missionary Society which was founded in Germany in 1730.

In 1821 the Basle Mission sent out Count Zaremba and Mr. Dittrich to the country lying between the Black and Caspian Seas for the purpose of finding a suitable field for missionary labor in that part of the world. They obtained permission from Alexander I to establish a Christian colony, and also to appoint to the pastoral office among the German colonies in the south of Russia ministers who had received their education in the Basle Seminary. In 1824 a missionary station was commenced at Shusha, a frontier town in the south of the Caucasus. The efforts of Zaremba and Dittrich were for some time held in check in consequence of uncertainty in regard to the action of the Russian government, hitherto friendly to missionary labors, but now assuming a hostile attitude. However, in 1828 they received permission from the Emperor to travel freely in the countries between the Caspian and the Black Seas to circulate the Scriptures, to establish schools, and to labor for the conversion of the Tatars in whatever way they chose. Three other missionaries were sent from Basle to Shusha, and it was arranged that two of the five should devote themselves to work among the Mohammedan population, the greater part of the year to be spent in travelling throughout the surrounding country, and the remainder in visiting the people in the bazaars at Shusha, or in preparing books and tracts in the vulgar Turkish dialect. In execution of this plan, Sheky, Shirwan, Baku, Daghistan, as far as Berbend, Nakhchivan, and Erivan were visited.

The missionaries, instead of seeking to gain the respect and good will of the people by paying liberally for their entertainment, went among them in the spirit of those who were commanded to "provide neither gold nor silver nor brass in their purses," and upon entering a village inquired who was willing to entertain them, and threw themselves on his hospitality. One consequence of this was that report never accused them of endeavoring to make proselytes by money.

The missionaries had originally Mohammedans chiefly in view as the object of their labors, but on becoming acquainted with the condition of the Armenians, were led to direct their labors principally to them. The large Armenian population they found without schools, and so ignorant that few could read the Armenian Scriptures, copies of which they had with them, and still fewer could understand them, while their character was so unchristian that they proved a great stumbling block to the Mohammedans, furnishing what appeared to them conclusive evidence of the falsehood of Christianity. Because of this deplorable condition, the missionaries resolved if possible, to do something for the Armenians. Their plan was to direct their efforts among the Armenians to the simple point of bringing them to be coadjutors with them in converting the Mohammedans, and then to place this department in the light of merely a subordinate branch of the original and primary object of the mission. They accordingly sought to enlighten and reform the Armenian Church, without drawing away its members. With this end in view, they endeavored to bring the fundamental truths of the gospel simply and clearly before the individuals as often as they had opportunity to do so.

Schools and the press were designed to be the principle means of effecting the reformation at which they aimed, but in the fomer a great difficulty was in the want of qualified teachers; and all attempts to establish a girls school proved unsuccessful. In the latter they were at first encouraged by receiving the approbation of the Archbishop of Tiflis, who then exercised the sensorship of the press as to books in the Armenian language, and several books were printed, chiefly for schools.

Mr. Dittrich also translated the New Testament into the modern Armenian language, the people not understanding the ancient Armenian in which the Bible is translated and public worship celebrated; but upon its completion, the printing of it was stopped by the veto of the Synod of Echmiadzin. However, the New Testament was later printed in Moscow and sent to Armenia. The teaching in the schools called forth the opposition of the priesthood, the patriarch going so far as to excommunicate those who sent their children to them. The missionaries were also represented to the Russian government as a set of persons who interfered, contrary to law, with the concerns of the Armenian Church, and in consequence received from the government an admonition to refrain from all attempts to exert any religious influence among the Armenians; hence they were obliged to confine their efforts entirely to the Mohammedans. But new and heavy complaints were brought against them by the Armenian clergy, and in 1835 the whole undertaking was stopped by a decree of the Russian government. The missionaries were prohibited from engaging in any kind of missionary labor. Having thus no prospect of further usefulness as missionaries, they left the country.[2] (The Armenian Lutheran congregation in Shemakha, between Tiflis and Baku, which came into being through Count Zaremba, still existed in the 20th century.)

### The Salvation Army in Russia

The first contact with Russia by the Salvation Army was made in 1888, when Major Rapkin visited the country and received the censor's approval for the Salvation Army publication.

In 1892 M. Paul Nardin, of the Department of Finances, St. Petersburg, sent official inquiries to local authorities throughout the civilized world requesting their opinion of the Salvation Army, essentially to find whether the organization was charitable.

Later, Prince Nicholas Galitsyn of Russia, a devoted Christian, investigated the evangelistic and social work of the Army in England. The Prince had also accompanied General Booth (1829-1912) on his campaign to Holland and returned to St. Petersburg prepared to defend the Army's work and methods; but by the end of 1904 no work had yet been opened up in Russia.[3]

In August 1908, Bramwell Booth (1856-1920), Chief of the Staff, travelled to Stockholm, Sweden, when by chance he met Mr. W.T. Staed (1849-1912), editor of "The Review of Reviews," in a railway compartment, who was on his way to St. Petersburg in hope of seeing M. Stolypin, the Russian Prime Minister.

Booth suggested to the editor to present the matter of Army's advent into Russia. The matter was put to Mr. Stolypin who, after receiving satisfactory replies, studied a copy of the Salvation Army Statutes handed to him and gave his approval for the Army's work. A friend of Emperor Alexander III and of Emperor Nicholas II had been converted in Paris through the ministry of the Salvation Army, and on her return to Russia had testified to her spiritual change.

A Salvationist from Hull Icehouse corps, temporarily falling out of employment, obtained a berth as foreman on board a ship bound for Russia. In Tallinn, Estonia, he met a Swedish evangelist. Together these two men were able to rent a building for meetings which was packed to hear the English Salvationist. Twenty-four were converted. Three more

2. Edwin M. Bliss, **Encyclopedia of Missions**, (New York, London, Toronto, 1891), Vol. I. p. 140.

3. Wiggins, **op. cit.**, pp. 76-77.

meetings were conducted by the Salvationist during his stay in Tallinn, and 100 more conversions were registered.

In 1908 Commissioner George S. Railtob (1849-1913) visited Russia and conducted crowded meetings in the capital.

In March 1909 General William Booth himself visited Russia and delivered his first address in St. Petersburg in the mansion of General and Madame Sabouroff. Present also was Her Imperial Highness, the Grand Duchess Constantini, with whom the General conversed about an hour.

In April 1909, Lieutenant-Colonel Gerrit J. Govaars (1866-1954) of Holland was selected by the General to open the work in the Russian capital. After four years of operation, the Council of Ministers decided in 1912 not to allow the Army to work in Russia anymore.[4]

However, about a year later the Scandinavian Salvationists were able to start a new work in the Russian capital. In the spring of 1913 the Salvation Army headquarters in Finland was visited by Mr. Oradd, superintendent of the state sanitation department. He informed them that on June 20, 1913, the hygienics fair was to be opened in St. Petersburg and encouraged the Salvation Army to place an exhibit in the Finnish pavilion.

In the Salvation Army booth in the Finnish pavilion the Salvationists arranged a display of pictures of their social institutions in Finland, samples of the beds used for men's hostels, a crib from one of the children's homes, handcrafts from their rescue home, and a model an Army slum officer, statistics of their work and large photos of their first two Generals. An illustrated brochure in the Russian language, describing the Salvation Army's work in Finland with its spiritual foundations, was provided. An officer was on duty at all hours the exhibition was open, answering questions and giving information. When the fair opened a Scandinavian officer, Captain Elsa Olsoni (1888-1969) was one of the Salvationists to supervise the Salvation Army booth. For her it was the beginning of her 10-year officership in Russia.

It was also decided to start the publication of their monthly magazine "The War Cry." By the help of Mr. Adam Piescheffsky, an office worker, the case was carried to the assistant printing inspector, who in turn brought the case to Prince Obolensky, chief of police, who had to approve all requests for printing new publications. Permission was granted and the Salvation Army's magazine was published and

4. Wiggins, op. cit., Vol. V: 1904 - 1914, (London and Edinburgh: Thomas Nelson Ltd., 1968), pp. 72-75.

entitled "The Messenger of Salvation." Adam Piescheffsky became the managing editor, and Baron Constantine Boije (1854-1934), a landowner in Finland, the registered owner of the new publication, because no magazine could be printed without a registered owner. The magazine was distributed at the exhibition and thus the Army secured subscribers from all parts of Russia. When the fair closed on October 8, 1913, the Salvation Army received first prize, an honor diploma, for the booth. When the second issue of the magazine was published in Russia, permission was sought to sell it on the streets. Permission was received and the Salvationists began to sell "The Messenger of Salvation" on the streets with considerable success.[5]

The Army's activities during the war was limited to visitations and small gatherings. The officers visited Vasyas Village, site of the worst misery in the midst of St. Petersburg's greatest affluence, where they witnessed to the outcasts and made some converts. The Salvationists had a place of worship at Gavanskaya Ulitza in the capital where meetings were held, producing conversions. Some of the saved enrolled as recruits to study God's Word. In 1917 the Salvation Army was officially allowed to operate in Russia. This freedom was utilized by the Salvationists to win the lost to the Lord Jesus Christ. The Army also had a hall on Petergovskij Prospect in the capital where many were converted.[6]

In 1922 the Soviets refused to grant permission for the Salvation Army activities, and all the Scandinavian officers had to leave.[7] In the year of 1922 the Salvation Army mission in Moscow was closed by the authorities. Captain Konstantinova, leader of the Moscow corps, was sentenced to prison for nine months for preaching the gospel.[8]

## Evangelization of the Jews in the Russian Empire

Russian Jewish Missions had a unique beginning, being first undertaken by Emperor Alexander I, who was more favorably disposed

[5] Karl Larson, **Ten Years in Russia,** (Chicago: The War Cry, July 19, 1969), pp. 12, 23.

[6] **The War Cry,** July 26, 1969. pp. 12-13.

[7] **The War Cry,** August 16, 1969. p. 23

[8] N. Saloff-Astakhoff, **In The Flame of Russia's Revolution** (New York: 164 Second Ave., Published by the Author, 1931), p. 281.

towards his Jewish subjects than were his successors. The Emperor employed Mr. J.C. Moritz, a converted Russian Jew, as an evangelist among his brethren from 1817 to 1825. He met with much success and many Jews were baptized into the Greek Church.

In 1817 when Mr. Moritz was commissioned, the London Jews Society obtained from the Emperor the assurance of his assistance in spreading the gospel among the Jews in Russia, and a letter of protection for Rev. Mr. B. N. Solomon, who was going to undertake the work.

In 1821 Alexander McCaul through whose ministry a number of Jews had been converted, established a mission in Warsaw, Poland. He was most successful among the Jews, but the strong opposition from the authorities forced him to retire to Germany in the following year. Concessions were soon obtained and Mr. McCaul was able to return to Warsaw with seven men to assist him. Nicholas I restricted the Mission to Poland, and in 1830 placed it under the Lutheran Church. Regardless of this restriction, the work prospered, new workers were added to the staff, and new stations opened in Lublin, Kielce, Kalisch, Suwlki and Zgierz, and a school established in St. Petersburg. From these centers the true gospel was proclaimed to many. The Crimean War (1854-1856) cut short this successful work. However, in 1875 permission was granted for the re-opening of these stations.

In Finland the small Jewish population was cared for by the Finland Missionary Society, having a mission school in Turku. The Swedish missionary, P. Wolff, preached the gospel in this region.

A Home for Jewish girls was established by Dr. Schuze in St. Petersburg in 1864. Not a few of the student girls were converted to Christianity.

South Russia was the scene of the labors of representatives of Central, Rhenish and other German societies.

Kischenev, in South Russia, became the center of two remarkable movements. The first was the work of Pastor Faltin, whose attention was turned to the Jews through the prayers of an old lady in his congregation. Since 1859 he devoted much of his time to the evangelization of the Jews in South Russia, baptizing many. Pastor Faltin established a home for the inquirers which was an important adjunct to his work. Gurland, Friendman and Rosenstraugh, spiritual sons of the Mission, assisted the Pastor in his work for a time. The London, British, Swedish, Central and Rhenish-Westphalian Societies aided his work among the Jews.

The other movement centered around Joseph Rabinowitz. He was brought to the knowledge of the truth of Christ Jesus while visiting Palestine (in the interests of a colonization society), sitting upon the Mount of Olives with a New Testament in his hand given him by Dr. Ellis of the London Society. He used it as a guidebook through which he became convinced that the destruction of Jerusalem was connected with the rejection of Christ. In 1884 he returned to Kischenev and began to preach to the Jews. Many turned to Christ, and a congregation "Israelites of the New Covenant" was formed. His printed sermons led thousands to Christ.[9]

The Zion Society for Israel, founded by the Lutherans on June 24, 1878, in Wisconsin, United States, sent its first missionary to Russia to work among the 6 million Jews in September 1882. The Rev. Mr. Mayershon settled down in St. Petersburg to start a work first of all among the 30,000 Jews who lived in the capital city. In the beginning of the next year, he reported the conversion of two Jews and two Jewesses. At the time there were about 2,000 Jewish proselytes in St. Petersburg. Pastor Ferhmann, a Lutheran Pastor in the city, suggested that a society of proselytes should be organized. The resolution was adopted in December 1882. At the first meeting only 10 proselytes were present, but these went out and secured other members. However, comparatively few joined the society; and the attendance began to decrease, resulting in dissolving the society in 1888. Instead of the proselyte-meetings, the Evangelical Christians of all nationalities would gather for "Bible evenings."

From 1882 to 1888 the preaching of the gospel by Mayershon had produced 225 conversions among the Jews, of which 167 were adults and 58 children, baptized.

In the summer of 1888 he visited Wilna, where his father-in-law, Dr. Adolf Althausen (1820-1895?), had opened a Bible Depot with a large supply of New Testaments donated by the Mildmay Mission, London, England, for free distribution among the Jews. Mr. Mayershon was deeply interested in this practical and successful mission activity among the Orthodox Jews in Russia, and decided to establish such a Bible Depot in Minsk as a most suitable place. In October the same year, he opened a Bible Depot in Minsk and received 1,000 Hebrew New Testaments from the Mildmay Mission for free distribution. He

[9] A.E. Thompson, **A Century of Jewish Missions,** (Chicago: Fleming H. Revell Company, 1902), pp. 145-149.

was soon able to report that a large number of the Jews, educated and uneducated, young and old, came to the Depot to receive New Testaments in the Hebrew, Yiddish, Russian and German languages. This gave him an opportunity to witness to them both in groups and individually about Jesus Christ. Within a month, the first 1,000 New Testaments were given out, but new supplies arrived steadily from England. Within eight months, 4,700 Hebrew New Testaments and 2,000 parts of the Testament in Jargon were distributed.

This soon aroused the fanatical Jews in the city who took concerted action to stop this progress of Christianity. However, the blessed work continued regardless of the strong opposition. Requests for the New Testaments came also from neighboring cities and villages.

Mr. Mayershon obtained permission from the government to distribute New Testaments also in other parts of the country. Instead of sending the Testaments by mail to the many people outside of Minsk who asked for them, he would make missionary journeys and bring them the bread of life in person, having thus opportunities to do personal work with seeking souls. On these journeys Mr. Mayershon and Dr. Althausen often travelled together.

In one city of 30,000 inhabitants, 8,000 New Testaments were given out in three days. Since 1888 when he settled down in Minsk, during the first 10 years he had distributed 156,119 New Testaments and parts of the Testament besides 25,000 gospel tracts. During the 33 years he had served as missionary of the Zion Society, he had baptized 438 sons and daughters of Israel.

Another missionary organization that was interested in the work among the Jews in Russia was the Mildmay Mission to the Jews in London, England (founded in 1876). The first man sent out to Russia by this organization was the Rev. Mr. James Adler (1830?-1895), who arrived in Russia in 1887. In Wilna he met Dr. Althausen and together they decided to attach themselves to the Russian Bible Society. They also obtained the permission of the Governor-General of the province of Wilna to distribute the Scriptures within the district. The distribution of the Scriptures by this organization began in 1887. The eagerness to possess New Testaments was great, and everyone was asked to give a small sum for the book. In one day, 128 copies were sold. The first depot in Russia was opened in Wilna on March 29, 1888.[10]

10. Rev. C. K. Solberg, **A Brief History of the Zion Society for Israel**(Minneapolis: The Zion Society, 1928), pp. 39-43.

Dr. Althausen, who was a physician in the Russian Army for 25 years, resigned in 1880 and was connected with the Mildmay Mission in 1887 as its first permanent work in Russia. From 1888 to 1896 he was the manager of the Depot at Wilna.

A great work among the Jews was performed by the Rev. Mr. Rudolph H. Gurland (1831-1900?). He was converted and baptized in 1864. In 1871 he received a call to become minister and missionary to the Jews at Mitau in Courland. From here he made mission tours, founded several Jewish mission schools and gave lectures at various places, which awakened interest and love for the Lord's people in Christian hearts. In 1875 he became Curate of the Church of the Holy Trinity at Mitau, and in 1876 when Pastor Neander departed, Pastor Gurland was asked by the people to be their next Pastor. In 1894 he resigned his pastorate in order to devote himself entirely to evangelizing the Jews. He became General Superintendent of the work in Russia, living at first in Riga, and visiting the other Depots from time to time.[11]

## The Young Men's Christian Association in the Russian Empire

The first Association was established in Russia by the Rev. Mr. Armin Findeisen (1831-1903) in 1869 in St. Petersburg, the Russian capital city.

**A large swimming pool has been built in the center of the former Roman Catholic Church on Leningrad's Nevski Prospekt.**

[11] Samuel Wilkinson, **In the Land of the North.** The Evangelization of the Jews in Russia, (London: Marshal Brothers, 1905), pp. 71-74, 81-83.

To understand the YMCA advance in Russia, its purpose and success in that country, it is important to have a little historical background of the YMCA movement and development in the central European countries, which later successfully invaded the Russian Empire.

As a student, Count Nicolaus L. Zinzendorf founded various societies of young men at Halle and at Wittenberg. The real importance of his work is the impetus he gave and the course he set for other similar small groups organized among the Moravian Brethren almost from the time the Moravian Church was established at Herrnhut. These groups, called "choirs" or "bands" were composed of persons of the same sex and met at least once a week. Personal faults and errors were pointed out. The meetings ended with an active intercession for the needs of the brethren. The "choirs" also held meetings for the purpose of edification, where hymns were sung and where the concern for missionary work soon became important.

The most important of these societies of young Christians during the 18th century was the Lediger Verein of Basle. Two Pastors of the National Church, Meyenrock (1733-1799) and John R. Burckhardt (1738-1820) – both members of the Moravian Church – had formed groups of young people and adults of both sexes on the pattern of what had been done at Herrnhut. The men's groups developed so rapidly that it was necessary to form a group for younger men, which became the Lediger Verein or "Bachelors Association" in 1768. This Lediger Verein of Basle was spoken of later as the first YMCA of that town.

Those who joined it were mostly strangers to the town. They were not very numerous, but they played a decisive role in the founding of the Deutsche Christentumsgesellschaft in 1780. This society played a leading part in the religious revival in German-speaking countries at the beginning of the 19th century in founding religious tract societies, Bible societies, and missionary societies of continental Europe. The permanent Secretary of the Christentumsgesellschaft, Christian F. Spittler (1782-1865), was one of the members of the Lediger Verein.

Towards the end of 1824, a young man of Basle wanted to found an association of young Christians, for which reason he was led together with Carl W. Isenberg (1806-1864), who had just entered the Missionhaus of the Basle Missionary Society to continue his studies. By Isenberg's help and advice, the young man together with his comrades founded the Evangelischer Junglingsverein of Basle on February 6, 1825. This association was involved in missionary work, and it wanted also to be a place of refuge, a home for young people, and a means of extending the kingdom of God. Many young men came from Germany, Switzerland and France to Halle to study. Also many of the students of the Basle Missionary Society belonged to this association.

In them Mr. Spittler saw men who, while practicing their own professions, would also serve the missionary cause. Some of the young men were not able to follow the full course of studies. For them Spittler devised a shorter course: a school for evangelists. This led to the Chrischona Institute, through which hundreds of YMCA members passed. From it also came many evangelists, some of whom went to Russia.

The YMCA movement in Russia was actually inspired by the German Junglingsverein in Paris, France. The Rev. Mr. Armin Findeisen, a German citizen, was Pastor of the Lutheran church in Paris from 1860 to 1865 and came into contact with the German branch of the YMCA. Four years later he had become the Pastor of St. Peter's Church in St. Petersburg. In 1869 he began to gather around him in his home a group of young men who formed the first YMCA in Russia. At first it was private because of police regulations, but later won official approval. The membership was about 30 young men of different classes, artisans, merchants and some students.

Various towns in Russia had followed the example of the St. Petersburg YMCA and adopted its statutes. Membership was restricted to congregations outside of the Orthodox Church. Mr. Findeisen, who started the work in Russia, continued to direct the work for 26 years. By 1887 the members of the YMCA in the capital city had increased to 130. In 1884 at the Berlin Conference, Mr. Findeisen was elected as the representative of Russia on the Central International Committee (CIC). He served in that capacity until death in 1903, when his son succeeded him.

The Central International Committee was also in correspondence with Warsaw, Poland, which at that time was a part of the Russian territory. The Rev. Mr. Paul Dworkowicz, who was in favor of having a YMCA established in Poland, related the many difficulties of the evangelical churches under police regulations which were much stricter than in Russia proper. It was not until 1884, after Mr. Fermaud's visit to Poland, that Mr. Dworkowicz was able to form a small YMCA, and he attended the Berlin Conference in the same summer as its representative.

In September 1883 Mr. M. Agricola from Moscow wrote to the CIC, encouraging Mr. Fermaud (1855-1937) to visit the Russian Empire, assuring him of a warm welcome but stressing that meetings and lectures could have only a strictly private character. In the spring of 1884 Mr. Fermaud sailed from Helsinki to Tallinn, Estonia, and from there to St. Petersburg where he stayed a few hours before he journeyed on to Moscow. Profiting by the fact that it was the period of the Russian Easter, the Moscow YMCA had secured police permission, and a meeting was held in a large beautiful salon of a Christian friend. A more intimate meeting followed this with a dinner together after the discussion.

At St. Petersburg he found a very active Association with a beautiful center and a library, which he considered as a model for other Russian YMCAs. It was celebrating its 15th anniversary, and delegates from the other Associations were present. Besides a meeting of the members, a large gathering was held in the big hall of the Protestant School. Tea alternated with the discussions and songs by a choir. The work in Russia grew steadily, and their connection with the World Movement strengthened it.

During the Easter season, 1893, the St. Petersburg Association celebrated its 25th anniversary and published a Silver Jubilee Report which revealed that the activity of the YMCA in the capital had not been without influence on other cities in the Empire. Little by little eight Associations had been established in different localities, and in 1893 they had 600 members, of whom 176 belonged to the YMCA in Riga, Latwia, and 113 at Mitau.

In 1896 Mr. Christian Phildius (1854-1937) visited Russia, Poland, the Baltic provinces and Finland. Both in Russia proper and in Finland he helped to organize the first national conferences, representing the international work and speaking of the broader fellowship existing outside the merely local and national interests. It was the first time Russia had been visited by the CIC since Fermaud's journey there 10 years earlier, and the first time that Finland had been contacted. In the latter country, the YMCA was started in 1876, and the work had progressed well. The national gathering brought 129 delegates of different towns of Finland.

During his travels of 1898 to 1902, Mr. Phildius had spent 58 days in Russia establishing 17 new Associations and 37 days in Finland establishing eight new Associations. By 1905, 44 YMCAs had been established in Russia in relation to the German Lutheran congregations; and in 1900 Finland had 14 Associations.

In 1910 Mr. Phildius reported to the Geneva Plenary on his visit to the 8th National Conference of the Russian Associations, that there were 103 delegates present, representing 26 Associations. These YMCAs were for the most part the outgrowth of the German Lutheran Vereine.[12]

There was also another YMCA development, called Mayak (the Lighthouse), which was authorized by the Holy Synod. This development was founded by an American philanthropist, Mr. James Stokes (1872-1960) of New York, in September 1900. It was supported by the Orthodox clergy and attracted mainly men of the Orthodox religion. Mr. Franklin Gaylord (1870?-1943), formerly from Paris, France, was its secretary. The meetings for prayer and Bible study attracted very large attendance, where in the excellent spiritual atmosphere young men were taught the Word of God. Six weeks after the opening of its doors, this YMCA had 350 members. The Council received many good testimonies from members who had profited by the meetings.

**Leningrad**

[12] Clarence P. Shedd, **History of the World's Alliance of Young Men's Christian Associations**, (London: 1955, Published by S.P.C.K.), pp. 5,11-12, 250-254, 329, 351, 366, 438.

"The Mayak transforms us," wrote one young man, "suppressing all that is unworthy within us and feeding our hungry souls with that which is reasonable, good, and eternal." "The Mayak opens to us many wonderful bright ideas," wrote another one.

"Mayak is my life!" wrote a third one. "Mayak, the name alone speaks for the building. It is a shelter in time of storm, an escape from the reefs and whirlpools of life that are so difficult for the young and inexperienced to avoid. I bless the name of him who had the idea to organize the society here."

Many other similar testimonies were given by the young men to the spiritual effect upon their lives because of the Young Men's Christian Association's development in the city which was attended by many of the Orthodox youth.

This institution exercised a great influence on the many young men who frequented the Mayak.[13]

**Dr. Friedrich W. Baedeker, The Prison Apostle**

The name of Dr. Baedeker (1823-1906), a German-born naturalized Englishman, will ever be associated with the prison work in Russia. The Czarist government encouraged the distribution of the Scriptures in the prisons, a work which was accompanied by the preaching of the gospel by the representatives of the British and Foreign Bible Society.

Dr. Baedeker travelled throughout Russia, twice traversed Siberia, stayed in the exile settlements, and used every opportunity to minister to the condemned victims. He carried a mandate from St. Petersburg stating he lay under special command to visit the Siberian prisons and to supply the convicts with copies of the Holy Scriptures.

He was given every official aid, and often a prison superintendent would stand beside him as he distributed Bibles and preached. Dr. Baedeker was always received with courtesy and appreciation for the object of his coming. He could converse in Russian, but preached through an interpreter, using English, French or German.

Dr. Baedeker brought encouragement to persecuted Christians, hope and comfort to convicts who embraced eternal life through his preaching. This man of God was not limited to the Siberian prisons, but

13. Latimer, *op. cit.*, pp. 43-44.

was allowed to visit all the prisons of Russia.[14] He enjoyed this privilege for 18 years, personally reaching 40,000 persons in prison and exile with the gospel and Bible distribution.[15]

In Siberia today many of the evangelical churches have their distant origin in the apostolic labors of Dr. Baedeker.[16]

### The Russian Student Christian Movement

Under the Czarist regime, the rule of the Empire was that every Russian who wanted to reach a place of worthy position must of necessity have a university education. Even the master of a provincial railway station had to have university credentials. This is the reason why the young people flocked to the great cities in hope of having an opportunity to get a university education with a potential future employment.

There were about 30,000 students in St. Petersburg before World War I belonging to various colleges – 21,000 men and nearly 9,000 girls. This great multitude of the young people presented a great challenge to the Evangelicals because the moral life of the students was very low.

The abundant publications of the cheap reprints of the ordinary infidel writings of the Western nations were widely read among the students. The influence of the infidel books became a destructive and degrading force in the student life, and suicide was committed frequently among the students.[17]

At that time God called a man who for thousands of students became the one who called them to Christ. This was the Finnish nobleman, Baron Paul Nicolay (1860-1919). He was an outstanding speaker and also an unusually gifted preacher for the student intelligentsia. His closest friend became Count Konstantin K. von der Pahlen, son of the Minister of Justice, one of the noblest figures in St. Petersburg before the First World War. Through him, while still a student, he was invited to Princess Lieven's palace and the Christian

14. Pollock, op. cit., pp. 71-72.

15. Durasoff, op. cit., p. 48.

16. Pollock, op. cit., p. 72.

17. Ibid., pp. 89-92.

circle there. It was at the meeting in the Lieven palace that Baron Nicolay was first asked to speak. In Finland he had often visited the family of Baron Wrede, and together with the famous Baroness Mathilde Wrede, visited the Finnish prisons.

Before he received the commission concerning the students, he visited Russian prisons with Dr. Baedecker. Once he found that a cab driver in Siberia was more grateful for the New Testament he gave him than for the fare.

In 1899 Nicolay left State service in order to be completely free for the service of the Lord Jesus Christ. For the door was now opening for his real life's work. During this year he met the American Secretary General of the World Student Christian Movement, Dr. John R. Mott (1865-1955). With him he discussed the question of bringing into being a Russian student Christian movement. He accompanied Dr. Mott to St. Petersburg. Here, as in Tartu and Riga, Mott spoke to small student groups. In a meeting at the Lieven home, it became clear to Nicolay that this was God's call for him.

Nicolay had no doubt that this ministry would not be easy for him – a spoiled aristocrat, with the hundreds of embittered students. For them, to be religious was to be a reactionary. But he set about the task of faith. He called Witt, the young secretary of the German Student Christian Movement from Germany to St. Petersburg, because Baron Nicolay hoped to reach the German students first.

The Russian Student Christian Movement (RSCM) was founded on November 18, 1899, in St. Petersburg in the home of the book dealer Grote. Apart from Nicolay, Grote and Witt , there were four German students present. Thus in the beginning, it had to work as a branch of the German YMCA. For two years the circle failed to grow. It was a spiritual struggle over each individual. When 50 students appeared on one occasion, they considered it as a victory. However, in 1902 the situation began to improve. A group of Russian Orthodox students joined the group so that the Bible studies were held in Russian. Outsiders were reached through discussion evenings. The purpose in all the meetings was to lead souls to Christ and a thorough conversion.

In 1903 the work began to grow when the women students were invited to the Bible study. Soon the work was bearing good fruit, and in 1903 the RSCM adopted its basis of faith. Fifteen students in St. Petersburg signed the confession of faith. Thus there came into being at the center of the work an active membership which continued to grow. After the revolution of 1905, the tolerance edict and the liberal policies of Witte, foreign evangelists and preachers were able to speak in student meetings, and Baron Nicolay served as interpreter because he was able to speak French, English, Swedish and German fluently.

In 1907 Baron Nicolay began a work among the students in Moscow. There he found a co-worker for the women students. In 1910 the work began at Kiev University. The Baron spoke twice there, each time before 500 students, on the themes: The Divinity of Christ, and How Does Christ Become a Practical Reality in the Lives of Men and of Women. Three student groups were the result of this pioneering work. The next place was Odessa – an unparallel mixture of peoples and religions. The decade before World War I may be described as the decade of revival among Russian students. Through Baron Nicolay, hundreds of lost, seeking souls found the way to a living faith in God.[18]

According to Nicolay, Miss Ruth Rouse, the Women's Secretary of the World's Student Christian Federation, held meetings for women students in St. Petersburg and in Moscow. The first meetings arranged in the capital city for the women students, with expectations of small attendance, attracted many of the young women to benefit themselves from the spiritual meetings. The services, which lasted for three weeks, drew increasingly greater crowds, until at the close of the meetings, the attendance reached 300 in St. Petersburg and about 1,200 in Moscow. The Baron was very active in this wonderful undertaking and utilized every opportunity to witness to the university youth.[19] After the death of Baron Nicolay in 1919, the work was carried on by Professor Vladimir F. Martsinkovsky.

### Revival in the Russian Universities

When Dr. John R. Mott, the American Methodist, visited Russia in 1899, he delivered only one public address, and that in the British-American Chapel in St. Petersburg. He was warned that the spies would be present. This led him to speak on the topic of "secret prayer." If he had spoken on any theme bearing upon organization, association, international relations, or propaganda, it would have ended all Dr. Mott's efforts to establish any Christian association or gaining access to the Russian students for the work of Christ.

18. Brandenburg, op. cit., pp. 136-142.

19. Latimer, op. cit., pp. 97-98.

In the early spring of 1914, when Dr. Mott again visited Russia, in striking contrast with his first experience, he was given great freedom to conduct public evangelistic crusades among the students and other educated classes in some of the principal cities. It was necessary to secure the largest halls in these centers to hold the multitudes of students. According to the Russian custom, all meetings were open to both men and women students, for in that land the students of both sexes insisted on having everything in common.

Admission to the meetings was by ticket, and a charge was made in order that the students might accumulate a fund with which to help fellow students who were in dire need. All the large halls and theaters were crowded. The meetings lasted for three hours.

Those who knew best the inner life of the Russian students said that the majority of them have contemplated suicide. Before World War I more students committed suicide each year in Russia than in all other countries combined. Nearly all the students of Russia were without religion, but they had thirst to find religious truth and to experience its power. Dr. Mott usually delivered two or three addresses in succession, pausing a few minutes between the two principal messages, during which interval the students according to their custom, drank tea and discussed the points of the address. As the meeting drew to a close, it was always difficult to get the other students to leave in order that the speaker and other workers could come into closer and more helpful relation to those who were ready to become serious inquirers. The students went to the hotel at announced hours for interviews, and they seemed to think that if they could draw near to Dr. Mott as the messenger of the Christian students of other lands, they might find something to quench their thirst to know the truth.

In some meetings the number of inquirers was so great that proper provision could not be made for them. In one university center the evening before the day of Dr. Mott's departure, he said to the audience: All those present who wanted to learn how to follow Christ as he had set Him forth, to meet him in the same hall at two o'clock in the afternoon the next day. Dr. Mott had chosen a difficult hour in order that there might be a more searching test. To the amazement of all, hundreds of students came to the meeting who were in dead earnest to discover and follow the truth. Nearly all of the large number who came decided heroically to become followers of Jesus Christ.

Those encouraging beginnings were followed by the establishment of scores of Bible classes or circles. Student Christian Associations were developed at the principle student centers. In some cases the work had become so extensive that suites or rooms properly equipped for the social and religious activities of the society were secured. Conferences of Christian leaders and workers were conducted from year to year, and several able Russian and foreign secretaries devoted their entire time to the leadership of the work.

In some cases the government had granted statutes to the newly formed Student Christian Associations. Most wonderful of all was the June 1913 new Christian movement in the universities of Russia – made up so largely of members of the Russian Orthodox Church – which was received into the World's Student Christian Federation.[20]

## A Training College for Pastors

Mr. Z.F. Zacharoff was a Christian and a member of the State's Duma (The Russian Parliament). He represented a constituency in the Taurida Province and was probably the only Evangelical in the Duma. His plan was to have the Evangelical Churches build a Bible College in South Russia for the training of the Pastors and preachers, but the permission was not granted until 1905 when religious liberty was granted.

In September 1905, after religious liberty was proclaimed, a college was founded in Astrahanks, Taurida Province. A house was donated for this purpose and furnished for use. An able spiritual young Lutheran Pastor was appointed as teacher. This work was of short duration because of World War I, which closed its doors.[21]

## Finnish Revivalists in the Russian Karelia

The Russian Kerelia is an area of about 67,720 square miles, including about 16,000 square miles of territory acquired from Finland following the Russo-Finnish War of 1939-1940. The area is bordered on the south by the Leningrad Region, on the west by Finland, and on the north by the Archangel Region. The Karelia was annexed by the Russian Empire in 1721 by Emperor Peter the Great. More than half the inhabitants are Slavs, with the next largest racial group being Karelians, a people similar to the Finns.

[20] John R. Mott, **The Present World Situation** (New York: Student Volunteer Movement for Foreign Missions, 1915), pp. 20-22.

[21] Latimer, **op. cit.**, p. 21.

This area became target of the Finnish preachers of the Finnish Free Church. Heikki Piiparinen (1878-1932) was saved in St. Petersburg in his early twenties and manifested a great zeal for the Lord. In 1906 the Finnish Free Church sent this young man as their missionary to the Karelia. Their work, which was started around 1894, had increased in numbers so that in late 1906 the Union of the Karelian Free Congregations was founded with Rev. Mr. J.A. Nyman as its President. In 1907 Pastor Nyman resigned and Pastor Piiparinen was elected president of this Union. Under his capable leadership, the work grew quickly.[22]

One of the top revival preachers was Tuomo Huuhtanen (1893-1975). His first visit to Russian Karelia in 1916 assured him of God's call to be a travelling evangelist to the Karelian people. An unusual anointing rested upon this humble servant of God. All the places where he preached were filled, and sometimes great crowds were outside listening through the open windows and doors. The Lord moved so mightily that altar calls were omitted as people came forward spontaneously, with thousands of souls being saved through his ministry.

According to his statements, a mighty revival swept through Karelia at that time. He personally baptized 2,822 people, with a total of 10,000 believers baptized. In August 1920 all the evangelical movements were united into one affiliation – the Union of Karelian Evangelicals – with Pastor Piiparinen elected president. Mr. Huuhtanen preached in Karelia until 1929 when the Communists initiated heavy persecutions. The union had 104 workers in 1929 and 41 places of worship. During World War II the Karelians were dispersed and the Union of Karelian Evangelicals ceased to exist.[23]

## The Activities of a Swedish Missionary Society in Russia Proper

In 1880 a Swedish Mission Society (Svenska Missionsforbundet) sent two missionaries to St. Petersburg, the Rev. Mr. Lars E. Hogberg (1858-1921), and the Rev. Mr. F.N. Hoijer (1857-1925), to open up a work in the Russian capital.

22. Tuomo Huuhtanen, **Vallankumouksen Vaiheilta,** (Tikkurila: Ristin Voitto, 1976), pp. 19-21. Translated from Finnish by Albert W. Olema.

23. **Ibid.,** pp. 78-79.

Because of opposition and difficulties, Mr. Hoijer went, in 1882, with Lydell to Baku on the Caspian Sea coast. The same year other missionaries were sent to Russia: Mr. Nygren to St. Petersburg, Mr. Sarwe to the Ural, Karlsson and Hammarstedt to Arkangelsk. In 1893 this Missionary Society had 14 missionaries in Russia proper. However, by 1914 only three of the original 14 missionaries labored in the land of the czars. Seven of them had died, and others returned to Sweden.

The Rev. Mr. F. N. Hoijer served and ministered in Russia for 40 years. In 1903 he founded the Evangelical Mission in Russia in Stockholm, Sweden. By 1909 the Mission had 50 native evangelists in the Russian field.[24]

In 1889 two Finnish Swedish-speaking Baptist preachers visited the Russian capital – the Rev. Mr. E. Jansson from Vasa, and the Rev. Mr. Eriksson from Nampnas – to establish a Swedish-speaking congregation. At that time there were about 7,000 Swedish-speaking Finns and 3,000 Swedes in the Russian capital. On March 14, 1889, a Swedish congregation was founded with 19 members, and within two months had increased to 55 members. Mr. Eriksson left St. Petersburg for Finland in 1890. Rev. Mr. O.E. Signeul (1858-1936) from Sweden took over the work, which then grew to a membership of 174. He was a fine leader of the Swedish Baptist church for several years. In 1896 he visited Estonia and preached to the Swedes living there, with visible results.[25]

## Evangelization of Russians in the Face of Opposition

Mr. Cornelius Martenes (1876-1940?) was born in the Province of Ekaterinoslav, in the village of Romanov, a Mennonite colony. He was saved at an early age and soon began to witness for his Lord and Savior Jesus Christ – which was blessed by the Holy Spirit – producing conversions. After severe persecution he left his native village and moved to another place where he got work in a factory, but there too he was mistreated by the foreman, who did not approve of his religious ways.

[24] L.E. Hogberg, **Skuggor och Dagar fron Missionsarbetet in Russland,** (Stockholm: Svenska Missionsforbundets Forlag, 1914), p. 37. Translated from Swedish by Albert W. Olema.

[25] J. Bystrom, **Sodd och Skodd,** (Stockholm: Svenska Baptisternas Mission, 1916), pp. 87-92. Translated from Swedish by Albert W. Olema.

He made the acquaintance of a Jewish engineer, who became interested in him and persuaded young Martenes to go to Kharkov, where for seven years he worked in a factory. During his first year in the city of Kharkov he preached and founded a Baptist church. This was before the Edict of Toleration proclaimed by Emperor Nicholas II in October 1905. Because of the strong opposition, he had to hold meetings in forests and fields, but the Lord blessed the work and many were converted.

In 1905 the Lord called him into a fulltime ministry, so he moved to the Cossack district of Melerovaw, with a savings of about 1,600 rubles. Together with his brother-in-law, who had saved about 900 rubles, he entered into a partnership and started a business in Defers.

There was not a single Russian convert in this place. He at once started to preach, and a number of people were saved. An elder of the Kharkov church came and baptized the converts and formed a Baptist church with a membership of about 60 people. The people unanimously voted to have Mr. Martenes for their Pastor; and after being ordained by the neighboring Pastors, he accepted the Pastorate. The work increased rapidly, and he started a number of mission stations in the district. Now fully recognized by the brethren, he was accepted as a member of the Baptist Union Council and later was appointed travelling preacher for the Union.

The poor village boy Cornelius Martenes was no more a poor worker in a factory, having to spend most of his time in toil. As an employer, he had more time to devote to the Lord's work. God prospered him so that before World War I he employed about 500 people in his factory. He sent large sums of money to Siberia to help the work of God in that distant land of horror. He and two other friends supported 11 preachers for two years in connection with the Baptist Union and the Mennonite Union.[26]

In 1920 and the following two years the Rev. Mr. C. Martenes was elected a member of the Council of the Baptist Union and was again appointed a travelling minister and empowered to spread spiritual literature by the Union. On his evangelization journeys in 1920, 1,000 souls were converted in a three-month period and a greater number were baptized. The meeting places were always too small to contain the audiences, and great crowds would listen to the preaching through the open windows in the summer months.

[26]A. McCaig, **Grace Astounding in Bolshevik Russia,** (The Russian Missionary Society, 43 Newington Butts, London, S.E. 1), pp. 9, 16-17, 21-24.

The Communists were also touched by the gospel. One day a man came to Martenes and said: "I have been a Socialist for three and a half years and have murdered thousands of innocent people, but now I have accepted Jesus Christ as my Savior and I will follow Him alone." At another time five Communists who were murderers and thieves were saved, as well as many Red soldiers. Some of the converted Communists were sentenced to three years imprisonment.

In the town of Grosno the authorities were friendly and allowed the evangelist to have meetings in the town hall which accommodated about 2,000 people. The auditorium was packed and the streets were filled with people who wanted to hear the gospel. Hundreds of people were saved in that town. One night two Red Army Colonels came to the meeting, and at the very close they surrendered their lives to Christ. Subsequently, when the two Colonels were baptized in the river, the banks were crowded with Red soldiers.

At a Cossack village about 86 people were saved and baptized. In another Cossack village about 52 people were saved and baptized in the first service. At the next place about 300 were saved. The Russian Orthodox clergy then packed their holy vessels and things from the churches and left with the words, "We haven't anything more to do here."[27]

At this time the people of Mr. Martenes' colony heard about his great revival and asked him to conduct a revival in his own village. Together with the adjoining colony, there were about 3,000 families. A hall was rented which accommodated about 900 people. The first night about 80 persons professed conversion. Many children were converted who attended an atheistic Bolshevist school. They started singing in the school until the schoolmaster drove them away. The children went into the courtyard and continued to sing and to pray. Driven from the courtyard, they went to the cemetery for their devotional exercises, but were ultimately driven from there also. This demonstrates the great desire in the hearts of the Russian people to serve God.

In 1925 there was a great spiritual movement in the city of Kharkov, in the Ukraine. Many educated and uneducated people were saved. The Lord used His servant, brother Martenes, in a great way while preaching in Russia – thousands were saved through his ministry. In 1927 he fled to the West where he lived and ministered until his death.[28]

27. Ibid., pp. 51-59.

28. Ibid., pp. 69, 81.

## The Christian Soldiers' Society

Many of the evangelicals were drafted with others into the imperial army, being scattered in various military units all over the country. These became missionaries to their fellow-soldiers in the army, and many of the military men accepted Jesus Christ as their personal Savior and Lord. This work was unofficial in the Russian Army, but it bore fruit, winning many of the lost soldiers to Christ.[29]

The Christian Soldiers' Society was organized in 1917 by Jacob J. Dyck (1885-1919), a man of splendid ability. This work under the able leadership of Mr. Dyck grew to such proportions that similar societies were established in all the larger cities of Russia where soldiers were stationed.

Mr. Dyck established lunch rooms for the poor, and with the help of the Christian young people from the Young People's Society at Moscow, street meetings were started. All these activities produced conversions.

At the conclusion of the war, the armies were demobilized, the soldiers from the front as well as the war prisoners from Germany came to their homes. The Christians among them were scattered across the country to preach the gospel of salvation in the darkest places of Russia. At the conclusion of the war, the Christian Soldiers' Society disbanded, but a Tent Mission was founded instead.[30]

## The Bible Christian Union's Activities in Russia

The founder of this missionary society was Gans P. Raud (1883-1953), son to the Estonian Pastor Pertel Raud. In his early years he travelled much with his father and his brother Wil. This young man was very eager to proclaim the gospel message to his fellow countrymen. Wherever he went in his native Estonia, he saw the need for gospel preaching. He saw town after town, village after village, with no regular preaching of the Word. He saw the need for Bibles, for preachers and meeting halls. He was especially touched by the plight of the peasants, who with many temporal burdens, desperately needed the Lord.

[29] N. Saloff-Astakhoff, **Christianity in Russia,** pp. 96-97.

[30] N. Saloff-Astakhoff, **In The Flame of Russia's Revolution,** pp. 13-14.

During the Christmas season of 1903, Gans Raud, his father, and brother Wil set out on a 10-day evangelistic tour to various villages in the Estonian countryside. In one place the police chief came with two men to arrest them. In that meeting the chief sat down to hear what the preachers were going to say. The Holy Spirit convicted the police chief, who surrendered his life to Christ. The other two policemen fled in great fear, and the meeting continued. At the conclusion of the gospel proclamation, about 40 people accepted Christ as their Savior and Lord.

After the service, when the people were praying, the Lord made it clear to Gans Raud that his life must be given for the people of Europe. This prayer meeting, which lasted through the night and the following day, has been considered the beginning of his later-organized work, the Bible Christian Union, which he founded in 1916 in the United States.

From 1905 to 1915 Mr. Raud divided his time among the following countries. Great Britain, Germany, France, Switzerland, Scandinavia and many parts of the vast Russian Empire, besides his native Estonia. In Germany Mr. Raud helped financially with two Russian students going through a Bible school in Berlin. These students went back to Russia in 1912, and one of them, Vasili Egoroff, subsequently became the director of the work of the Bible Christian Union in the Ukraine.

At the conclusion of World War I the Russian masses were very receptive to the gospel message because of four factors:

1. The general war in Europe of 1914-1918.
2. The violent revolution of 1917.
3. The Civil War of 1918-1920.
4. The tragic famine of 1921-1922. All of these factors worked together to break down the spiritual resistance of the Russian people. Often the meeting halls were crowded for gospel meetings and numerous conversions resulted.

By 1923 the Christian Bible Union was supporting 35 workers in the Soviet Union, 29 of them in the Ukraine. Between 1912 and 1930 Rev. Mr. Egoroff and his co-workers had established about 300 groups of believers in various parts of the Ukraine.[31]

[31] Ibid., pp. 27-41, 54-60.

**In obedience to their leaders, Russian masses demonstrate in Moscow on anniversary of Red revolution. (1969)**

## CHAPTER X

# COMMUNISM AS A NEW POLITICAL SYSTEM AND RELIGION IN RUSSIA

### The New System Hailed as a Redeemer

The year of 1917 was a period of upheaval, revolutions, and turmoil. Waves of confusion and agitation raged in the country before the new regime was able to stem the wave of turmoil. The February revolution overthrew the hated Czarist system, without giving power to the Communists; but the October Revolution put the Bolsheviks in power.

At first Communism was acclaimed enthusiastically as a redeemer by the workers, peasants, the army and the navy, believing this to be the resolver of problems and the creator of a new good life. The peasantry, which constituted about 70 percent of the Russian population, were in need of land and improved social conditions.

The propagators of the new system promised the people land free of charge for agricultural use. This land was to be confiscated from the oppressors of the people and divided among the peasants. This won about 60 percent to 70 percent of the peasants for the new regime. Under the Czarist rule, the factory workers had to work from 10 to 11 hours a day, receiving a very low salary. The average wage for unskilled labor was 25 cents to 50 cents a day, and skilled labor received about 50 cents to $1.50 a day.

For the masses of workers, the Communists declared: "The factories are the products of the workers and belong to them. Therefore, the factories must be confiscated from the capitalists and used and managed by the workers themselves."

The soldiers were not respected in the imperial army but were treated like animals by the officers. To them, the Communists promised to abolish all rank and military distinction. The leaders of the army must be elected by the soldiers themselves, peace must be made and the troops disbanded and sent home. About 75 percent of the army and navy joined the Communists. The Bolsheviks promised freedom of speech and of the press. Thus, the workers were allured to follow the new system and their leaders, who promised the people good times to come.

There were further promises made by the Bolsheviks: On the strength of the fact that in the socialist state everything belongs to the people, the latter must utilize all privileges free, and on equal rights. All railroad fares were abolished. Electric energy, water, medical help – all was to be used free of charge – and many other promises were made. Such prospects enticed masses of people into Communism without giving thought to the real consequences.[1]

**The Kazan Cathedral, completed in 1812. Now a Museum of Atheism.**

## The Communist Rule Precipitates National Catastrophe

To win more support, the Communists liberated all the criminals throughout Russia, while the political prisoners had been already set free by the Provisional Government. The prisoners were armed and merged with the Communists, giving them unquestionable aid in their struggle against capitalism. These prisoners usurped the political offices in all localities and became the main acting force in the new system.

[1] N. I. Saloff–Astakhoff, **Real Russia From 1905 to 1932 and Communism in America**,(New York: Published by the Author, 1932), pp. 20-23.

Former politicians, land owners, and managers of industry were delivered into the hands of angry masses of workers and liberated criminals. Those who could not escape were exterminated and properties destroyed.

Former common laborers, and all kinds of criminals, now became directors of factories, mines, oil wells and railroads. Common soldiers became commanders of regiments of the Red army. Deserters from the imperial army became policemen and chiefs of police.

Thus, the uneducated and inexperienced elements of the lower masses became leaders of a nation on the verge of bankruptcy. These conditions produced a complete collapse of industry and transportation, destruction of former supplies, followed by an unprecedented famine which starved millions of people to death.[2]

## The Dissatisfied Proletariat

The new system did not bring the expected "Utopia," nor did it end the disastrous war. The Civil War, with its devastations, brought indescribable suffering and distress to the people instead of peace and opulence. Passing armies robbed the people of all the agricultural products as supplies for the troops. No one could count anything his own, for the soldiers of the Red army had to supply their own needs.

Much of the land was unattended, followed by a drought and famine. Millions had perished in the war; disease was now taking its toll. All the people were waiting for the end of the war to devote themselves to peaceful occupations and to enjoy the benefits of the revolution. Instead they experienced a miserable slavery. When the open warfare concluded, the new rulers became more firmly established in power; and people in Russia commenced to realize that they were the victims of deliberate deception. All classes saw that instead of being liberators, the Communists were the most monstrous oppressors.

An American Communist who visited Russia gave testimony in New York City in December 1931. He spoke of some of the dissatisfied peasants who wished that God would send them some kind of war; then in one night, they would dispose of all the Communists.

The same Communist spoke of an American who went to Russia after the revolution in 1922 and did not know how to escape from the

2. Ibid., pp. 23-24.

U.S.S.R. The American was to be arrested and exiled to Siberia, but he decided to flee regardless of the consequences.[3]

## Communism Versus God and Religion

In the fall of 1917, the Communists were in possession of Russia. The Bolsheviks were militant atheists who rejected God and considered every religion an enemy to be exterminated as quickly as possible.[4] The doctrine of Communism is a comprehensive philosophy of life which includes an epistemology, a metaphysics as the material foundation of Communism. Matter and its motion is all that actually exists, consciousness is determined by material existence and is its product. According to Karl Marx (1818-1883), religion cannot be separated from the class structure of society. The "liberation of humanity" from this structure is the ultimate end of socialism; therefore, religion must be destroyed.

All contemporary religion, churches, and every kind of religious organization has always been viewed by Marxism as instruments of bourgeois reaction, serving as a defense of exploitation and the doping of the working class.[5]

According to the principles of Marx, capitalism can be defeated only by:

1. Abolition of God and all religion.
2. Abolition of all private property.
3. Abolition of all family relations.
4. Abolition of the right of inheritance.
5. Abolition of patriotism.[6]

Communism affirms that the teachings about God and religion are the foundation of capitalism, the pillars on which it rests. Hence, these must be done away first of all. The Bolsheviks say: Until the whole idea of God is eradicated from the mind of man, the creation of a society based on equality, equity, and justice is impossible.[7]

[3]. **Ibid.**, pp. 32-59.

[4]. N.S. Timasheff, **Religion in Soviet Russia, 1917 — 1942.** (London: The Religious Book Club, 1943), p. 1.

[5]. **Ibid.**, pp. 10-13.

[6]. Astakhoff, **op. cit.**, p. 95.

[7]. Sidney Dark and R. S. Essex, **The War Against God** (New York, Cincinnati, and Chicago: The Abingdon Press, Inc., 1938), p. 12.

## The Bolshevik Attack on the Orthodox Church

Religion, being one of the chief cornerstones of the old Czarist order, was to be exterminated. But, what was the best means to achieve this end? Too quick an action might revive the decaying fabric of the Church and make it a formidable enemy. The state religious system was merely an instrument used by the oppressors of the people; liberated from the bonds of capitalism, people would understand that religion was their enemy and would rid their minds of religious superstition.

It was, therefore, understandable that in the beginning the logical procedure was to separate religion from the political support, from the economic support, and undermine its material existence. Anti-religious strategy was not much debated during the elaboration of the new State's first Constitution. In the Constitutional Committee, the moderate members prevailed and the Committee introduced into its draft the formula:

"Religion is a private affair of the citizens."

Lenin was not satisfied with this kind of statement and ordered it to be replaced by another clause which guaranteed the freedom of religious and anti-religious propaganda. This became Article 13 of the Constitution of the Russian Socialist Federal Soviet Republic of July 10, 1918, the archetype of all later Soviet Constitutions. [8]

The clause introduced by Lenin was quite moderate because it equalized religious and anti-religious propaganda. The only difference was that religious propaganda was left to a weak Church, and anti-religious propaganda was to be furthered by the new State with the strong Communist party as its backbone. In fact: The formula in the new Constitution was a declaration of war on the Orthodox Church.[9]

In reality, the purpose of the Communists was to destroy her as soon as possible because it embodied in its social teaching and influence all the tendencies most characteristic of the Czarist regime.

Mr. Dark says that according to the decree issued on January 23, 1918: The Church is hereby separated from the State, and the school is separated from the Church. The teaching of religious doctrine is not permitted in any state, public, or private school where general educational subjects are taught. No religious society whatsoever has the

8. Timasheff, **op. cit.**, pp. 21-22.

9. **Ibid.**, pp. 22-23.

right to own private property, the property of the existing religious societies in Russia becomes the property of the people.[10]

During the first period of four years (November 1917 – February 1922), the Communists employed three features in anti-religious policy in their fight against the Church.

1. To deprive churches of material means and legal existence.

2. To reduce priests and other ministers to a status of social inferiority.

3. The destroy the Church's influence on various phases of life, especially on education.

**This former Russian Orthodox church in Moscow, U.S.S.R., is being used as a public toilet.**

The spirit in which these regulations were applied appears in a reply from the Department of Justice of the Kremlin territory to an application, made by a town to have religious education restored in its schools. "It is obvious that religious education results in stupidity. As the Soviet Government is responsible for the children of the country, it must prevent the minds of these children from being darkened by religious superstition."[11]

10. Dark, op. cit., pp. 106-108.

11. Timasheff, op. cit., pp. 24-27.

The Family Code of October 22, 1918, refused Church marriages and divorces legal recognition.

The regulation of the Communists made marriage a precarious union to be dissolved whenever one of the parties desired to be liberated from the marriage bond. It was a "postcard" divorce. If one of the marriage partners told the registration office of his desire to have the marriage dissolved, the divorce was immediately signed and the other party informed by a postcard.

Anti-religious work which was not so vigorous before, was becoming one of the main branches of the Communist propaganda.

On February 7 a new organization was established called the Militant Atheists League. By 1928, the League numbered only 123,000 members. From 1926 on, anti-religious propaganda of the most vicious character was systematically disseminated by it. The lines of attack were chosen.

1. A demonstration that religion, in all its forms, has always been the enemy of the workers.

2. Natural science explains everything and leaves no room for religion.

3. Religious belief is disloyalty to the Soviet State, for religion is incompatible with socialism.

**Palace of Peter the Great**

Anti-religious performances and carnivals became one of the League's main functions. On December 26, 1922, the priests were obliged to submit their sermons to the censor, because religion was declared to be "a brutalization" of the people.

In 1928, the sale of Easter foods and Christmas trees was forbidden. Christmas ornaments were displayed no more in the shop windows; they were replaced by anti-Christmas literature.[12]

**Confiscation of Churches and Ecclesiastical Properties**

The property and wealth of the Orthodox Church was enormous. During her 1,000–year history, the church had become possessor of vast areas of land, of buildings, and of a tremendous bank account.

According to the information supplied by Mr. Casey, based on the report of the Holy Synod in 1914, there were about 85,791 religious edifices in the Russian Empire.

| | |
|---|---|
| Churches | 55,173 |
| Chapels | 29,593 |
| Total | 84,766 |

These churches were served by 112,629 priests and deacons. There were about:

| | |
|---|---|
| Monasteries | 550 |
| Convents | 475 |
| Total | 1,025 |
| Plus | 84,766 |
| Total number of edifices | 85,791 |

The monasteries and convents were served by 95,259 inmates, says Mr. Casey. The church owned about 20 million acres of land and had many commercial enterprises and houses. Its annual income was estimated to be about 500 million rubles. At the time of the nationalization of the banks, its deposits were 8 billion rubles.[13] According to the decree of January 23, 1918, on the separation of the

12. Ibid., pp. 27-37.

13. Casey, op. cit., p. 91.

State and Church and of Church and School, all property owned by the churches was nationalized and forfeited to the government without compensation.[14]

### Reaction of the Orthodox Church Results in Persecution

After the confiscation of churches and ecclesiastical properties, the Orthodox Church people with the clergy began to defend their places of worship. On Febraury 26, 1922, a decree was issued which ordered all articles of gold, silver, and precious stones to be surrendered to the State.

Patriarch Tikhon, who at that time was the head of the Russian Orthodox Church, replied with a message on February 28, 1922, in which he declared that it was impossible to give away sacred vessels. The government ordered their removal by force despite the offers of the people to pay the full value. Some 1,400 bloody fights around the churches were reported in the Soviet press. An incident took place in March 1922 in Shuya, where the people congregated in the Cathedral Square before the service. A detachment of infantry with machine guns was ordered to the Square. The people met them by a rain of stones and revolver shots. After the first volley in the air, the second was directed at the crowd. Four people were killed and 10 were seriously injured – then the crowd dispersed. About 120 pounds of silver were requisitioned.

Many of the clergy were brought to trial and some of them were shot. The Patriarch himself declared that in accordance with the canon law, he condemned the confiscation of the sacred vessels. The court ordered the Patriarch to be tried at once. The trials and executions were an attempt to break the resistance of the Orthodox Church.

The Patriarch was imprisoned; many churches were turned over to The Living Church, a church which was started by a group of priests inconsistent with the policies of the Patriarch. Eighty-four bishops were deposed from their positions and more than 1,000 priests were expelled from their parishes to make room for the new organization. The new organization promised to cooperate with the Soviets and outlined plans for new reforms. The State hoped that through this dissention, the Orthodox Church would receive a further devastating blow. The

[14] Timasheff, op. cit., p. 24.

Patriarch, who had been in prison since May 1922, was released by the Soviets on June 27, 1923.[15]

**Kiev, capital of the Ukraine.**

## Communism as a New Religion

Religion (as a profession) is a system of belief in an object of adoration. Communism is just that. It is a religion of science, of technique, and adoration of State.

The Bolshevists stated that the Church, as a system of religion, had been a willing instrument in the hands of the Czarist State and of capitalistic society to keep the people in slavery and to oppose their liberation. Therefore, the proletariat needed a new religion which would liberate him from the tyranny.

Atheism was recommended as a necessary stimulus of revolutionary activity and as an antidote to the opium of religion. Religion, or superstition, could no longer exist in modern culture based on science. Revolutionary atheism was proclaimed as the dawn of a new religion of science and technique.[16]

15. Ibid., pp. 28-31, 33.

16. Dark, op. cit., pp. 136-137.

The study of Communism reveals that it has its trinity consisting of three persons:

1. Karl Marx (1818-1883), the father of Communism.

2. Friedrich Engels (1820-1895), a German revolutionist and the great collaborator.

3. Vladimir Lenin (1870-1924), the practical demonstrator of Communism in Russia.

The philosophy of these three men remains the cohesive force which keeps Communism intact. Communism, then, is a pseudo religion which, in its highest ideal, believes that the State is God, work is worship, and a better social order is the promised land.

The Pope's Encyclical Letter on Atheistic Communism, published in April 1937, stated: "The Communism of today, more emphatically than similar movements in the past, conceals in itself a false Messianic idea. A pseudo-ideal of justice, of equality, and fraternity in labor."[17]

The supreme dialectical laws of life all converge on the Bolshevist Party, investing it with ultimate right, making it the final depository of truth, commissioning it to take up the authority already given to it, permitting it to disregard any opposition, encouraging it to crush all enemies. No autocratic ruler ever wielded greater power, nor has any monarch ever more elaborately appealed to philosophy and science to justify his rule.[18]

## Communism as a Perverted Worship

Mr. D. Benson calls the Soviet atheistic system a perverted worship, which is carried by the Russian Communists to such a degree that Lenin is all but worshipped by his followers. And, if it be not Lenin, then the Party, or the State, is exalted as an object of ultimate belief.[19]

The shrine of Communism is in Moscow, the capital of world Communism. It is the dark-red mausoleum in the Red Square where the remains of the "communist saint" Vladimir Lenin lie. Visitors to the mausoleum say that even in the coldest winter days, one often has to

17. **Ibid.**, pp. 136-137.

18. David V. Benson, **Christianity, Communism and Survival**, (Glendale: Division of Gospel Light Publications, 1967), pp. 61-62.

19. **Ibid.**, p. 16.

wait three or four hours before passing the guards and descending in reverent silence the steps leading to the crypt. At the spectators file past the hermetically sealed glass-covered coffin in which – dressed in black, arms at his sides, his features well preserved by embalmer's art – lies the body of Lenin, the famous demonstrator of Communism in Russia.

It is well known throughout the world that to keep up the image of Lenin's popularity, organized groups from factories and from the schools visit the mausoleum every day. For this is the essential shrine, the symbol above all others that holds the cult of Communism up to the people's gaze with its history as a sacred history to the Communists.

The Pushkin Museum is arranged to resemble an ancient temple with a large hall decorated with classic columns and polished floor. Entering through a door at the opposite end from the altar, one is struck with awe. Then walking the length of the room, one sees the astounding incongruity of design, for there upon the sacred altar, where in classic times a statue of some deity would have stood, sits a bust of Lenin. Communism has all the trappings of an organized religion: its messiahs and saints – Marx, Engels and Lenin, with a host of other figures who wax or wane in popularity as the ruling priests decide; its sacred scriptures – writings of these men; a band of apostles and prophets – the Communist Party; an elect nation – the Russian people; a sense of predestined authority – the immutable course of the dialectic working in history; a millennial period of transition – socialism; which leads to the endless state of bliss. It is a religion, and as such its transgressions of logic and consistency, its narrowminded prejudices, its violence and fanaticism are all essential parts of its make-up. For no man-made religion in all recorded history has ever been impregnated with a sense of a holy war of deliverance more than has Communism.[20]

### Communism, God's Judgment

A number of European theologians have taken the view that Communism is the rod of God's anger. Some of the theologians have lived under Communism, and they find a parallel between their

[20] Ibid., pp. 1-3.

situation as Christians living under the Soviet rule and the Northern kingdom of Israel during the second half of the eighth century B.C.[21]

The kings of Israel with their people lived in idolatry, killing the prophets and provoking the Lord. The Lord says: "O Assyrian, the rod of mine anger, and the staff in their hand is mine indignation."[22] This is a startling statement because the Assyrians, a heathen nation, instead of being regarded as despised by God, are regarded as instruments of God for purification of His people. In 722 B.C., Assyria deported the 10 tribes to Assyria, and the Northern kingdom of Israel came to an end. God used the heathen to punish His people for their sins.

The study of Russian Church history reveals waves of persecutions against God's people, the believers in Christ. The Church in Russia was in a way an idolatrous system which recognized God by name, but rejected Christ as their Savior, substituting ikons for the Savior.

Mr. N. Berdyaev, a Russian philosopher and Orthodox Christian, exiled by the Communists from his native country, says that the sins of the Christians and of the historical churches have been very great, and these sins bring with them their just punishment. Communism is the fruit of Christian failure. The calamity of Communism is something which the Christians have helped through their sins to bring down on our own heads.[23]

21. Paul Geren, **Christians Confront Communism,** (Nashville, Tennessee: Convention Press, 1962), pp. 125-126.

22. Isaiah 10:5

23. Geren, op. cit., p. 127.

**Leningrad. The old stock exchange.**

## CHAPTER XI

# EVANGELICAL AGGRESSIVENESS DURING WORLD WAR I

### A Period of Religious Alleviation and Harvest of Souls for the Evangelicals

In 1917 the Provisional Government under the leadership of A. Kerensky, a member of the Parliament, proclaimed religious liberty to the citizens of Russia to confess their faith according to their own conviction. This decree gave all denominations and creeds equal rights. The Communists, when assuming power, issued a decree that all who refused to take arms because of religious convictions were exempted from the draft. This kind of policy of the Communists won the favor of the Protestants, who had been persecuted for centuries by the State Church, believing that through this new government they finally had attained religious liberty.[1]

The Orthodox Church, having lost the support of the State, was no longer able to oppose the Evangelicals, which made the Christians rejoice that at last the time had come when they could preach the gospel of Jesus Christ everywhere in the Russian language.[2] The Christians lost no time in utilizing the religious freedom, going and witnessing everywhere.

On the streets of the cities, in the parks, in public halls, in theaters, at railroad stations, or trains, on board ships, in factories, everywhere, could one hear the singing of the gospel hymns and good evangelical preaching.[3]

A nation exhausted by war, weary and tired of internal and external conflicts, longed for spiritual rest and reality. After the collapse of the autocratic rule, the Evangelicals demonstrated on the

1. Astakhoff, **op. cit.**, p. 93.

2. Astakhoff, **Christianity in Russia** p. 101.

3. **Ibid.**, p. 98.

streets with red flags, carrying banners inscribed with Bible texts: "We preach Christ crucified," "The blood of Jesus Christ cleanses us from all sin," and many other Scripture verses.[4]

Mr. Astakhoff tells about an episode of those days of profound preaching and evangelical enthusiasm which shows great spiritual hunger in the hearts of the Russians.

A group of young people carrying banners with various Scripture verses like, "The blood of Jesus Christ His Son cleanseth us from all sin," went singing to the city park. In the park a large crowd gathered around the evangelical group, including thousands of soldiers. As the speaker stood there on a box to speak, there was a sea of human faces before him, all listening with intense interest. At the end of the gospel message, the speaker asked the question: "Today, you have heard about the Lord Jesus Christ, His claims, and His call. Who of you desires and would be willing to follow Him whole-heartedly from this minute on?" There was a great response as thousands of hands went up, signifying their need of a Savior, the Lord Jesus Christ.[5]

### The Soviet Toleration of the Evangelicals

The first wave of the persecution hit the Orthodox Church because of its enormous wealth and anti-revolutionary spirit. The Orthodox clergy were utterly discouraged by the awful opposition and suffering which had befallen them, but the Evangelicals were spared for a time. The Protestants had no magnificent cathedrals and buildings, nor any huge land holdings to be confiscated.[6]

After the Revolution, the Evangelicals supported the government for granting them religious liberty. The Soviets welcomed the Protestant support, hoping that the sectarians would be more successful against the power of the Orthodox Church than the State could be.

This was justified on two grounds: (1) The attack on a church regarded in the West as corrupt, was being at least partly carried on by Protestant bodies. (2) If persecution could be made to appear as a contest between two rival types of Christians, the government would not be branded by the Protestant nations as anti-Christian. In

4. Astakhoff, **Real Russia**, p. 93.

5. Astakhoff, **Christianity in Russia**, pp. 100-101.

6. **Ibid.**, pp. 102-104.

accordance with the Soviet policy, the government paid for the Protestant support by handing over to the Evangelicals a number of Orthodox churches, and by permitting their ministers to preach in the market places and on the steps of cathedrals.[7]

Why was the Soviet government so friendly to the Evangelicals? The government was most actively fostering sectarianism as a means to its own ends. The result was that the Orthodox Church grew weaker and the Evangelicals grew stronger.[8]

### All-Russian Evangelical Tent Mission Organized

At the conclusion of World War I, when the Christian Soldiers' Society disbanded, the question arose: How to continue the evangelical work under the new conditions?

Mr. Dyck felt now that God was opening up a new effective door for the evangelization of the Russian masses. There were many capable workers present, just released from the army, willing to go out with the Tent Mission under the leadership of Mr. Dyck as soon as it was organized. The brotherhood prayed to God for a tent, which petition was speedily answered, for in a few days 5,000 rubles were received for the tent. In the spring of 1918 this consecrated band left Moscow to open meetings in Kazlov in the province of Tambov. The tent had a seating capacity of about 200.

The Tent Mission continued through the whole summer, until the severe winter forced the tent evangelists to cease their activities for the winter season and go home to return again the next spring, the Lord willing. In the beginning of 1918, Mr. N. Astakhoff went south and was encouraged by the Christians to join the work of the Tent Mission, which Mr. Astakhoff also accepted. The work was concentrated primarily in the Ukraine, both among the Russians and the Germans.

In early spring of 1919, Jacob Dyck invited new workers into the Lord's vineyard, and in response many brothers and sisters consecrated their lives to God's service. In the middle of May, 20 young people, joined later by 13 others, divided into four groups. With hearts burning with zeal to win souls for the Lord, these young soldiers of the cross started on their journey.

7. Dark, op. cit., pp. 113-114.

8. Casey, op. cit., p. 45.

The members of the Mission team used every opportunity to preach the gospel truth to the unconverted everywhere. The Civil War in the south forced the people to flee from the Communists. At some places around the railway stations were thousands of homeless refugees. To these multitudes, the gospel was preached by some of the evangelists. The people manifested great hunger for the living Word and received it with open hearts, standing for hours to listen to the glad news.[9]

The summer of 1919 was a busy and successful period of the time in winning souls to Christ. Late in the fall when the rain and fog made walking difficult from village to village, the party decided to have a general missionary concourse at the headquarters at Panutino, for a grand thanskgiving service. From far and near came newly converted Christians to be present at this occasion. All the new converts loved and desired to serve the Lord with all their hearts. A number of young men and women decided to join the Mission for the next summer campaign.[10]

By the fall of 1920, the Soviets had gained full control of Russia. Pillage and murder from marauding parties had also decreased considerably. The Mission concurred to secure full permission to extend the Mission's work over all the land. Some of the Communists replied: You should not receive permission for such an undertaking, but should be taken to the Death Tribunal and shot as a counter-revolutionary.

At length, Mr. Astakhoff was able to register the Mission and continue with the work. By 1923, every religious organization had to re-register, but the new law made it impossible to obtain permission, and the Tent Mission ceased.

During seven years of activities, the Mission proved to be a great help and blessing to multitudes of the suffering Russian people. Eleven members of the Mission had also died, including Mr. Dyck, who was killed with his group by a marauding party in 1919. The tremendous increase of Evangelicals during those years was due to the fact that every born-again Christian was a missionary, a witness for Christ.[11]

[9] N.I. Saloff-Astakhoff, **In the Flame of Russia's Revolution.** pp. 15-22, 25.

[10] **Ibid.,** pp. 57-58.

[11] **Ibid.,** pp. 183, 182.

## The First Gospel Mission to Communist Siberia of 1922 Fails

The first attempt to reach Communist Siberia with the gospel from the United States of America was made by Pastor Hajer of Seattle, Washington, in 1922. The Pastor and his assistant built a boat to sail to Siberia from Alaska. The first missionary group consisted of six workers who were eager to win souls to Christ in that infamous land.

The men who made the daring and heroic gospel mission across the sea to Siberia were greeted on the shore by friendly Communist troops and native Siberians. The missionary group built the first mission station at East Cape, Siberia, in 1922. Both the Communist soldiers as well as the natives were open to the gospel message. The preaching of God's Word produced good results. Many were converted to Christ, both of the troops and of the natives, and they each received a New Testament.

After several months, orders arrived from Moscow to banish the Americans. The Siberian believers were arrested and their New Testaments burned. The non-Christian soldiers were furious, and one of the officers shot and killed a missionary. The rest of them were escorted back to the boat and expelled from the Soviet Union.

On their way back to the United States, they all concurred that they would return at a later date to evangelize in Siberia. Pastor Hajer returned later with another boat to Siberia, but the boat sank in icy seas off Siberia, and Pastor Hajer died of pneumonia after being rescued. The fate of the converts of the first gospel Mission remains unknown.[12]

## The Rapid Evangelical Growth

The Christians took advantage of the great liberty for religious propaganda in 1917 to 1928 and spread rapidly, establishing efficient organizations and building publishing houses. In 1923 at the Baptist World Congress in Stockholm, Sweden, the Russian Baptists reported that they had about 5,000 Sunday Schools in the Soviet Union attended by about 300,000 boys and girls. In 1927 the Russian Baptists joyfully declared that they were blessed by religious liberty to preach

12. "Christ in Russia," Underground Evangelism

the gospel of Jesus Christ in overflowing halls and to baptize converts openly in rivers and seas before great crowds of people.[13]

In 1928 the Evangelicals numbered about 2.2 million. In 1929 in the heat of the religious persecution, about 3,219 evangelical

**The first mission station in Siberia — at East Cape, Siberia — in 1922.**

13. Durasoff, op. cit., p. 79.

congregations were still functioning, but in 1940 only 1,000 congregations remained active.[14] During the early '30s in the midst of severe persecutions, the Baptist Union suffered great losses. A large portion of believers broke entirely with religion, and many transferred to the Evangelical Christians, who were stronger and better adapted to the new conditions; so that by 1935 the Baptist Union almost discontinued its work.[15]

During World War II, some religious liberty was granted, which motivated the Baptists to propagate their faith. They advanced considerably. In 1944, when the All-Union Council of Evangelical Christians and Baptists (AUCECB) was organized, possibly over a million Evangelicals did not join the Union merger. Between 1941 and 1947 the membership of the United Baptists declined from one million to 300,000.[16]

The same statistics are mentioned by Dr. W.O. Lewis, the Secretary of the Baptist World Alliance.[17] The Union had experienced a steady growth in numbers. During the first half of the summer of 1946, about 30,000 newly converted persons were baptized and another 30,000 were expected to be baptized during the second half of the summer, making a total of 60,000 new born-again members. In 1948 the local communities of the Evangelical Christian Baptists numbered about 350,000 members, all of whom were over 18 years of age and baptized by immersion; by 1958 they increased to 530,000.[18]

By the close of 1947, there were about 4,000 Evangelical Christian Baptist communities; in 1958 the number of congregations reached 5,400. The membership is less than 100 per congregation. Only 168 communities were listed the same year with membership exceeding 100.[19] In 1964, the Moscow congregation had 4,818 members.[20] The churches are served by Pastors.

14. Ibid., pp. 87, 99.

15. Ibid., p. 114.

16. Ibid., p. 118.

17. Bolshakoff, op. cit., p. 122

18. Durasoff, op. cit., p. 119.

19. Ibid., pp. 133-138.

20. Ibid., p. 307.

As early as 1946, the Moscow headquarters of the AUCECB issued 3,000 presbyter's certificates and mailed them to its member Pastors. In the Kiev, Roven and Kur oblasts, the Pastors superintended from 120 to 200 churches.[21] At some places spiritually mature and wise women serve the churches by conducting prayer meetings and preaching. But the Lord's Supper and other ordinances of the Lord are administered by presbyters of the neighboring churches, who visit periodically for this purpose.

"Bratski Vestnik" (Fraternal Messenger) is the official organ of the All-Union Council of Evangelical Christians and Baptists and has served essentially as a correspondence Bible school for the thousands of evangelical Pastors. The 3,000 copies of the magazine have been published on Soviet presses in Moscow, usually six times annually. With some 500 copies sent abroad to satisfy its foreign readers, the remaining 2,500 copies somehow must meet the needs of more than 5,000 churches and over 25,000 preachers.[22]

### The Pentecostal Movement in South Russia

The Pentecostal message was brought to South Russia by Ivan E. Voronaev (1886-1950) in 1922.

He was born in Russia and served with the Cossacks in the imperial army. Shortly after his conversion in 1908, he ministered in Baptist churches in Irkutsk and Krasnoiarsk. Religious persecution forced him and his family to leave Russia via Harbin, Manchuria, in 1911. Arriving in San Francisco, California, he pastored a Russian Baptist Church and worked as a typesetter and proofreader. Three years later, he moved to New York and pastored a Russian Baptist Church on Henry Street.

By a neighboring Pentecostal family, his daughter – and later Voronaev himself – was led to the Glad Tidings Assembly of God church on 42nd Street, where he received the Pentecostal experience with speaking in tongues. To avoid any misunderstanding, he resigned and founded an independent Russian Pentecostal work in 1919 in New York City, which he pastored for two years. During a prayer meeting held in a member's home, an utterance in another tongue was followed by its companion gift, the interpretation of tongues in the Russian

21. Ibid., p. 128.

22. Ibid., pp. 133, 154.

language stating: Voronaev, Voronaev, Go to Russia. This was repeated three times.

Later, while privately at prayer in his apartment, the Lord spoke to him, "Voronaev, Voronaev, Go to Russia." On July 15, 1920, the Voronaev family left for Bulgaria to minister in that country before journeying on to the Ukraine.[23]

In 1922 the Soviets allowed missionary Ivan E. Voronaev to enter the Soviet Ukraine. He was described by his fellow-preachers and religious friends as a great preacher and a born organizer with great wisdom who had good success among the Baptists and Evangelical Christians.[24]

Voronaev was under appointment of the American Assemblies of God, and monthly support came from the Glad Tidings Assembly in New York City and from the Russian Eastern European Mission in Chicago. Missionary I. Voronaev proclaimed his Pentecostal message with great success in Odessa, drawing half of his congregation from the Baptists and Evangelical Christians who eagerly embraced the Pentecostal doctrines. His work grew rapidly; and in Odessa alone, the membership of the Pentecostals reached about 1,000.

**Odessa**

23. Ibid., pp. 68-70.

24. Kolarz, op. cit., p. 332.

Voronaev travelled extensively, visiting many places including even Leningrad and Moscow. He travelled and preached for two or three months at a time, opening up new assemblies across Russia, while the Odessa church and the Pentecostal headquarters were administered by his co-workers. As word spread rapidly about the Pentecostal phenomena, all-day meetings were held in village after village as the Pentecostal missionary preached and ministered successfully in praying for the sick and afflicted. In 1924 the Rev. Mr. Voronaev organized the Union of Christians of Evangelical Faith in the Ukraine, having Odessa as his Pentecostal headquarters. By 1926 the movement had spread throughout the Ukraine with 350 assemblies, having a membership of about 17,000.[25]

In 1928, Voronaev began to publish a Pentecostal magazine, "Evangelist," which was shortlived. The wave of persecution which descended on the Ukraine put a stop to the Pentecostal activities.[26] In 1936 the late Donald Gee, editor of the magazine "Pentecost," wrote on the basis of available statistics that there were about 80,000 Pentecostal believers in Russia.[27]

On August 24, 1945, about 400 Pentecostal congregations joined the Council of Evangelical Christians/Baptists, and the Council was to include in the future a member of the Pentecostal denomination. An unknown number of the Pentecostals in the Ukraine refused to join the Council. This movement has become an important religious force in the Soviet Union after its formal amalgamation with the Baptists and Evangelical Christians. This faith, which was first confined to the Ukraine, has during the past few years invaded many other parts of Russia. The Soviet press has revealed that the Pentecostal groups have been functioning in a large number of provinces in European Russia and the Maritime Provinces of the Soviet Far East.

The spread of the Pentecostal faith is the result of deliberate migration of entire Pentecostal groups and families. Because this movement is banned in the Soviet Union, it takes courage to associate oneself with the Pentecostals. Nevertheless, many young people have attended meetings of this charismatic movement which are held in the

25. Durasoff, op. cit., pp. 70-73.

26. Kolarz, op. cit., p. 332.

27. Durasoff, op. cit., p. 73.

mountains, some in the forests, or in rooms on the periphery of a city. At these secret meetings the youngsters with others sing Christian hymns with great enthusiasm.

In January 1957 the leaders of Baptists, Evangelical Christians, and more moderate leaders of the Pentecostals convened in Moscow to discuss theological problems. The conference lasted a week and produced a new profession of unity. However, many of the latter faith did not join the Union and decided to form an independent Pentecostal Church.[28]

D.I. Ponomarchuk, a former leader of the Christians of Evangelical Faith and the only Pentecostal member in the presidium, published the figure of 25,000 as the total number of the Pentecostals who entered into the Union; 14,000, or 36 percent, of the Pentecostals rejected the August Agreement of 1945. Because of doctrinal controversy, the Pentecostals who had become members of the union, later withdrew in increasing numbers.[29]

28. Kolarz, op. cit., pp. 332-336.

29. Durasoff, op. cit., pp. 138-139.

# CHAPTER XII

# PERSECUTION OF THE EVANGELICALS UNDER COMMUNISM

## Reasons for the Molestation

This study has revealed that the Evangelicals from 1917 to 1928 enjoyed comparatively great freedom for religious propaganda. This liberty was granted by the Communists with the purpose of using the evangelical bodies to their own ends, especially in the destruction of the Orthodox church. However, this expectation did not materialize; and the Christians, as a religious force, had to be eliminated.

Already in 1927 Stalin declared that the Party could not be neutral towards the religious prejudices. The suppressed reactionary clergy, which was to be eliminated, had not yet been completely liquidated. Anti-religious propaganda is a means by which the complete liquidation of the reactionary clergy must be brought about.[1]

The reason which triggered the fierce Soviet opposition to the Evangelicals was the supposed counter-revolutionary spirit among the sectarians, but for the sake of better understanding, I will deal with three aspects as basic reasons for the persecution.

1. Evangelicals branded as a counter-revolutionary force.
2. The Mennonite problem.
3. The Baptist refusal to support the Soviets in the formation of collective farms.

## Evangelicals Branded as a Counter-revolutionary Force

The Soviet criticism of the sectarians as a social force revealed itself in the complaint that the records of the sectarians had been consistently anti-revolutionary, and they had done nothing to help in the class struggle. When the proletarian revolution broke out, it owed nothing to the initiative of the dissenters; instead, the sectarians impeded it.

[1] Durasoff, op. cit., pp. 86-87.

Leningrad

At the sectarian religious conferences of 1905-1907, strong protest was made against revolutionary action and loyalty pledged to the Emperor and his imperial government. In 1905, the Protestants arranged no uprising against the landlords and the officials of the imperial government. As a result of the struggle, the Evangelicals were granted freedom of conscience; in response, the Christian leaders assured the Emperor of their devotion. Sectarians were among the government spies, and Baptists served as jailers in the Peter and Paul fortress prison and even fought faithfully in the imperial army in the 1914–1917 war.[2]

The Bolsheviks noticed the resolution of the Baptist congress in 1905, which encouraged its adherents to serve loyally in the imperial army; and Mr. Prokhanov's decision in 1917 to form a political party under the provisional government was not forgotten by the Soviets. However, the real Bolshevik complaint was that all Christian ethics were opposed to revolution and did not cooperate in the creation of a godless society.[3]

2. Casey, op. cit., pp. 48-50.

3. Ibid., pp. 52-53.

The Communists say that the Christian who looks to Christ as the one who can set the world to right by the force of His personality and purity of character, is looking for a spellbinder, not a revolutionary leader. In case of a social crisis, the Christian is definitely reactionary and counter-revolutionary, a tool in the hands of the anti-social forces.[4]

**The Mennonite Problem.**

The Mennonites, especially the wealthiest of them, were accused of refusing to take arms during the 1905 uprising; and again in 1917, they failed to aid the revolutionary cause. The Mennonites were also accused of being armed with rifles and pistols in 1917 to help the Emperor in suppressing the uprising.

During the Civil War, bands of bandits in the Ukraine grew to such proportions that they attacked the wealthy German-speaking colonies. So great was the suffering and dangers that the Mennonites were obliged to break their binding tradition, and armed men joined the colonies to protect their women and children. They were now charged with having been the enemies of the Red army.

In 1924 the Mennonite Congress convened in hope of recovering some of their former religious liberties and submitted an eight-point petition which enraged the Bolsheviks. They demanded freedom from military service, requested permission to teach the laws of God in the school, permission for religious meetings, choirs, and Bible courses. This petition miscarried and only one of the eight points was taken into consideration – permission to import some Bibles.

This stern Communist reaction to the petition triggered a second Mennonite migration; and between 1923 and 1927 some 21,000 left Russia for Canada. After 1927 the Soviets discontinued issuing passports, and Mennonite emigration ceased.[5]

During World War II, the Ukraine was occupied by the Nazis. In September and October 1943, when the German army retreated, about 35,000 Mennonites took advantage of the German occupation and left the Ukraine to accompany the retreating Germans. Many of the sick people and children perished on the way, some of the Mennonites were overtaken by the advancing Russian armies and deported to Siberia. Of the survivors, 8,000 were absorbed by Canada and 5,000 by Paraguay.[6]

4. Dark, **op. cit.**, pp. 118-119.

5. Durasoff, **op. cit.**, pp. 82-83.

6. **Ibid.**, p. 103.

Nothing further was heard of them in Russia until 1956, when two of the American Mennonite leaders found some of them in Siberia in the region of Altai and Kazakhstan. About 125 Mennonite villages were discovered in those regions, with a possible Mennonite population of about 20,000 – 1,000 of them in the town of Karaganda alone.[7] The total number of Mennonites in Russia in 1967 was about 45,000. In spite of difficulties, the Mennonites are increasing. Every member tries to make Christ known through personal conversion with those around him. Originally, the sect was German-speaking; but it is rapidly adopting Russian.[8]

The Mennonites joined the Union of Evangelical Christians and Baptists in 1953, and the first numerical account listed 18,600 members who merged.[9]

### Baptist Refusal to Support the Soviets in the Formation of Collective Farms

The main charge brought against the Evangelical Christians and Baptists was their acceptance of foreign support from abroad because some wealthy Americans supported the cause of Christ in Russia. New fuel was added to the Communist wrath by the Baptists in 1928-1929 when collective farms were in process of formation. The Baptists' desire to form collectives out of their own church members led to a misunderstanding and produced the suppressive law of 1929, which was primarily against the Evangelical Churches.[10]

### The Law of 1929, A Death Blow to the Evangelicals

The Law of April 8, 1929, proved to be a major blast against all believers in Russia, but especially against the demanding Mennonites who drew the fire of the Soviets. The Law denied legal existence to all churches, but allowed the performance of worship only. The Department of Justice issued about 60 Articles as an elaborate

7. N. Struve, **Christians in Contemporary Russia,** (New York: Charles Scribner's Sons, 1967), p. 231

8. **Ibid.,** pp. 231-232.

9. Durasoff, **op. cit.,** p. 138.

10. **Ibid.,** pp. 84-86.

codification of the laws on religion. From the Revolution to 1929, about 2,000 churches were closed, whereas in 1929 alone about 1,370 churches and synagogues ceased to function. The Dom Evangelia built by Pastor Fetler in St. Petersburg was confiscated by the Bolsheviks in 1928 and turned into a dance hall and a Communist club.[11]

The number of Evangelicals in Russia prior to 1929 is impossible to ascertain. Mr. Durasoff thinks that the most reasonable total for the

**This humble sanctuary in Minsk, U.S.S.R., was confiscated by the authorities without any compensation. The believers, who had worshipped there for many years, "exiled" to the city's outskirts and permitted to occupy an old building which they remodeled at great expense. Evangelist John Panko, who stands in the pulpit, died in 1965 of ruined health from nine years' exile at hard labor in Siberia. (1968)**

11. Ibid., pp. 85-86.

1928 membership was 2.2 million – derived by comparing the statistics printed in "Bratski Vestnik" with the Soviet estimate of a decimation of 78 percent of the Evangelicals since 1928.[12]

### The Bolshevist Opposition to the Evangelicals

In the beginning of 1928, cruel persecutions were inflicted in the Soviet Union upon all who professed any religious belief. For several years, Communists had fought against the Evangelicals through organized public debates in the hope of exposing the deceit of religion and the nonexistence of God. But the Communist agents frequently were defeated by the Christians, who won the moral victory; and some of the unsaved people who attended the public debates were converted to Christ.

The persecution brought thousands of Christians to the prisons and concentration camps, where the believers continued to witness to the glory of God. Many suffering and despairing people in the slave camps accepted the gospel truth and found peace in Jesus Christ. Secret Bible studies and prayer meetings were held in private homes, but the government issued a law forbidding all such gatherings in the homes. Next, the Christians began to gather at homes for supper, which had not been forbidden. There at the table, with a cup of tea before them, the believers held their prayer meetings. Later on, the Soviets began to arrest all those that participated in these suppers. In addition to that, the government began to place their agents as spies among the believers, but that method produced very little results because the spy was easily discerned by the Christians.[13]

### The Bolshevist Method of Recruiting Protestant Spies

The method used to enlist such agents was a very cunning one. Once, Soviets selected a prominent church member and invited him to their office. The church member was very cordially received by the Communists, who commented about his Christian steadfastness and successful Christian life. Next, a question was introduced to the member: Did he believe everything written in the Bible? The poor Christian, not realizing the trap, replied, "Yes!" This pleased the

12. Ibid., p. 87.

13. Astakhoff, Christianity in Russia, pp. 108-109.

Communists because now they could use the Scriptures to their own profit, saying: "Peter and Paul say all government is from God and that we should be subject to it; therefore, on the authority of God's Word, we command you, citizen, to give us a detailed account of everything that is spoken, or prayed about, in your service."[14]

If the Christian refused, promises of good remuneration were made. If bribery and flattery did not induce the Christian to comply with their request, the Communists resorted to another method. A paper, with a few words on it, was presented to him for his signature. The Christian reads: "On this date I was summoned to the office of the Secret Political Government Police, to which I testify with my signature." The Christian signs and leaves the office, rejoicing that the matter was ended. After a time, the same church member was again summoned to the police office where the paper which he had signed before is brought to his attention, to which had been added this statement. "I solemnly agree to be a faithful co-worker with the Secret Police." The church member is demanded to cooperate with the Bolsheviks or face the consequences. He must choose one of two alternatives:

1. Prison and death.
2. Become a traitor to his fellow Christians.

Some were trapped in that way, because refusal would mean loss of life of the entire family. Some of the believers did not return to the police office any more but left their homes and fled. Wandering around as vagabonds, clad in rags, they let their hair and beard grow long, living on what was given to them by kind-hearted people. During the daytime, these pilgrims hid themselves, but at night they preached the gospel and comforted the believers. From 1928, persecutions of the Evangelicals increased up to 1935, when the Bolsheviks began to retreat and Christians enjoyed a little respite of the seven-year period of molestation.[15]

Approximately 14,000 ministers and deacons were occupied with the preaching of the gospel until the last great wave of persecution swept over the country.[16]

14. N.I. Astakhoff, **Christianity and Communism,** Second Edition (New York: Published by the Author, 164 Second Ave., 1931), pp. 44-45.

15. Astakhoff, **Christianity in Russia,** pp. 109-110.

16. **Ibid.,** p. 113.

Mr. Astakhoff, reflecting upon the late '20s and early '30s, wrote in 1932 that most of the clergy and religious workers were either in prison, exile, or killed. Many died in places of exile, while others, under inhuman tortures, lost their minds.[17]

A few cases of suffering of the Christians in the Soviet Union will be included to introduce the inhuman molestation of the innocent victims, whose only crime was their love for Jesus Christ.

### Arrest and 500-Mile March of a Widow Woman

At one town, several Communists broke into the house of a widow at night, searched the house and confiscated the Bibles and New Testaments they got hold of. The mother was arrested and forced to walk heavily guarded about 500 miles to Moscow where she used to live. Her two little children were left alone, without mother and father, being in the most horrible circumstances. The mother was to be exiled to Siberia for three to five years, while her younger sister had been already sentenced to Siberia for three years for attending a prayer meeting at a private home.[18]

### Torture of Rev. Mr. Odentsov, President of All-Russian Baptist Union

Rev. Mr. Nikolai Odentsov (1870-1939) lost all property to the Communists and was thrown out on the street. Later he was arrested, sentenced to death, and cast together with other condemned men into the death cellar to await execution. One day the president, with others, was led out to be executed. They were lined up against the wall to face death. All his fellow prisoners were shot in his presence, whereas Odentsov was led back into the death cellar. This ordeal was repeated three times. At this time, the president of the Baptist Union collapsed and became insane. He was brought to an asylum where he recovered. He died in Siberia in 1939.[19]

17. Astakhoff, **Real Russia**, p. 98.

18. Astakhoff, **Christianity and Communism**, pp. 99-100.

19. Ibid., pp. 100-102.

## 25 Believers Executed by Freezing Them to Death in a River

In 1961 in Brazil, South America, a sad but victorious story was related to me by a fine Christian gentleman who lived in Russia himself for many years. In one region in eastern Russia about 25 believers were condemned to die in ice-cold water in a river. It was about 30 degrees below zero. A hole was made in the thick ice, and all the Christians were stripped of their clothes and placed in the cold water.

The condemned were given an opportunity to deny Christ and go free. In the nearby building the steam bath was heated that in case of "repentance" on the part of some stubborn believer, he would be pulled out of the water and warmed up in the hot steam.

On the riverbank was a tower in which a Communist policeman with a machine gun had orders to shoot anyone who tried to run away. As the Christians were slowly freezing in the cold water, the Communist suddenly saw crowns descending slowly from heaven on the heads of the Christians. The policeman was staring at the phenomenon with increasing confusion and realization that this was something supernatural – not produced by man.

One crown descended very close to the head of one believer, but then stopped and began to ascend slowly. After a few seconds it descended again slowly close to the head of the believer, then went up and disappeared. This man denied the Lord. He was taken out of the water and rushed to the steam bath, but it was too late. Before he died, the backslider confessed that he saw how his crown of life was given to another. When the Communist saw this remarkable phenomenon, he came down from the tower, laid his machine gun aside, accepted Christ, took the man's place in the river who had denied Christ, and died with the group.*

## Christians Suffocated in Hot Stifling Air

Sometimes believers were locked in rooms in hot stifling air. After the victims were half suffocated, they were thrown into an ice-cold house to freeze. After a period of time, the suffering victims were given an opportunity to deny faith in God and to sign a paper which declared that Communism allows freedom of worship to the believers. They

*Name withheld for security reasons.

could go without being tortured any more. Some of the Christians died during such tortures, others became schizophrenic. Some denied their faith, signed papers and were released.[20]

## World War II Induced Some Religious Alleviation

The Russian Orthodox Church in the late '30s presented a picture of total desolation. Throughout the Soviet Union, less than a hundred churches remained open for worship. Rostov-on-the-Don, a large industrial city with a population of 600,000 had only one chapel open in the Armenian cemetery, but had no services because there were no priests. In the whole province there was only one single church functioning, served by a very old priest.[21]

On June 22, 1941, Germany attacked Russia. By the end of November the Germans were only 30 miles from Moscow. In this unprecedented exigency, Stalin realized that only religion could unite and encourage the people to fight for the country and made his famous remark: If the people won't fight for socialism, perhaps they will fight for Holy Russia. Stalin re-established the Patriarchate of Moscow with pliant clergymen and called off the vestiges of the anti-religious campaign.[22]

The great Patriotic War against the Third Reich prompted the Communist Party to channel the nation's religious forces to serve general Communist policies. Concessions granted by the Party to religious groups were matters of expediency and not law. In September 1941 the publication "Bezbozhnik," the newspaper of the League of the Militant Godless, and "Antireligioznik," the League's monthly organ, were discontinued. The Soviets, maintaining that these publications were not managed by the Party but by special agency, disclaimed its anti-religious propaganda activity. Thus, without admitting any changes in government policy toward the religious bodies, the anti-religious movement could be terminated conveniently.

The religious force united the Russian people in the great Patriotic War against the Nazis. Common patriotic activities united the evangelicals more closely in spiritual relations, and the unity among the

20. **Ibid.**, p. 41.

21. Struve, **op. cit.**, p. 57.

22. F.B. Randall, **Stalin's Russia and Historical Reconsideration**, (New York: London: Collier-Macmillian LTD, 1965), p. 258.

Evangelical Christians and Baptists was greatly accelerated during the German invasion. Joint services of both evangelical bodies were held before the war in Moscow, Leningrad, and Novosibirsk. In May 1942, I. Goliaev and N.A. Levindanto, as representatives of the Baptist Union, appealed to the legally existent Union of Evangelical Christians to serve the Baptist communities as they served their own Union.

From then on, the unofficial united effort commenced which culminated in the 1944 merger of the two bodies of believers. In May 1942 the Evangelicals jointly appealed to the world to help the Soviet Union in the struggle against the German forces. During the war, many of the Evangelicals served with distinction, some as officers, decorated with medals. Over a quarter of a million war orphans were adopted by the homes, many of them in homes of believers as a result of the direct appeal of their churches. Thousands of present-day Evangelicals have emerged as a result of this response.[23]

## The Bolshevist Charges Against the Pentecostals and Baptists

In 1959, A.I. Klibanov led a Soviet government expedition to Lipetsk Oblast, in the city of Voronezh, to study the contemporary state of religious groups and their movements, the ideology and tactics of sectarianism, and ways of overcoming religious survivals and growth. The historical ethnographic method, combining the study of the activity of the local religious groups, personal encounters with individual believers, and an investigation of archive sources was used in the study by the expedition. Klibanov was baffled over the doctrines of the Pentecostals, especially over the assertion of the accessibility of God to man via the sense organs. The leader of the expedition listed the Pentecostals among the most "virulent species of religious opium." The Soviet writer, Garkavenko, in writing on religious sects referred to the leaders who followed Voronaev, the founder of the Pentecostal movement in Russia, as epileptics and hysterical prophets and prophetesses. Garkanenko stated further that healings and prophecies were manifested in the prayer meetings in order to reinforce the religious rites of the psychology of believers.[24]

23. Durasoff, op. cit., pp. 99-102.

24. Ibid., pp. 165-166.

The anti-religious press constantly published articles accusing the sectarians of negativism in the social upbringing of their children: "The Baptists mutilate their children and educate them in a reactionary spirit by not permitting the youngsters to wear the Pioneer tie nor to enter the Komsomol. Children who have fallen into the Baptist net are made sullen, unsocial, depending upon God's will for everything, whereby they have lost their capacity for independent thinking." More involved than the independent Baptists and Evangelical Christians were the Pentecostals, who were often accused of forbidding their children to join the Pioneers. The believers' violation of the Soviet Constitution as it applied to the separation of Church and State, and the School from the Church, invited the wrath of the officials.

The Soviet leaders believed that faith would die if parents did not rule the souls of their offspring, and that children of tender years who sat with parents in prayer meetings suffered from weakened psyches and became emotional cripples in such a fanatical religious atmosphere. A Pentecostal preacher named Godyshev, dismayed by the impact the Communist youth group had made upon his youngsters, removed his two sons from the Pioneers. Pressured by the Crimean school director, Zharskaia, Godyshev stated: "Your business is to teach my children,

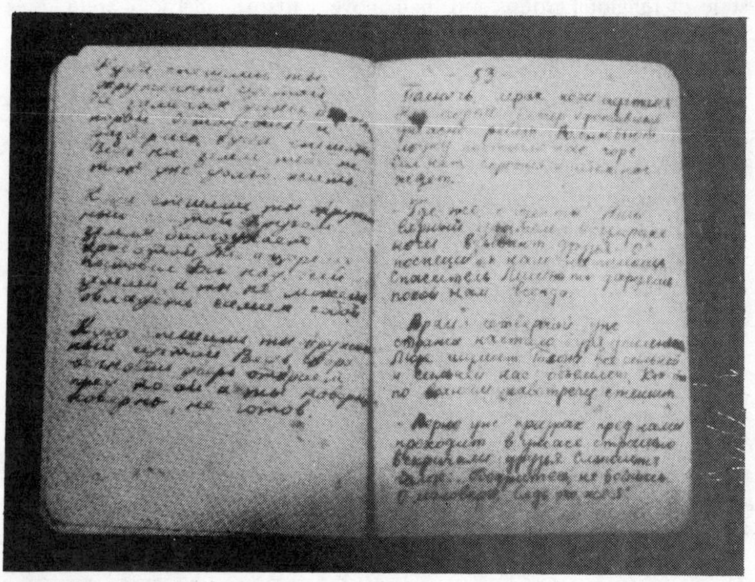

**Because of Bible shortages in Russia, many Christians copy Scriptures by hand.**

but I myself will train them as I need to. I will give myself as a sacrifice if you unteach my son. You honor a struggle – then let's struggle."

Pentecostal ministers were stereotyped as fanatics forbidding the reading of newspapers, journals, and books (except the Bible), the attendance at the theatre, concerts, dances, and social organizations. Some ministers were accused of having encouraged their people to refuse service in the Red army and not to participate in Soviet holiday demonstrations.[25]

### Soviet Youth and Evangelical Parents

The Bolshevist Pioneer rules included a love for the Communist Party and a program to train the youngsters for the Komsomol candidacy. The members of the Komsomol possessed a code of conduct resembling many qualities which are compatible with the Christian ethic such as obedience to parents, care for the young, and aid to the old, self-discipline, love for labor, and care of public property. The Komsomol members are called upon to help the Bolshevist regime in its political indoctrination, general education, industry, agriculture, social relations, military activities, and world affairs. The youth, as yet idealistic and not disillusioned, were trained to acquire quality of character including a loyalty to Party chiefs, inflexible discipline, self-sacrificial bravery, ideological purity, firm conviction, incessant vigilance, uncompromising militancy, and a hatred toward all enemies.

A.V. Karev (1894-1971) revealed the AUCECB headquarters' awareness of the concern and apprehension of Christian parents for their young. He wisely dispatched a message of encouragement to Christian parents to faithfully train their children despite the opposition and trials of life in the Soviet society by drawing a parallel from the life of Moses. Mr. Karev reminded his fellow believers that Moses spent the formative years of his life with his parents, during which time the fundamentals of faith, hope, and love were deeply implanted. Later in the palace of Pharaoh, the temptations and allurement could not overcome the young Hebrew man. Today we see the power and greatness of God as indicated before the king of Egypt and all his people; the power of darkness contending with the power of light.

25. Ibid., pp. 191-192.

Mr. Mitskevich, member of the AUCECB presidium also encouraged the believers that the Christian home was a great school in which the children were to be brought up in honor, nobility, morals and culture. In reference to the charges of the anti-religious articles so often aimed at sectarian parents, he warned the Evangelicals against antagonizing their children by physically compelling them to read their Bibles or forcing them to pray at length. In acknowledging a Christian's beating of a child which necessitated the attention of a physician, Mr. Karev asked the parents to exercise parental self-control; to train their children to be industrious; to teach the children to read, and to keep them from immoral books, to instill love for the people and for the nation; so that the effect of the teachings of Christ can be seen in the Christian home.

Party members were alert for any such instances of sectarian beatings of children. A report was followed by the action of the Soviet People's Court, depriving believers of their parental rights and committing the children to a State Children's home. The Bolshevik Party also demanded that parents must serve as models of political and social activities, industriousness, unselfishness, and optimism. They believed that children become emotionally alienated from parents who do not act in accord with the precepts and ideals which the children learn in school and in the Pioneer of Komsomol organizations.[26]

### Persecution of the Pentecostals During the Khrushchev Era

Pentecostal activities in Russia are prohibited. The Soviet Union has banned the charismatic movement as a fanatical and dangerous force which has attracted some of the Russian young people. The Bolshevist Press describes the Pentecostals and their leaders and preachers as skillful propagandists of their faith, who spread their faith and doctrines through personal work or by the help of written letters to be copied and passed on.

The Soviet police has found it easy to convict Pentecostal leaders in various parts of Russia as political criminals. The regime disregards the religious aspect of the Pentecostal movement and considers it as a hostile group to the State, the army, the Party and Soviet education.

26. Ibid., pp. 188-191.

During the Khrushchev era, trials of Pentecostals occured in many parts of the Soviet Union as in the Ukraine, Byelorussia, Moldavia, the Crimea, in the Moscow region, and other areas. The authorities accused the charismatic movement preachers of religious fanaticism, alienating young people from the Soviet life, commiting crimes against the State, and indulging in all kinds of debauchery. The defendants were sentenced to 10 years in the slave camps.

In addition to the judicial trials in the late '50s, great use was made of propaganda. Anti-pentecostal newspaper articles appeared, and Communist teachers in the villages organized discussion groups with Pentecostal peasants to convert them to atheism.[27]

**Struggle of the Dissident Group**

In August 1961 a dissident group emerged as a divisive force within the All Union of Evangelical Christians and Baptists. At the height of this drive against AUCECB, the dissident movement, led by A.F. Prokofiev and G.K. Kriuchkov, spearheaded the withdrawal of some 26,500 Christians or about 5 percent of the membership. On October 15-17, 1963, the AUCECB summoned a conference in Moscow, to which 450 ministers responded. This convention was called especially in response to the challenge of the dissident group. The agenda included the examination and confirmation of the AUCECB rules and regulations of the presidium by the valid voting delegates, and the problem of unity.[28]

Researcher W.C. Fletcher, through his study and findings, concluded that the schism apparently began as a result of an instruction issued by the AUCECB to its senior presbyters ordering them not to preach when requested to do so by churches in their territory, and to instruct their churches not to baptize candidates under 30 years of age, and no longer to seek new converts. However, on examination, the Statutes of the AUCECB indicated no increase in the minimum age of 18 for church membership by means of baptism.

In 1946, Zhidkov defended the Soviet law because it enables a candidate for water baptism to be sufficiently mature for this important ordinance. He strengthened his argument by referring to

27. Kolarz, **op. cit.**, pp. 335-337

28. Durasoff, **op. cit.**, pp. 197-198.

Christ who received baptism at the age of 30, which is full maturity. It is possible that a similar expression could have been misconstrued to mean that the minimal age for baptism had been increased to 30. The dissident group is determined to remain independent and to challenge more believers to secede from the AUCECB, a union they were convinced was a tool of the Soviet rulers.[29]

Writers in the "Underground Evangelism Magazine" give more relevant information about this struggle between the AUCECB and the dissident group. Their information is based on a document or letter signed by "62 relatives of Evangelicals imprisoned by their faith," and smuggled out from Russia to the free world.

Evangelical Christians in Russia faced a Communist ultimatum in 1944: Conform to a cunningly conceived, government-supervised organization, or face the consequences. The directorate of the brotherhood of the Soviet Federation of Evangelical Christians-Baptists chose the way of compromise. The Communist-sponsored evangelical group in order to retain its status quo, bowed to the State. In spiritual questions they did not compromise – and until today they do not fulfill the commandment of Christ, but let themselves be governed after the prescriptions of outsiders, and by this, ruining the church inside. These measures led to a state of Laodicea in the church. Many believers, seeing this obvious destruction of the work of God, sought for a way out. Many arose from their spiritual sleep and stepped out on the way of true service for the Lord. At this time the reformers broke away from the Communist-dominated All Union Council of Evangelicals and Christian Baptists and formed their own group.[30]

This information, just quoted above, is relevant and authoritative. This study has shown that about 700,000 believers never joined the Union in 1944. To this group can be added the independent Pentecostals. There were unrelated independent groups of Evangelical Christians in the Ukraine, Belorussia, Siberia, and the Urals. Some independent Baptists have been accused of conducting illegal anti-social activities, including the opening of illegal houses of prayer. Other independents, called Pure Baptists and Compelte Evangelical Christians, condemned the AUCECB leaders for achieving the historic unity, calling it instead dirty work.[31]

29. Ibid., pp. 107, 199, 202.

30. "They Worship Underground," **Underground Evangelism Magazine**, (May 1970), pp. 7, 12.

31. Durasoff, op. cit., pp. 196-197.

The split resulted in severe persecutions and many of the believers were incarcerated.

A new storm of persecution was unchained. The honest children of God were expelled from the communities of the official church. They were obliged to hold their services in private houses, in forests, and in the open air, while the elder church which had entered upon the broad way of compromise, assembled quietly in their church houses. A wave of arrests followed. Police descended on meetings all over the country.

From the year 1961 on, more than 500 brothers, mainly servants of the church, presbyters, and preachers, have been arrested and thrown into prisons.

The children of Evangelicals are taken before the public prosecutor and subjected to brutal questioning regarding their Christian education. Often they are forced against their will to testify against their parents. Many of these children have been forcibly separated from their parents by the People's Court. More cruel persecution is the result of their uncompromising faith in Christ. Increasingly, the believers find themselves confronted with the apostolic decision to obey God rather than men. During the latter part of 1969, arraignment of Evangelicals was stepped up sharply.[32]

### Soviet Controlled Official Church System

Many people are confused about the state-run church system in the Soviet Union. After years of control and subversion, The Ministry of Cults controlling the churches is selecting young Communists, Komsomols, to go into training as future Pastors. These young Communist-trained Pastors are put into pastorates by the Bolshevist government. The goal is a totally controlled, subverted church system. With such men in control they are turning the church system into an actual extension and branch of the government itself as a control over the Christians, and to deceive foreign tourists who go there, see open churches, and think in Western terms. The Bolshevist goal is the subversion, control and slow strangulation of Christianity from within. Thus, the subverted church system becomes:

32. "They Worship Underground," **Underground Evangelism Magazine,** (May 1970), p. 12.

1. A window through which to watch the Christians, and a tool of control over them.

2. A vehicle through which to carry out the slow strangulation of Christianity from within.

3. A tool of deception for naive foreign tourists who look at a Russian situation with American eyes.[33]

Mr. Paul B. Peterson, editor of the "Gospel Call" magazine of the Eastern European Mission, says the 1944 merger agreement lured the leaders of the Evangelical Christians and Baptists into taking this step by the promises of greater liberty, the lifting of certain restrictions, and official recognition that was to improve their precarious standing. This agreement was reached when Stalin needed the moral support of all the people. Mr. Peterson was acquainted with several of the evangelical leaders who signed the agreement; but a close friend of one of them during the last 35 years, said to Mr. Peterson that the agreement which the Soviet government subsequently published was not the one that he had signed. After obtaining the signatures of these men, it published above their names whatever suited it best.

By July 1960 the Soviets evidently considered that the leadership of the Union had been subdued to the point where it would do the

**This picture of a large gathering of Christian believers in the open air "somewhere in Russia," taken in the summer of 1966, demonstrates at least two things: (1) that the new Free Church movement is composed of a younger, more virile generation, and (2) that their meetings and struggle for recognition by the government are open (not secret or underground).**

33. "Russia's Counterfeit Church," **Underground Evangelism Magazine**, (May 1970), p. 10.

bidding of the authorities in dictating to the evangelical churches regarding the conduct of their services. At this time, a letter of Instructions, which probably was prepared by the Soviets, was sent to all the churches in that denomination. Among the directives were these:

1. Not to seek to gain new members.

2. To restrain unwholesome evangelistic activity.

3. Applicants for membership to be placed on probation for not less than two to three years, for the purpose of discontinuing the unwholesome practice of competing for a larger membership.

4. To give no invitations in public service.

5. Insistance that the baptism of believers in the age group between 18 and 30 years be reduced to a minimum.[34]

These points constitute the law or laws the Pastors must enforce to be relicensed the following year. Until a few years ago, the Communists searched out and found cooperative Pastors to license from within the older body of Pastors. The uncompromising believers departed from the compromising churches and spread the gospel secretly or underground. Most of Russia's underground preachers are former Pastors whom the Bolshevists refused to license because of their love and faithfulness to God.[35]

**The church in the Soviet Union in which this group makes a joyful noise to the Lord doubtless considers itself fortunate. The musical instrument at left, as well as the three in front, appear to be homemade.**

34. P.B. Peterson, "The Churches in Eastern Europe Today," **The Gospel Call,** (November 1969), p. 4.

35. **Underground Evangelism,** (May 1969), p. 11.

Mr. Sven Svenson, editor of the Swedish Baptist Union weekly newspaper, visited the Baptist churches in European and Asiatic Russia in 1971. During his three-week tour he observed that the dissident Baptists and the regular Baptists through continuing discussions with government authorities, have both improved the climate in which religious bodies must operate in Russia. His observation is that the Christians in the free world cannot really comprehend the conditions under which believers live in the Soviet Union, and therefore must not sit in judgment on the Russian Christians. The main problem which has divided Baptists in Russia into two camps is the question: Should one openly resist restrictions on religious work, or should one theoretically accept restrictions, but then try to improve matters.

The dissidents did not pull out of the registered union over doctrinal differences, but over a difference in opinion on how to react to government restrictions on religious work. The dissidents are an underground church in the sense that they operate outside the framework drawn up in the Soviet law for religious organizations, but they have not deliberately tried to conceal themselves from the government. To conclude that some Baptists have betrayed their faith or that others have been perfect representatives of true Christianity would be a most unfair oversimplification of a deeply rooted issue that has far-reaching implications that most Westerners cannot grasp.[36]

[36] "Dissident Baptists and Regulars Striving to Get Along in Russsia," **The Baptist Courier,** (May 1969), p. 20.

**Millions like this lady in Russia depend on the Russian radio gospel broadcasts for spiritual food from abroad. (1976)**

## CHAPTER XIII

# EVANGELIZATION OF THE RUSSIANS IN THE SOVIET UNION

### A Great Hunger for the Word of God in Russia

Jesus said: "... man shall not live by bread alone ..."[1] The soul of man hungers for spiritual food, no matter what nationality he is.

In 1957 a true story was related in a sermon by the late Pastor Baisil Malof, a Russian preacher, who between the two world wars pastored a large evangelical church in Riga Latwia. One day he met a Russian seaman in Riga who was working on a Russian boat moored in the harbor.

In the conversation, Pastor Malof encouraged him to smuggle a number of Russian Bibles on board the ship to bring them to the Soviet Union. When back in his country he was to go to the nearest marketplace and give the Bibles out.

In Russia the seaman went to the marketplace in a city. When there were no police in sight, he lifted up a Bible and proclaimed: "Who wants a Bible?" The people stopped gossiping; the merchandise on their respective tables was forgotten. People rushed forward with outstretched hands to get a Bible. In a minute the precious Bibles were gone. Only one was left. The seaman tore a few pages out of the Bible at a time to give the living Word of God to the spiritually hungry people. When a person got a few pages of the Word of God, the one kissed the pages and joyfully walked away. This illustrates the great hunger in the hearts of the Russian masses.[2]

### The Russian Radio Gospel Broadcasts

The most effective means for the evangelization of the people in the Soviet Union are the radio gospel programs. Communist forces cannot stop the gospel message that travels through the air into the Soviet Union.

1. Matthew 4:4

2. Baisil Malof, A sermon preached in Vancouver, British Columbia, 1957.

**Baptismal candidates. Church of Evangelical Christians—Baptists, Minsk, August 1977.**

At the present (1983), several missionary organizations are involved in broadcasting the gospel into the Russian Communist empire. One of the most advanced in this phase of the evangelization program is the Slavic Gospel Association, Inc., with more than 600 gospel broadcasts a month into Russia. Millions of Russians listen to these programs. Statistics show that more than 40 million shortwave sets are in use in the U.S.S.R.[3]

Eastern European Mission Inc. began its Russian gospel radio broadcast on March 5, 1967. Today they sponsor four weekly broadcasts in the Russian language to the Soviet Union and are planning to begin a fifth Russian broadcast in the near future. It is estimated that as many as 7 million people listen to these programs. Christian leaders in Russia express the opinion that about 1 million people have been saved through the combined evangelical radio broadcasts.[4]

As early as 1968 it was evident that the gospel broadcasts were listened to by great multitudes with many conversions. Mr. Paul Semenchuk of Trans World Radio's Russian Department with Roy Hertzog, Trans World Radio's Chief Engineer in Monte Carlo, Monaco, visited Russia in October 1967 in order to make an accurate study of available frequencies, atmospheric conditions, and technical interferences. They met the people and learned about the great effect on their three daily broadcasts on the lives of the Russian people. The seed sown over the past several years had begun to bear precious fruit.

3. "Shouldn't Russians Have a Choice," **Slavic Gospel News,** (July 1976), p. 1.

4. "Millions of Russians for Christ," **The Gospel Call,** (March-April 1977), p. 5

They learned that the Russian youth were turning to the Russian gospel broadcasts in epidemic proportions! Intellectuals, professional people, executives, officials and party members have bowed their knee to Christ! First one member of a family and then the rest have accepted the Lord Jesus Christ as Savior as they have listened to the broadcasts day after day. The Christians were exceedingly happy for the gospel broadcasts. At one time in the evening there were about 20 people listening to the broadcast, and when the radio speaker admonished his audience to bow their heads in prayer, all 20 people as one man rose to their feet and prayed. Many of the Christian university students thanked them for the Word of God aired over the radio.[5]

**The photograph below was taken shortly after these 25 happy people in the Soviet Union had followed the Lord in baptism. It may surprise some of our readers to know that most of the converts in Russia are young people. They are zealous, courageous and daring. (1970)**

The letters received by Trans World Radio Russian Department indicate a spiritual awakening in the Soviet Union. A Christian couple from Russia visited Poland in 1968 and wrote to the Russian Department in Trans World Radio, Monaco. The radio broadcasts have awakened the Russian people. Many new converts have been added to the churches. Also many backsliders have come back to the Lord after 10 to 15 years of indifference.[6]

A letter was sent to the Gospel Call by Rev. Earl S. Poysti, speaker on the Russian broadcast, Monte Carlo. When he visited Prague,

5."Let the Skies Pour Down Righteousness," **The Gospel Call,** (January 1968), pp. 3-4.

6."Numerous Conversions Through Radio Broadcasts," **The Gospel Call,** (June 1968), p. 13

**Russian believers enter the water for a baptismal service conducted by the Evangelical Christian—Baptist Church in Olschansk, District of Brest, U.S.S.R.**

Czechoslovakia, information left there by a visiting Christian from western Russia revealed that in some places many people had been saved; in some instances, almost entire villages had turned to the Lord through the radio ministry. Many of the people have acquired tape recorders and record the broadcasts for their own personal study. Again the information reveals that not only the Christians but also worldly people, Communist Party people, young and old, listen to the broadcasts, resulting in many conversions.[7]

The results have proven that radio is the most effective means for evangelism. The door is closed to any missionary activity from outside the country. The vast area of the Soviet Union can be reached from abroad only by shortwave radio.

Consider what the Communist world is doing to spread its propaganda of lies. The Soviet Union's powerful transmitters are broadcasting about 1,400 hours a week; China beams 1,027 hours of propaganda weekly. The total output of international broadcasting by all Communist countries makes a total of about 4,901 hours a week in 76 languages.

[7] "Gospel Radio Broadcasts Awaken Russian Villages, **The Gospel Call,** (July 1968), p. 11.

Since World War II in the Ukraine alone more than 800 congregations have been disbanded, and large numbers of church buildings have been closed, confiscated, or destroyed. It is therefore part of the duty of the Christians abroad to expound Scriptures by means of radio for the benefit of thousands of Christian homes. Radio is the most effective means there is for evangelizing a country like the Soviet Union which for so long a time has been a victim of incessant atheistic propaganda and indoctrination. Information reveals again and again that not only Christians but also unbelievers, atheists, Communists, Party members, intellectuals, youth, children and people in high places listen.

The greatest response is among the young people – the product of Communism. One report from the Soviet Union revealed that there had been instances where large numbers of people had been converted through hearing the message of salvation over the radio. In a particular stronghold of Communism, a town in which there was no gospel witness or Christian, 13 people believed the gospel and accepted Christ and were born again. How? By listening to the broadcasts from Monte Carlo which was their only spiritual contact. Today (1969) there is a nice assembly in that town, having about 40 members.[8]

The revival fires are burning in many parts of the country, and the radio ministry is having a vital part in this awakening. In 1968 in the Ukraine alone, some 12,000 Communist youth were saved. The majority of the converts are men and young people, which is very significant for that country.[9]

An elderly man from Russia wrote to Trans World Radio Russian Department: "How are you, dear, holy fathers? I send you a hearty thank you for your dear holy Word, which to me is more precious than anything else in the world." He was 88 and got saved through the radio ministry.[10]

The radio programs are heard not only in countless homes in the Soviet Union, but also in church services. Not to miss the programs that are broadcast during the time of the services, the believers incorporate them as a regular part of their meetings, after which they kneel to pray. Cassette recordings of the programs also are used in church services.

8 "Blanketing the Soviet Union with the Gospel," **The Gospel Call,** (January 1969), pp. 7-8.

9. "A Spiritual Awakening in Russia," **The Gospel Call,** (May 1969), p. 1.

10. "Inspiring Messages from Behind the Iron Curtain," **The Gospel Call,** (July 1970), p. 16.

**A representative of Trans World Radio's Russian Department listens to gospel program from Monte Carlo in the home of a Christian engineer in a city in southwestern Russia. (1970)**

Thousands of cassettes containing the Russian programs aired in Monte Carlo have been prepared by two missionary organizations, and eventually will find their way behind the "Iron Curtain."[11]

In 1941 there were no Russian broadcasts in existence. In 1976 there were about 1,800 broadcasts per month reaching the Soviet Union from 10 missionary radio stations. Russian listeners from 88 countries have written letters to the station.[12]

### Christian Literature and Bibles Smuggled into Russia

In Russia, the average Christian would gladly pay a month's salary for a Bible – if he could find one to buy. No Protestant seminaries or Bible training schools operate in the entire Soviet Union. Sunday Schools and Christian youth activities are not officially allowed. Some Christians have gone to prison for conducting Sunday Schools and other evangelistic activities. These are just a few of the problems and

11. "Russian Radio Programs Used in the Church Services," **The Gospel Call,** (July-August 1976), p. 11.

12. Slavic Gospel News, (July 1976), p. 7.

persecutions that Christians face in Russia. The Slavic Gospel Association, Inc., is involved in this good work in several ways.

1. The Association buys and delivers thousands of pocket-size Russian Bibles and Christian books every year.
2. Prints Russian Bible concordances.
3. Life of Jesus Christ pictorial Bibles.
4. Self-study Bible courses for Russian Christian workers.
5. Evangelistic booklets for university students.
6. Hymnals, and other Christian literature.

The purpose of ministers of this Association is to reach the millions of non-Christians in the U.S.S.R. and to encourage the Russian Evangelical Church, with a current membership of at least 6 million.[13] (There are many other organizations and evangelical groups involved in this work of smuggling Bibles into the Soviet Union.)

The need for Christian literature is very great. More than 75,000 lay preachers in Russia minister with almost no Bible study books. Most ministers and church leaders have never received systematic theological training. The majority of Pastors are lay preachers. They plead for help in their ministry. The Slavic Gospel Association is sponsoring a Bible Training School by correspondence that was developed by the staff of the Russian Bible Institute in Buenos Aires, Argentina, South America. By 1976 seven courses were complete:

1. Introduction to the Old Testament.
2. Introduction to the New Testament.
3. The Life of Christ.
4. Christian Apologetics.
5. The Book of Genesis.
6. The Gospel of John.
7. The Epistle to the Romans.

These courses are produced in book form to be taken into Russia. Approximately 15,000 of the correspondence books have been delivered into East Europe for Russia. The just-mentioned Association will also reprint 5,000 pocket-size Russian Bible Concordances to help meet this need. In 1976 the Association was preparing 25,000 Bibles to be sent into the Soviet Union. They have also prepared 300 Sunday School lessons and sermon outlines to provide valuable assistance to

[13] "Shouldn't Russians Have a Choice," **Slavic Gospel News,** (July 1976), p. 1.

**The gigantic radio towers in the Alps Mountains above Monte Carlo on the Mediterranean Sea near the French-Italian border give the winds a mighty voice. Through these facilities the Eastern European Mission broadcasts the gospel message in Russian to the Soviet Union twice weekly. The signal of Trans World Radio's 100,000 watt, short wave transmitter is heard as far east as Japan, blanketing Russia and Siberia with the good news that "Jesus saves!" (1971)**

Christian teachers and preachers in the U.S.S.R. About 5,000 of these books were to be printed.[14]

Many people have taken upon themselves to bring Bibles into the Soviet Union in one way or another. The following story will supply sufficient illustration to show how the Lord is calling His servants in various countries into this unique ministry, making it possible for them to get into Russia with the precious bread of eternal life.

In a Scandinavian country a young man made his first trip to the Soviet Union, having 25 Bibles in his suitcase. At the border, all were ordered to go through the customs inspection. However, to his great relief his bags were not even opened.

[14] "Christian Literature Projects for Russia," **Slavic Gospel News** (July 1976), p. 6.

In his briefing a few days earlier the young Bible courier was instructed to take bus number 25, which would take him to a certain area where he was to go to a certain farmhouse and deliver the Bibles. But he could not find the right bus. In despair he took another bus, number 27, thinking that that bus would also go to the same area. This one brought him to a different location. At the last stop he got off the bus and soon realized he was lost. The farmhouse he had to go to was not in sight. In despair he walked until he was tired and sat down on a stone to pray.. After the prayer the saw the light of a farmhouse. He went to the house and rapped on the door. The lights went out and the door remained locked. He sat down on the well and prayed again. He could not leave Russia with 25 Bibles. An idea struck him. He wrapped the Bibles in a plastic bag and stacked them under a wooden bucket which was on the well.

Back in Scandinavia, he learned that another courier had just returned from the same area. He had learned that a woman who had prayed for several years for a Bible had found 25 under her bucket. Yes. God is a good God! The Lord answered her prayers in a unique way. The young courier's mistake was God's way to supply the request of His handmaid, not with one Bible, but with 25 Bibles.[15]

A dear brother from Florida, who was born in Russia, sends Russian Bibles in quantities to a certain city in Western Europe. A gentleman there who visits Czechoslovakia quite often takes these Bibles with him into the latter country. Then brethren there use devious methods in getting them across the border into the U.S.S.R. Some of the Bibles were in the spare tire of the car he was driving. He placed the Holy Books in the tire, inserted the tube and then inflated it. He also removed the interior panels of the car doors and, after inserting Bibles, replaced the panels. As these hiding places for the Scriptures were not discovered, he drove into Russia with his treasure.

The elderly gentleman from Florida carried one Bible and eight New Testaments across the border. He fastened four Testaments to each lower leg with the aid of twine. They remained unnoticed because of his loosely fitting trousers. When the Russian customs official noticed the large family Bible that he carried, he protested. The American replied that it was used for his devotions, and so he carried it with him wherever he went. He needed it for his daily meditation. So

[15]. "The Wrong Farmhouse," **In Action**, (April-May 1974), p. 3.

the customs official wrote "Bible" on his passport and made it clear that he was to bring it back with him when leaving the Soviet Union.

So when the customs officer saw the word Bible written in his passport, he inquired about it. The American said some relatives had been without a copy of the Scriptures for so long that he could not resist leaving it with them. "I was warned that you would be angry if I didn't have the Bible with me, but that really doesn't worry me. My real concern is my wife. I fear what she will say." With that they laughed and let him go."[16]

The Earl S. Poysti family of Trans World Radio, Monte Carlo, Monaco.

### The Results of the Combined Efforts of the Christians

Our study has already shown that the Russian gospel broadcasts, the Christian literature, Bibles and personal witness in the Soviet Union has resulted in the conversion of about 6 million souls. According to the Soviet magazine "Molodoy Kommunist (Young Communist), two to three percent of the 14-30 age group in the U.S.S.R. declare themselves believers. Research among selected groups of young people indicates 1.2 to 1.8 million young people are willing to say openly they believe in God. Collective farm and unskilled workers show the highest

16. "Taking the Scriptures into Russia," **The Gospel Call,** (November 1968), pp. 3-4.

percentage in the believer category – about 15 percent and 13 percent respectively.[17]

## Bibles Printed in the Soviet Union

In December of 1976 the Orthodox Church in Russia printed 50,000 Jubilee Bibles and 75,000 New Testaments to celebrate the 100-year anniversary of the first printing of the Russian Bible in the common language of the people. A second printing of 50,000 Bibles was scheduled for 1977. The majority of the copies were distributed through the Russian Orthodox Church, with 10,000 copies made available to Protestant churches.

Russia had been officially Christian for almost 900 years before the entire Bible was translated into language the people could readily understand. The translation was complete in 1875 and printed for the public in 1876. The Jubilee Bible is an updated edition of the 1876 version with the archaic words changed to more modern language. However, this token printing of 50,000 does not even begin to meet the need for Bibles among Soviet Christians starving for God's Word. The Soviet government has allowed several Bible printings previously.

But in a country of 270 million people, the approximate total of 250,000 authorized Bibles, including New Testaments and portions printed between 1956 and the Jubilee printing, amounts to less than one Bible per thousand people. Even if one considers only the religious sector of the population – approximately 50 million Russian Orthodox, 6 million Protestants, and 3.5 million Catholics – only one person out of 240 would receive a Bible.

The few Bibles that have been printed have been cautiously distributed under the supervision of the Soviet government and have not necessarily been given to the Russian citizens. Some of the 1957 printing was shipped by the government to Russian emigrants outside the country as proof of Soviet religious freedom – the "freedom of religious worship" theoretically guaranteed in the U.S.S.R.'s constitution.

According to the book, "U.S.S.R. Questions and Answers," published by Novosti Press Agency, an official publishing house in Moscow: "Religious bodies have the right to publish journals, prayer

17. "Research Discovers Many Young Believers," **Slavic Gospel News**, (July 1976), p. 8.

books and other religious literature." In practice, however, Christians find that these rights are often violated.

Because of the Bible shortage Christians sometimes have resorted to printing their own Bibles and books on secret presses. If Soviet officials discover these printing operations, they shut the presses down, and the Christians involved may face long prison sentences.

Some Russian Christians visiting in a satellite country recently reported the publication of 40,000 Bibles and devotional leaflets on a clandestine press in southern Russia. It is impossible to estimate the exact number of Bibles being printed on hand presses, but the amount is obviously insignificant in comparison to the need.

Knowing of this scarcity of Bibles in the U.S.S.R., helpful tourists often try to take Bibles into Russia as gifts for Christians they might meet. Soviet laws do not require entering tourists to list Bibles among items that must be declared. Nevertheless, when customs officials, checking through a tourist's luggage, see the Bibles, they often confiscate them. One summer, an American tourist of Ukrainian heritage visited the Soviet Union, carrying Bibles in his suitcase for his numerous relatives in the Ukraine. At the border, a customs guard confiscated the American's Bibles and commented wryly, "There are two things we fear most in this country – China and the Bible."

The Bible may be the book the Russian government fears most, but it is also the book the Christians in the Soviet Union love and cherish above all others.[18]

The question may be asked: Where are the official Bibles in Russia? Have they been distributed to the people? Underground Evangelism Magazine says that this is not the case. On a recent special assignment, a group of Russian believers visited churches in major cities across the Soviet Union, including Moscow and Leningrad. A number of the group learned of the alleged printing of 100,000 Bibles and their distribution among the believers of Russia. He was asked whether he had heard anywhere about this "Jubilee Bible." His answer was: "The arrival and distribution of even a few Bibles would represent a great event in the life of the believers anywhere in the Soviet Union. During the whole trip, in all the cities and towns visited, we did not hear of one single case of official Bible distribution."

18. "Russian Bible Supply Never Meets Demand," **Slavic Gospel News,** (July 1977), p. 8.

There is only one report of official Bible "distribution." A senior official minister recently was selling Bibles at prices from 30 to 50 rubles.[19]

**The World's Most Unique and Courageous Christian Press**

In basements of Russia, crude presses made from bicycle chains and handmade parts are turning out hundreds of New Testaments and other Christian literature. A picture was taken in a hidden basement somewhere in Russia on movie film and hand carried to the West at great risk. The quality of the picture suffers, because of the difficult circumstances and extremely dangerous conditions under which the picture was taken. Yet this picture documents in a way more eloquently than words, what the spiritually starved and oppressed Christians of Russia are doing that they might have God's Word. The need of Bibles in the Soviet Union is desperate.

Just recently, one authority of the Bible situation in Russia said: "At least 70 million Bibles are needed in Russia right now!" The believers in Russia are working day and night secretly, in hidden basements across the Soviet Union. They willingly risk up to five years in prison to try to meet their desperate need for Bibles and Christian literature. This is almost certainly the most courageous and heroic Bible-printing effort in all Christian history.

The presses are hand made from parts and materials cannibalized from other pieces of equipment, such as chains taken from bicycles, and various parts from other simple everyday tools and equipment. Both presses and materials are "standardized," so that printing operations can continue smoothly should the secret police locate any one of the several presses operated by "Khristianin" (Christian) publishers. If one press is closed down, another cranks up to continue. Tens of thousands of New Testaments already have been printed in secret locations in Russia.

After printing, the New Testaments are arduously and laboriously hand assembled by devoted Christians eager to make God's Word available to their fellow believers. Thousands of the New Testaments, bound and stacked, are ready for distribution. Since Christian publishers began secretly publishing Christian literature in 1968, their total output is reported to be 350,000 books, among which are tens of

19. "Newsline," **Underground Evangelism**, (September 1978), p. 11.

**This complete Bible was produced in Russia on a secret Bible Press. At right is the secret press. (1978)**

thousands of New Testaments. Their ultimate goal is to print the complete Bible, with as many as 10,000 copies per printing.[20]

However, at last in 1978 the first complete Bible was printed on the underground Christian press in the U.S.S.R. This Bible carries the highest price tag ever placed on a 20th century book – the same kind of martyrdom other generations have paid to have it in other God-hating lands in other days, on down to today's suffering Church in God-hating Communist Russia. The Bible is large, of necessity, because of the strenuous conditions under which it has been printed: 2 inches thick, 9 inches long, and 6 inches wide. The completion and publication of the Bible is a monumental and remarkable achievement, by the grace of God.[21]

### The Union of Evangelical Christians-Bapists of U.S.S.R.

More than 120 new Pastors of local churches were elected and ordained in 1977. Churches in Khazakhstan, the Ukraine and

20. "The World's Most Unique and Courageous Christian Press," **Underground Evangelism,** (April 1977), pp. 7-8.

21. "Complete Bible Produced on Russia's Underground Press," **Underground Evangelism,** (September 1978), p. 8.

Byelorussia reconstructed old buildings and built new prayer houses. The Pentecostal churches in Brest and Novovolynsk erected prayer houses. The Pentecostal church in Chernovtsy was given a spare building for a prayer house free of charge, which has now been reconstructed.

The church of Evangelical Christians-Baptists in the same city was also given a building for a prayer house, and this building is now being renovated. The Pentecostal church in Minsk has finished building a prayer house. The Darnitsa area church in Kiev has finished its reconstruction program.

In certain areas of the Russian Federated Republic, the Ukraine and Byelorussia, there were opened new congregations of Mennonites, Pentecostals and Evangelical Christians-Baptists. Two new churches were opened, for example, in Lvov city. The congregations of Evangelical Christians-Baptists and Pentecostals of Rovno, Ternopol, Volyn and Chernovtsy areas opened new churches, as well as Baptists in Ashkhabad.

More than 6,000 new souls were won for Christ and were baptized, among them a large number of young people.

Regional meetings of Pastors took place in the Far East, Byelorussia, Latwia, Ternopol, Chernovtsy, Rovno, Omsk, Kiev and in some other cities.[22]

[22] "The Union of Evangelical Christians-Baptists of U.S.S.R." **Action** (May 1978), p. 14.

**A baptismal service in White Russia, U.S.S.R. White Russia with Minsk as its capital extends westward from a point about 200 miles west of Moscow to the borders of Poland and Lithuania. Only part of the audience is visible.**

## CHAPTER XIV

# CONCLUSION

In A.D. 988, Prince Vladimir of Russia accepted Christianity for political purposes and imported Greek Orthodox Christianity into Russia as a ready-made religious system. Subsequently the Russian heathen masses were forced to accept the Greek Orthodox religion as their own, resulting in a forced mass-conversion to the latter faith.

The Greek Orthodox religion did not produce any true internal conversion in the hearts of the heathen masses, and the influence of its Christian principles was rather slow among the recalcitrant Russians. However, after several centuries, the new religion became an aggressively political and economic institution, gathering unto itself vast material resources.

After the fall of Constantinople in 1453, the Church in Russia separated itself from the Greek domination and enabled Russia to develop a truly national Church free of foreign political influence, owing allegiance to no one but the national State and Emperor; and in due time this nation was called Holy Russia.

The clergy assured the people that God had chosen Orthodox Russia to be the bearer of the only true faith, while all the Westerners were heretics. Thus the Russians had the only true and superior religion, which no one could forsake. The Orthodox concept of a supreme religion forbade any evangelical activity in the Russian Empire, considering any such movement as a revolutionary ferment.

However, there was also a widely held belief that in order to remain a great power, Russia must preserve intact its unifying spiritual force, the Orthodox Church and its centralized autocratic government. From this point of view in conjunction with the Orthodox conception of a supreme religion, all sectarian movements among the Russian Orthodox people were dangerous and all religious separatists were destroyers of their spiritual and cultural unity and were potential traitors. The Evangelicals in Russia have the misfortune to be associated with a wide spectrum of sectarians, some of which have truly been quite weird and extreme in various ways and deserved the opposition they received. The Evangelicals being closely connected with the West, were most obnoxious to Orthodoxy and to the Emperor. With all power, the Orthodox Church and the autocratic governments persecuted the Evangelicals. This poses a paradox: A religious nation opposed to true, vital, evangelical faith. Why?

The Russian Orthodox Church was a state-controlled and operated religious system which was led by unregenerated men, bound by the power of sin. II Corinthians 4:4 applies well to them: "In whom the god of this world hath blinded the minds of them which believe not, lest the light of the glorious gospel of Christ, who is the image of God, should shine unto them."

The Evangelicals were born-again children of God. As Children of Light, they could not be tolerated by the power of darkness as witnesses for Jesus Christ and destroyers of the kingdom of darkness. Thus the history of Evangelical Christianity in Russia during the autocratic rule reveals a great struggle between the power of darkness and the power of Light.

When Communism took over Russia, the Evangelicals soon experienced opposition and persecution. This materialistic atheistic system of Russia is itself a type of religion. The study of Communism reveals that it has its trinity consisting of three persons: Karl Marx, the father of Communism; Friedrich Engels, the great collaborator; and Vladimir Lenin, the practical demonstrator of Communism in Russia. The philosophy of these three men remains the cohesive force which keeps Bolshevism intact. Communism then is a systematic religion which, in highest ideal, believes that the State is god, work is worship, and a better social order is the promised land.

Communism is a revolutionary movement with totalitarian undertones which has become the right arm of Russian imperialism. As such, the Communist movement is a threat to the freedom and spiritual values of man. The Evangelicals who serve God with all their heart are considered as a revolutionary force and must be removed.

Here is a parallel between the former autocratic government of Russia and the present government of the Soviet Union. The former considered itself as the only supreme religion in the world to be brought to all nations. The latter also considered itself as a supreme government with supreme ideology to be brought to all nations.

The youth in Russia are at present at the throes of a serious spiritual and intellectual crisis. The personality cult, the deification of the State in the person of a single man, has not been able to satisfy the spiritual needs of Russian youth. The Russian people need the gospel of Jesus Christ. At present the gospel is being beamed into Russia over several radio stations, producing a considerable number of conversions. If a change should take place in the Soviet government so that preachers could go to Russia, a great harvest of souls could be gathered.

*　　*　　*

Dear Reader:

The world is reported to be spending more than $300,000 a minute, $18 million an hour, or $432 million a day on armaments. It has been reckoned that its present stockpile of nuclear warheads is sufficient to destroy today's 4.5 billion population 50,000 times over.

Since we have no promise of tomorrow, humanly speaking, we shudder at what a possible tomorrow may bring; but we who know our God should be strong and do exploits. These may be the last days of a period during which the gospel has been beamed into Russia unhindered. Millions of them have heard the gospel, but hundreds of millions of the lost souls have not yet heard the message of salvation once.

A 24-page booklet, "Look: How Simple," has been translated into the Russian language. This strong gospel message will be brought into Russia. In due time we want to print 10 million copies. Please pray also that the Lord may supply all the needs.

# BIBLIOGRAPHY

## Copyright Acknowledgments

The following have been consulted or quoted in the preparation of this publication. Every effort has been made to locate the owners of copyrighted material used. Upon notification, the Publisher will make proper correction in subsequent printings.

Some of the books in this bibliography are not copyrighted, or are out of date.

## Books

Astakhoff, N. I. *Christianity in Russia,* Chicago: Loizeaus Brothers Publishers, 1941. Used by permission.

– *Christianity and Communism,* New York: Published by the Author, 1931.

– *In the Flame of Russia's Revolution.* New York: Published by the Author, 1931.

– *Real Russia from 1905 to 1932 and Communism in America.* New York: Published by the Author, 1932.

Benson, Davis V. *Christianity, Communism and Survival.* A Division of Gospel Light Publications. 1967. Used by permission.

Bliss, Edwin M. *Encyclopedia of Missions,* New York: 1891.

Blumit, Oswald A. *Sentenced to Siberia.* Washington, D. C. Mayflower Publishers, 1946. Quoted by permission of the Russian Bible Society, P.O. Box 6068, Ashville, N.C. 28816.

Bolshakoff, Serge. *Russian Nonconformity.* Philadelphia: The Westminster Press, 1949. Used by permission.

Brandenburg H. *The Meek and the Mighty.* London & Oxford: A.R. Mowbray & Co., Ltd., 1976. Copyright © Used by permission.

Byford, Chas. P. *Peasants and Prophets.* London: The Kingsgate Press, 1914. Used by permission.

Bystrom, J. *Sodd och Skodd.* Stockholm: 1916.

Casey, Robert P. *Religion in Russia.* New York: Harper Brothers, 1946. Used by permission.

Dark, Sidney & R. S. Essex, *The War Against God.* New York: Abington Press, 1938. Used by permission.

Duin, Edgar C. *Lutheranism Under the Tsars and the Soviets.* Ann Arbor: 1975.

Durasoff, Steve. *The Russian Protestants Evangelicals in the Soviet Union.* Rutherford: Fairlaigh Dickinson University Press, 1962. Used by permission.

Geren, Paul. *Christians Confront Communism.* Nashville: Convention Press, 1962. Used by permission.

Harmon, Nolan B. *The Encyclopedia of World Methodism.* Nashville, 1974. Copyright © Used by permission.

Hogberg, L.E. *Skuggor och Dagar fron Missionsarbetet; Russland.* Stockholm: 1914.

Huuhtanen, Tuomo. *Vallankumouksen Vaiheilta.* Tikkurila: Ristin Voitto, 1976.

Kaups, Richard. *Hea Sonum ja Eesti Baptisti Kogudused.* Santa Barbara: 1974.

Kolarz, Walter. *Religion in the Soviet Union.* New York: St. Martin's Press, Inc., 1961. Used by permission.

Kuosmanen, Juhani, *Heratyksen Historia,* Tikkurila: Ristin Voittu, 1979. Used by permission.

Laks, John. *Arkamistuuled Kodumaal.* Toronto: Ortoprint. 1966.

Latimer, Robert S. *With Christ in Russia.* London: Hodder and Stoughton, 1910. Used by permission.

Makinen, Anti. *Vapaakirkollinen Liike Suomessa.* Helsinki: 1910.

Malof, Basil A. *100% For Kristus.* Orebro: Evangeliipress, 1955.

McCaig, A. *Grace Astounding in Bolshevik Russia.* London:

Mott, John R. *The Present World Situation.* New York: 1915.

Pollock, J. C. *The Faith of the Russian Evangelicals.* New York: McGraw Hill Company, 1964. Copyright © Used by permission.

*Quaker Biographies.* Issued by the Representatives of the Religious Society of Friends for Pennsylvania, New Jersey and Delaware. 1916.

Randall, F. B. *Stalin's Russia, and Historical Reconsideration.* New York: The Free Press, 1965. Copyright © Used by permission.

Rushbrooke,, J. H. *Some Chapters of European Baptist History.* London: The Kingsgate Press, 1929. Used by permission.

Salter, Doris. *The Story of the Bible Christian Union.* New York: 1968.

Scott, Richenda C. *Quakers in Russia.* London: Michael Joseph Ltd., 1964. Used by permission.

Shedd, Clarence P. *History of the World's Alliance of Young Men's Christian Association.* London: Published by S.P.C.K., 1955.

Smith, Oswald J. *Tales of the Mission Fields.* London: Marshall, Morgan & Scott, 1966. Used by permission.

Solberg, C.K. *A Brief History of the Zion Society for Israel.* Minneapolis: 1928.

Struve, N. *Christians in Contemporary Russia.* New York: Charles Scribner's Sons, 1967. Used by permission.

Thompson, A. E. *A Century of Jewish Missions.* Chicago: Fleming H. Revell Comp., 1902. Used by permission.

Timasheff, N.S. *Religion in Soviet Russia: 1917 – 1942.* London: The Religious Book Club, 1943. Used by permission.

*The Holy Bible.* Authorized King James Version.

Wiggins, Arch. *The History of the Salvation Army, 1886 – 1904.* Edinburg: T. A. Constable Ltd., 1964. Used by permission.

Wilkinson, Samuel. *In the Land of the North.* The Evangelization of the Jews in Russia. London: Marshal Brothers, 1905. Used by permission.

**Periodicals**

"The Wrong Farmhouse," *In Action,* April-May, 1974.

"The Union of Evangelical Christians-Baptists of U.S.S.R." *Action,* May 1978.

"Shouldn't Russians Have a Choice," *Slavic Gospel News,* July 1976.

"Christian Literature Projects for Russia," *Slavic Gospel News,* July 1976.

"Research Discovers Many Young Believers," *Slavic Gospel News,* July 1976.
"Russian Bible Supply Never Meets Demand," *Slavic Gospel News,* July 1976.
"The Hutterian Brethren, 1528 – 1928," *The Mennonite Quarterly Review,* January 1928.
– *The Mennonite Quarterly Review,* April 1928.
– *The Mennonite Quarterly Review,* January 1929.
– *The Mennonite Quarterly Review,* January 1930.
"Dissident Baptists and Regulars Striving to Get Along in Russia," *The Baptist Courier,* May 13, 1971.
"Let the Skies Pour Down Righteousness," *The Gospel Call,* January 1968.
"Numerous Conversions Through Radio Broadcasts," *The Gospel Call,* June 1968.
"Gospel Radio Broadcasts Awaken Russian Village," *The Gospel Call,* July 1968.
"Blanketing the Soviet Union with the Gospel," *The Gospel Call,* January 1969.
"A Spiritual Awakening in Russia, *The Gospel Call,* May 1969.
"Taking the Scriptures into Russia," *The Gospel Call,* November 1968.
"The Churches in Eastern Europe Today," *The Gospel Call,* November 1969.
"Inspiring Messages from Behind the Iron Curtain," *The Gospel Call,* July 1970.
"Russian Radio Programs Used in Church Services," *The Gospel Call,* July-August, 1976.
"Millions of Russians for Christ," *The Gospel Call,* March-April 1977.
"Russia's Counterfeit Church," *Underground Evangelism Magazine,* May 1970.
"They Worship Underground," *Underground Evangelism Magazine,* May 1970.
"The World's Most Unique and Courageous Christian Press," *Underground Evangelism Magazine,* April 1977.
"Newsline," *Underground Evangelism Magazine,* September 1978.
"Complete Bible Produced on Russia's Underground Press," *Underground Evangelism Magazine,* September 1978.
Larson, Karl. "Ten Years in Russia," *The War Cry,* July 19, 1969.
– *The War Cry,* July 26, 1969.
– *The War Cry,* August 16, 1969.

## INDEX